Warfare!
Strategies of the Enemy

Collegium Books

Mark David Shaw
Kathryn Colton Shaw

Spiritual Warfare Series

Unless otherwise indicated all Scripture quotations are taken from *New American Standard Bible : 1995 update*. 1995. LaHabra, CA: The Lockman Foundation.

Some Scripture quotations are taken from the following:

The Holy Bible : King James Version. 1995 (electronic ed. of the 1769 edition of the 1611 Authorized Version.). Bellingham WA: Logos Research Systems, Inc.
The Everyday Bible : New Century Version. 2005. Nashville, TN.: Thomas Nelson, Inc.
The Holy Bible : English standard version. 2001. Wheaton: Standard Bible Society.
Peterson, E. H. (2002). *The Message : The Bible in contemporary language*. Colorado Springs, Colo.: NavPress.
The Revised Standard Version. 1971 Oak Harbor, WA: Logos Research Systems, Inc.
Young, R. (1997). *Young's literal translation* Oak Harbor: Logos Research Systems.
Stern, D. H. (1989). *Jewish New Testament : A translation of the New Testament that expresses its Jewishness* (1st ed.). Jerusalem, Israel; Clarksville, Md., USA: Jewish New Testament Publications.

Warfare!
by Mark David Shaw and Kathryn Colton Shaw
ISBN 978-0-9801865-3-6

Copyright © 2009 by Mark David Shaw

Published by Collegium Books
410 Dakota Street W.
Cannon Falls, MN 55009

Printed in the United States of America. All rights reserved under International Copyright Law. Written permission must be secured from the publisher to use or reproduce any part of this book, except for brief quotations in critical reviews or articles.

To reach us on the Internet:

www.collegiumbooks.com
www.collegiumbibleinstitute.com

Warfare!
Strategies of the Enemy

1 Peter 5:8

Be of sober spirit, be on the alert. Your adversary, the devil, prowls around like a roaring lion, seeking someone to devour.

"This is perhaps one of the greatest lessons to learn as a Christian; who the enemy is and his tactics. To many, I think this is still a vague concept."

-Susan Snelling

This Book is Dedicated To:

To my daughters, Jennifer and Elizabeth, when you were young we would have a discussion about what you wanted to be when you both grew up and I remember telling you, "You can be whatever you want to be, just be careful that no one takes the dream away from you." Look at you both now; I am so proud of your hard work and the success you have demonstrated through the pursuit of your dreams. I love you both dearly and I am excited to see how your futures will unfold.

To the market place ministers and evangelists, because you are often on the front lines of spiritual warfare, we dedicate this work to you. You are in the world and around people with a regularity that is unequaled with regard to the other callings. As a result, you are encountering all of the philosophies and doctrines that the devil can muster which serve only to put people into bondage.

Armed with the truth, the market place minister and the evangelist are able to reach those souls that would never darken the doors of a church. They are located in the front lines of the battlefield and are in a unique position to set the captives free. We commend you for your service and exhort you to carry on in your ministry as it is crucial to the expansion of the Kingdom of God.

Acknowledgements

To our Lord Jesus who won the fight destroying the works of the devil!

I would like to thank my father whose many conversations about our family helped to join together the ideas which are revealed in this writing. It has opened the door for every one of us to become all that God has created us to be. I love you Dad, thank you for the years of reminiscing.

Love,

Kathryn

We would like to acknowledge the Colton's of past generations who prayed for us to be filled with the Spirit of God. Their foresight and obedience to the Spirit are manifest in the work we are able to accomplish today for the kingdom of God.

A big thank you is owed to Susan Snelling, a true friend, for her tireless work of reading, re-reading, proofing, and re-proofing. Without you we would not have been able to complete this work in such a timely manner. Thank you so much.

Table of Contents

This Book is Dedicated To:... vii
Acknowledgements ix
Introduction xiii
Journey Into the Enemy's Camp 1
In The Beginning – Warfare! 17
Faith Academics 37
Perception vs Reality 52
The Road To Freedom 76
Rules of Engagement 94
Building A Philosophy For Life 116
Can a Christian be Possessed? 175
Soul Ties 201
Generational Curses 209
Word or Spoken Curses 224
The Fruit of Adultery 239
The Jezebel Tactic 252
Preparing for Warfare 277
About the Author 291

Introduction

At the age of seventeen I was asked to watch my two-year-old nephew as my sister and her husband went out to dinner. They had just arrived in Florida and were living with us in our family's home. My brother-in-law was a minister who had just been removed from the Nazarene Church because they would not accept that he had been baptized in the Holy Spirit and was now speaking in tongues.

I started out that night watching TV in complete boredom. After a while I began to look for some rock music to play. My brother-in-law had brought this big reel-to-reel tape player so I began looking through his tapes hoping to find some rock music. What I found changed my life forever. The tapes were labeled, but I really didn't understand what the labels were saying.

I took one of the reels and began to thread it into the player. I turned it on and it wasn't long until I realized that I had loaded a tape of an exorcism. I sat there spellbound as I listened to this story unfold.

I do not remember the entire story, only that a little girl was possessed and would have bite marks appear on her arms. Once she was set free from this demonic torment she was declared sane and released from the asylum. I remember the minister telling her that if that spirit ever tried to come back just cry out the name of Jesus. Then upon leaving, witnesses saw her being dragged across the lawn of the asylum, but whatever was dragging her was invisible to them. All they could tell was that something had a hold of her hair and was dragging her across the lawn. Then the little girl yelled the name of Jesus and it stopped—this time for good.

She had not received Christ until that moment when she cried out to Jesus to save her.

I have no idea as to who this was or when it took place. All I knew at the time was that it ended in the girl being delivered and in her right mind. For me, however, it ended with the sudden awareness that I have an enemy, and more importantly, that I was serving on the wrong side. I had a Christian family, but I had not made the decision to receive Christ. My Christian upbringing is what allowed me to see that I was on the wrong side.

When my sister and brother-in-law got home I waited for an opportunity to talk to him alone. When that moment came, I told him what I had done and the blood drained from his face. He apologized I had gotten a hold of the tape and that it was only meant for those who were mature Christians. I told him it was okay, but that listening to it I realized I am on the wrong side. *"What should I do?"* I asked. It was then that he led me to Christ and I became a Christian. This would mark the beginning of a life long journey; an adventure that would have many experiences.

Little did I know it would be thirty-seven years later that I would be writing a book which is meant to bring understanding to the battle we are in. There are many in Christian circles that do not even believe there is a devil. They think he is just a figment of someone's imagination made up to make the story interesting. *"What good is a story without a villain?"* they say. Yet, if we are to believe our Bibles, he is a very real entity who has set himself to destroy the object that has God's passion and attention—mankind, whom He made in His image. On the other side of that pendulum we have those who believe they see devils in everything around them. They are consumed with the notion that there is a demon behind every tree. They utter, *"I rebuke you Satan!"* many times throughout the day.

Don't take me wrong, I am not making fun of these people. Most of them love God and want to do right; they have just accepted a message that is not in agreement with the Bible. I would love for both these groups to grasp the principles laid out in this book so they would have what is necessary to defeat their enemy. I am a truth seeker. I do not write these things with the expectation that people need to take what I say at face value. I fully expect you to test what I say, compare it to other positions, and then take that which stands out as being true. If you will do this you are well on your way to stopping the enemy in his deceptions.

I want to make some sense of what is real concerning the devil and what is not. We will also look at his devices—those things he uses to trick Christians into giving up on their purpose and destiny. I will be challenging you with the notion that either Jesus did a half way job on earth and that He is not the great Savior everyone makes Him out to be, or He thoroughly defeated our enemy the devil from the cross and is every bit and more of a Savior to mankind.

There are some practices in the Body of Christ with regard to our enemy that are making him out to be a spirit equipped with all the weapons, power, and authority to destroy Christians. The problem with this idea is that if Christians believe these things it will actually empower the devil to destroy them. Our fight is a fight of faith. We either have faith in the power of the devil, or we have faith in the power of God.

This book is much more about the power of God than it is about the power of the devil. Many of my brothers and sisters have ascribed powers to the devil that he does not have over the Christian. I write this book in the hope that all believers would see the error of some of these doctrines so that it would set them free to be used of God for the glory of God.

The layout of this book is to first describe for you where we stand with regard to warfare; who are we fighting against, how do we fight, upon what battlefield does this war take place, and how do we prevail every time. After you have a complete understanding of these things, we will then move on to deal with those beliefs which have crept into the Church; beliefs that only serve to put people in bondage while promising them that it will release them from bondage. Then we end with our protection as Christians. My prayer is that you will find knowledge in this book that will take you into a greater freedom than you have now! God's Church is militant with regard to the spirit world, you are a warrior in the fight, you are commissioned to the battle, you have your armor, you have your weapon. Now, let's take a journey into the enemy's camp!

Journey Into the Enemy's Camp

Chapter One

Much of what we see today that is called spiritual warfare needs to be tested to see if it is, or if it is just a ruse of the enemy to get us to wage war with counterfeit weapons on counterfeit battlefields. We are going to take a biblical look at this subject. What I will not do is enter into subjective so-called *"moments of revelation"* by people who have had an experience and then go to the Bible to look for evidence to support it. This is a sure way of entering into false beliefs.

What I am saying is that we cannot try to make the Bible fit our experiences. We need to measure the experience with the Word of God. If our experience seems to violate Scripture then we need to discard the experience as phony. I will be sharing an experience, but we will use the Bible to measure the experience instead of using the experience to measure the Bible.

I remember one instance when I was an associate pastor and the senior pastor came back from a seminar saying that we Christians can be possessed. I immediately asked him for biblical reference. He told me that he didn't have it yet but would study and then happily provide it.

Later, I asked him again for the evidence and he still did not have any biblical reference. So I asked him where the speaker who revealed this information got these things. He told me that he was casting out demons and in the process was communicating and asking questions of the demons. The demons revealed this information to the minister about being able to possess Christians, to which I responded, *"Well, that is a good source."* Of course, I was being facetious. Jesus calls Satan the "father of lies," not exactly an endorsement as a reliable source of information.

Battle Lines

I love to allow the Word of God to speak for itself. The problem is that we often get taught certain interpretations of particular passages which cause us to instantly apply those interpretations every time we read or hear those passages. For that reason, the first thing I want to do is shake up your predetermined interpretations of certain Scriptures dealing with spiritual warfare. We do this by grouping. What do I mean by grouping? Grouping is a process that I practice to help in correct interpretation. Because the Bible interprets itself, I will gather passages of the same subject and read them as a group in their individual contexts. This will help to pull out the actual meaning of the subject.

Since we are going to be talking about warfare, I am going to group scriptures that deal with warfare. I will use keywords like warfare, victory, weapon, sword, shield, battle, fight, and overcome. This will give us a good general idea of the battle that we are in. Of course, I cannot put all of the references into this writing as it would be too large. What I will do is quote the most pertinent ones with regard to spiritual warfare.

> ***Hebrews 11:32-34*** *And what more shall I say? For time will fail me if I tell of Gideon, Barak, Samson, Jephthah, of David and Samuel and the prophets, who by faith conquered kingdoms, performed acts of righteousness, obtained promises, shut the mouths of lions, quenched the power of fire, escaped the edge of the sword, from weakness were made strong, became mighty in **war**, put foreign armies to flight.*

I want to draw your attention to the connection that war or warfare has with faith. This will be a recurring theme throughout the Bible. If I am to understand this correctly, we become mighty in warfare by faith! If I want to be a mighty warrior, I must have faith. Yet, so much of what we see with regard to advancing as a soldier in the fight against the devil has nothing to do with faith. You know the stories, *"Buy this vial of oil for it was acquired in Israel and anoint the walls of your house and demons will be unable to cross it"* and many more like it.

> *2 Corinthians 10:4-5 for the **weapons** of our **warfare** are not of the flesh, but divinely powerful for the destruction of fortresses. We are destroying speculations and every lofty thing raised up against the knowledge of God, and we are taking every thought captive to the obedience of Christ…*

We deal exhaustively with this passage in another chapter so all I want to mention is the connection with the knowledge of God and the weapons of our warfare.

> *1 Timothy 1:18-19This command I entrust to you, Timothy, my son, in accordance with the prophecies previously made concerning you, that by them you **fight** the good **fight**, keeping faith and a good conscience, which some have rejected and suffered shipwreck in regard to their faith.*

This seems to be saying that we fight by the personal prophetic messages given to us. What does this mean? Since most personal prophecy is in regard to a person's destiny, it is this information that drives us to continue in the fight. Anything that would come in between us and that revealed destiny would then be identified as hostile and dealt with. Without destiny, we would lack the motivation to continue fighting in the face of opposition.

> *John 18:36 Jesus answered, "My kingdom is not of this world. If My kingdom were of this world, then My servants would be **fighting** so that I would not*

> *be handed over to the Jews; but as it is, My kingdom is not of this realm."*

From this we can see that our fight is not a physical fight because the kingdom we are fighting for is a spiritual kingdom. Since it is a spiritual kingdom, then our fight is a spiritual fight.

> ***1 Timothy 6:12 Fight** the good **fight** of faith; take hold of the eternal life to which you were called, and you made the good confession in the presence of many witnesses.*

Again, faith surfaces with regard to the fight we are in. What does a fight of faith look like? Is it a struggle to keep faith or a struggle to advance faith? Is it a struggle to maintain truth in the earth? Or is it all the above? Let's keep looking.

> ***2 Timothy 4:7** I have fought the good **fight**, I have finished the course, I have kept the faith.*

There seems to be somewhat of a connection with fighting and maintaining faith. Yet, we cannot make too strong of a connection here. Paul could have been listing three distinct things that were not necessarily connected with each other, but it is curious that faith and warfare show up together again.

> ***Ephesians 6:17** And take* THE HELMET OF SALVATION, *and the **sword** of the Spirit, which is the word of God.*

> ***Hebrews 4:12** For the word of God is living and active and sharper than any two-edged **sword**, and piercing as far as the division of soul and spirit, of both joints and marrow, and able to judge the thoughts and intentions of the heart.*

Our weapon in this fight is a sword, that sword represents the Word of God. Now let's look at our shield.

> ***Ephesians 6:16*** *in addition to all, taking up the shield of faith with which you will be able to extinguish all the **flaming arrows** of the evil one.*

The weapons used against us are flaming arrows. I figure the devil does not want to get close enough for a real fight. If the sword is the Word of God, what do the flaming arrows of the enemy represent? If we were to use logic we would say that they represent the word of the devil.

> ***Psalm 120:2-4*** *Deliver my soul, O L*ORD*, from lying lips, From a deceitful tongue. What shall be given to you, and what more shall be done to you, You deceitful tongue? Sharp **arrows** of the warrior, With the **burning** coals of the broom tree.*

Yes, the burning arrows are the deceits and lies the enemy throws at us. No wonder that the weapon God has given us is truth and the defense that God gives us is faith. Keeping with this, faith is what protects us and the Word of God is what attacks the enemy.

> ***1 John 5:4-5*** *For whatever is born of God **overcomes** the world; and this is the **victory** that has **overcome** the world—our faith. Who is the one who **overcomes** the world, but he who believes that Jesus is the Son of God?*

Since we are in a battle we must be trying to overcome something. According to this passage, we are overcoming the world. The world is the manifestation of the kingdom of darkness.

> ***Ephesians 6:12*** *For our struggle is not against flesh and blood, but against the rulers, against the powers, against the **world forces of this darkness**, against the spiritual forces of wickedness in the heavenly places.*

From these verses we get a strong sense of what spiritual warfare is. Knowing what it is can also identify what it is not. Some of the doctrines that have been presented concerning spiritual warfare are suspect in light of these passages. In later chapters we will deal with things like generational curses, word curses, soul ties, possession, and so on.

For now, I want to share with you an experience. Before I do, however, I reiterate that this experience does not determine doctrine. Instead, we measure the experience by the Word of God. It will be a good exercise to use this experience to show how one would use the Word of God to test it.

One morning in August 2004, I had finished breakfast and was joking around with my wife, Kathryn. I left to go down stairs to my office to do some work. She went to her computer to check for emails from people that requested prayer. She was replying to one when she suddenly started not feeling well. She hit the intercom and told me to pray for her because she was feeling sick.

Kathryn went to the bathroom and began to sense she was losing consciousness. She realized that she was not going to make it so she stood up, yelled my name, stomped on the floor, and began to run for the bedroom. I knew something was wrong and I ran up the stairs. When I came into the bedroom she was half on and half off the bed. Her eyes were wide open and she was staring straight ahead. Her eyes had changed color. Instead of the dark brown that they are, they were lighter in color, more of a green color. Her breathing was very shallow.

I yelled her name and she did not respond at all. For a split second I thought she might be joking with me because of the kidding around we were doing right after breakfast. It didn't take me long to realize that this was really happening. Then she stopped breathing and her face smoothed out. I knew she had just died. I called 911 and began frantically giving my address to the dispatcher. As he put me on hold to call the ambulance, I grabbed a hold of her ankle and yelled, *"Kathryn, get back in your body in the name of Jesus right now!"* As soon as I finished that prayer, the 911 operator came back on and Kathryn shuddered and yelled, *"Where am I?"* The following is what she experienced.

Kathryn's Journey

The first thing I saw was a path leading up to the North. I don't know how I knew that I was going up North, I just knew. The path ahead was lit and had an amber golden glow. I appeared younger to myself, probably about late 20's to early 30's, and I had long hair like I used to. I was wearing a fancy dress like you would to a wedding and it was about ankle length. I was walking and swinging my arms and I knew that I had a destination to reach. I had never felt so free and secure before.

At the beginning of the path and to the right were some indiscriminant objects that had no real meaning or design that I could tell. They were, however, coated with a thick shiny red substance. It reminded me of red acrylic paint. You know how, even though it is dry, it still looks like it is wet? This substance was not applied smoothly, but as if it had been poured over the objects and then allowed to dry with the natural flow of ripples.

As I began to walk up the path, I heard noises that were clamorous. There was immense darkness on either side of the path that I was on. As I looked to my right, I could see these dark silhouettes moving in the darkness. As I began to look more intently, I could see them clearly and I could also hear that they were chanting.

What I saw was a group of about a dozen large demonic leaders that were chanting scriptures. The problem was that they were chanting them correctly, but with a twist. What I mean by that is they are quoting scripture, but adding something to it that amounted to false doctrine, a false interpretation.

I could also see a massive group of smaller demons that were assigned to the larger ones and each one had to repeat the chant of their leader. Each leader was saying a different scripture, and then that leader's underlings would repeat that scripture. Because all of the beings were speaking at the same time, it was loud and very irritating.

Behind the group of smaller demons there stood an assembly of Christians. This group of demons would have a hold of the Christians by their belly through what appeared to be an umbilical cord of sorts. The demons would chant their perverted scripture and immediately the Christians would jump up and down with glee as they chanted the same scripture with a warped interpretation. All the while the Christians were chanting, the demons continued to have a hold of them. The Christians were delighted in what they were saying and believed it was from God. Some of these Christians I knew, but I was not given their identity, except for one.

All of this was taking place at the same time and the noise was most irritating. At no time was I afraid. I had such peace as if a great load or burden had been lifted from me. However, I could sense how evil and dark these beings were. I could tell they were very determined and they were incredibly busy with their tasks. It was as though time was a factor in getting their work done so they were in a hurry. I could feel the tremendous hatred of these beings and the desire they have to murder and destroy. Yet, I knew they could not get to where I was at on the path. There are really no words to describe how evil they were and the great hatred they have for us.

As I heard the twisted scriptures being chanted, I pointed toward the crowd of demons and Christians and said very nonchalantly, "That's not right!" As I said this, all the chanting immediately stopped and the demons all looked toward me. Then the head demon leader pointed his finger at me and began to speak accusations against me. As the demon spoke, I could see the words as they came out of his mouth.

Then between me and the demon's words there appeared in giant letters, three words. They were: Accuser, Accuser, Accuser. These words were the same red as the objects at the beginning of the path. As these words appeared, the words spoken by the demon could not pass the larger words of Accuser, Accuser, Accuser. These three words were backwards from my point of view so that the leader that was shouting the accusations could read them; to me they were reversed.

Then, beyond this and to the left of the path were other demons who were chanting different phrases. I could see the letters of these phrases as they were being chanted. As a demon would chant a phrase, he would jump up and down on the letters, and as he did, the letters would get bigger and bigger like they were gaining energy and power in their meaning. Then these phrases were being stored to the side, waiting to be sent to earth to be used on Christians.

These are the phrases we all hear when the devil is trying to discourage us. They were phrases such as "I am no good." "I can't make it." "There is no use in trying." "No one loves me." These phrases were so powerful and they were sent with so much evil intent that the only way they could not harm us is if we were to reject the thoughts.

At this point, I continued up the path. I was just about to leave the area where all the chanting was when I heard my husband yell "right now!" Immediately, I started moving backward down the path. As I did, the clamoring that I had heard got louder and louder. It was accompanied by great clanging and banging noises that were unbearable. Then I jerked and came back into my body. Even though I was in my body, for a moment I could hear both my husband shouting to the 911 operator and the clamoring of the demonic hoard. At this point, my mind was split between both realms and the one with the path seemed more real than this one. Because of this, I was trying to go back to the path. Finally, I screamed and then shouted, "Where am I?"

It was the most terrifying feeling to have your mind in two places at once. I will never forget how frightened I was in that condition. Since then I have been afraid this will happen to me again. I was angry for awhile, perhaps for a couple years after I had this experience. I felt that I had already experienced enough trials in my life. If God wanted to show me something, why didn't He just tell me instead of making me go through this experience? Twice I asked God, "Why did this happen to me?" Both times God has replied with, "I am blessing you." Not finding this answer to be comforting or humorous, it was not until sometime later that I realized how strong the message was for His children to understand how the enemy tries to deceive us. I will never, ever forget how hateful and angry the enemy is towards us!

This place I was passing through on the way up North was so very, very dark. It was so dark that when the crew members carried me outside to the ambulance, the sunlight hurt my eyes so badly. To this day, I cannot stand a bright light over my head; it immediately reminds me of this journey. I was depressed for quite awhile after having to go through this. It took almost four years before I could speak about it publically without crying. What makes me so upset is the hate and the darkness that I saw, and how the enemy knows he is running out of time. He has one thing on his mind, and that is to destroy us before Christ comes for us. His purpose is to stop us from doing the will of God in our lives; to prevent the works of Christ from going forward by deceiving us so *that we stop listening to the Lord with the end result being a failed Christ.*

Kathryn really did go through a tough time with this. By the way, the hospital sent her home that same day unable to find anything sufficiently wrong to keep her. That was a healing by God. When I got her home, I noticed that she had become quiet. I was thinking she might be mad at me for calling her back. Then I began to question her about what she saw. As she recalled to me what happened I took notes, and the Scriptures started to come to my mind as I wrote.

There are some details in this account that we cannot verify by Scripture. We must also note that none of these details disagree with Scripture either. When we think of demonic entities, we are not necessarily thinking about where they have set up their authority. Since they do not have access to the third heaven which is the point that is outside of space and time, they have access only to the first heaven which represents earth and its atmosphere, and the second heaven which would be space.

> ***2 Corinthians 12:2-5*** *I know a man in Christ who fourteen years ago—whether in the body I do not know, or out of the body I do not know, God knows—such a man was caught up to the* **third heaven.** *And I know how such a man—whether in the body or apart from the body I do not know, God knows— was* **caught up into Paradise** *and heard inexpressible words, which a man is not permitted to speak. On behalf of such a man I will boast; but on my own behalf I will not boast, except in regard to my weaknesses.*

The assumption by many is that if paradise, which is in heaven beyond time and space, is the third heaven, then the second heaven must be space and the first heaven would be earth's atmosphere. All of this is to say that when a Christian's body dies, the spirit of that person begins a journey to be with Christ.

> ***2 Corinthians 5:8*** *we are of good courage, I say, and prefer rather to be absent from the body and to be at home with the Lord.*

Of course, if God wanted to translate us to heaven without having to travel He is certainly powerful enough to do that. However, if we have to travel to heaven, this would explain the dark tunnel and the light at its end. This would mean that upon death, the Christian would traverse the first heaven and the second heaven before arriving at the third heaven. The second heaven would be that dark tunnel many have reported to have walked through. The fact that demonic authorities operate in this area is not strange. They operate in darkness and they have authority.

> ***Ephesians 6:12*** *For our struggle is not against flesh and blood, but against the rulers, against the powers, against the world forces of this darkness, against the spiritual forces of wickedness in the heavenly places.*

The fact that Kathryn appeared younger is by reason of being a spirit without a body. The ravage of age upon our bodies is the effect that sin has upon them. Being born again, the spirit becomes ageless and without sin. She was also dressed in a wedding dress. This also is in keeping with the idea of being the Bride of Christ. We are going to a wedding.

> ***Revelation 19:7-9*** *"Let us rejoice and be glad and give the glory to Him, for the marriage of the Lamb has come and **His bride** has made herself ready."* It

*was given to her **to clothe herself in fine linen**, bright and clean; for the fine linen is the righteous acts of the saints. Then he said to me, "Write, 'Blessed are those who are invited to the marriage supper of the Lamb.' " And he said to me, "These are true words of God."*

The concentration of the demonic hordes is for the purpose of deceiving Christians in particular. We are their greatest threat and if they can keep us neutralized from fulfilling our destiny in the power of God, they can keep the world under Satan's control. Interestingly, God only let her know the identity of one of the Christians that she saw. Why this is interesting is that we had no idea of any deceptions being in this person's life at the time. Shortly after this event, we were scheduled to travel to Florida to visit family. We had received some tapes a year earlier from this person who was identified as being in deception, so we figured we had better listen to them.

As we were listening to the tapes of her pastor, we almost drove off the road when we heard some of the things he was saying. Things like, *"I am Holy Spirit, you are Holy Spirit."* He even told the ushers to lock the door so that no one could leave. He stated that we do not need to evangelize our families as they will not be in hell forever. Once their punishment is over they will join us in heaven. What nonsense! Then he began to espouse the doctrine that we are gods which was why he was calling himself the Holy Spirit.

In light of what Kathryn saw, we were stunned. We had no idea this person was in a church like this. God was validating Kathryn's journey with that information.

I had been developing our lessons for the Bible institute on spiritual warfare and this experience confirmed what I was writing. Our warfare is an ideological one where deceptions are the weapons of the enemy and truth is the weapon of God. This will become quite clear as you proceed through this book.

When the demonic leaders began to accuse Kathryn, those accusations were of things she had done wrong. They could not, however, reach her by reason of the three instances of the word "accuser."

> ***Zechariah 3:1-4*** *Then he showed me Joshua the high priest standing before the angel of the* LORD, *and* ***Satan standing at his right hand to accuse him****. The* LORD *said to Satan, "The* LORD *rebuke you, Satan! Indeed, the* LORD *who has chosen Jerusalem rebuke you! Is this not a brand plucked from the fire?" Now Joshua was clothed with filthy garments and standing before the angel. He spoke and said to those who were standing before him, saying, "Remove the filthy garments from him." Again he said to him,* ***"See, I have taken your iniquity away from you and will clothe you with festal robes."***

> ***Revelation 12:10*** *Then I heard a loud voice in heaven, saying, "Now the salvation, and the power, and the kingdom of our God and the authority of His Christ have come, for the* ***accuser*** *of our brethren has been thrown down, he who* ***accuses*** *them before our God day and night.*

Satan is constantly trying to pit your Creator against you through the accusation process. Remember that God is the great Judge and if an accusation is leveled against someone, the Judge, being a just Judge, must hear the accusation. We also have an Advocate with the Father which is Christ our Lord. This is our Lawyer in heaven fighting our case for us.

1 John 2:1** My little children, I am writing these things to you so that you may not sin. And if anyone sins, we have an **Advocate with the Father, Jesus Christ the righteous.

Be aware of continually how this battle is forming in your mind. The devil arranges opportunity and tempts you to sin. Upon sinning, he then runs to the Judge in heaven to accuse you of sin so that he can force God's hand to be against you. As a Christian, however, your Savior Jesus steps up to the bench of that court room in heaven and defends you before the Father based upon His blood being poured out to cover your sins.

Based upon this revelation we see that Satan is fighting Christians on three fronts. They are:

1. Deceptions through the twisting of Scripture.
2. Discouragement through a constant bombardment of discouraging thoughts to our minds.
3. Temptation, accusation, and judgment against the Christian.

Three battlefronts are revealed. We must guard the word of God and not allow it to be polluted with demonic interpretations. We also need to have a clear-cut picture of what God has called us to do. This will help us to guard against discouraging thoughts. The word devil is *diablos* in the Greek and it means to strike repeatedly. The enemy is taking those discouraging thoughts and constantly sending them to our minds. If we keep the Word of God pure in our hearts, we will have a defense ready for the attack of discouragement.

Finally, the enemy tries to undermine you with sin. He will tempt you and set you in places where you are not able to overcome because of your flesh. Then upon falling, he will use discouragement while attempting to get God to come against you for it as well.

Here we have the battle plan of the enemy. As you can see, he cannot strike you directly. This is why much of what we know to be termed spiritual warfare is actually a ruse of the enemy to get us to fight a battle that is nonexistent. Kathryn's journey revealed those three fronts as well; the demonic leaders twisting the scripture, the demonic discouraging word factory, and the accusation of the enemy.

Kathryn did see the light at the end of that journey and God did speak to her. Speaking from that light ahead, He said, *"Do you see all of this? I am way more powerful than they are."* God is God and He is able to defend and protect those that belong to Him. You have nothing to fear as a child of God. You are victorious through Him and He will set you above your enemies! Now I invite you to take a journey and allow the Bible to define for you and me the battle we are in.

In The Beginning – Warfare!

Chapter Two

> **Genesis 3:1** *Now the serpent was more **crafty** than any beast of the field which the Lord God had made. And he said to the woman, "Indeed, **has God said**, 'You shall not eat from any tree of the garden'?"*

To understand our enemy we need to look at the first encounter that man had with him. Right from the beginning we note that he is crafty. His craft? Deception! The first thing the enemy does is to try to bring doubt concerning what God has said.

The word "crafty" is the Hebrew word *aruwm* and is from the root word for "to be naked" or "to uncover." The idea is the revelation of the malevolent mind. In that revelation we find a sinister nature that has been around from the creation of man to present. That is a long time to study human behavior.

We need to take note of the fact that truth had to be spoken first. That is, if there were no truth, there could be no deception. Deception can only thrive when there is a truth for it to hide. The hiding of truth is the great end goal of any deception. Truth will always bring freedom to the upright and exposure to the wicked. Truth had been established and that wonder, the Word of God, had brought life.

Through his word which is always deception, Satan and his malevolent mind brought death. Not a death inflicted through an action of demonic strength or ability, but a death that is self-inflicted through, and here is the rub, trust in the devil. It was trust in the devil that brought death to mankind. You can slice it anyway you want and you still wind up with that simplistic end result, trust in an evil malevolent creature. Not only trust in him, but trust in his words as superior over a trust in the Creator who is benevolent.

How awful, you say. Yes, and you too are guilty! How many of us have believed that God did not love us at some point in our lives? You may have been going through a rough time. There may have been a death, the loss of a marriage, persecution, or abuse. This left you feeling abandoned and as if God did not care. Right? You heard the words as they formed in your mind, *"God does not care about me,"* or *"God has abandoned me."* There could have been a thousand different combinations of words all with the same outcome—the diminishing of your worth in the eyes of God. You believed—and at that moment you too trusted the words of Satan as superior to the words of your Creator.

It could also take on a much more subtle nature, but the outcome is still the same; either the diminishing of yourself, another, or God. It could be as simple as you saying, *"I can't do that"* after realizing God has given you a task to do. Explore that for a second. Do you think the Creator of all things would give you a task that you could not accomplish? Thinking that God would do this makes Him out to be without knowledge, or incapable of working through you. Why do you think the anger of the Lord burned against Moses when God had given him an assignment and he responded with, *"I can't talk right?"*

As much as can be noted about the attack of an enemy, there is so much more that can be noted by what the enemy did not do. Observe that Satan revealed no other power but that of deception. This is not to say he had no other power, but that all he revealed was the power of deception. Could it be that Satan was holding out, was not revealing all of his cards?

In the power of deception there must be a convincing of the victim to accept what is said as truth. Since it is opposed to reality, the truth must be masked or hidden. This is what was done to the first man and woman God created.

We must understand some things that can give us insight into the enemy's restrictions. Adam and Eve are still in relationship with God, and because of this Satan is unable to harm them. In fact, even after the fall there are some things that the enemy cannot do. Think about this, if the enemy, according to the words of Jesus, only comes to steal, kill, and destroy, why did he not just kill Adam and Eve himself? Again, we can learn a lot by what our enemy does not do here.

Why does Satan talk to Eve instead of destroy or even possess her? I raise these questions because a lot of what we hear regarding spiritual warfare in our Christian churches only serves to magnify the power of Satan beyond what he is capable of, rather than enforce the victory won by Christ. Apparently, Satan is restricted in his ability to harm God's creation. I want the reader to understand this. This is not underestimating Satan, it is revealing him.

> ***Genesis 2:17*** *but from the tree of the knowledge of good and evil you shall not eat, for in the day that you eat from **it** you will surely die."*

I highlighted the word "it" because in the Hebrew "it" is a **him**, not an it. This is how the Hebrew reads according to the Lexham Hebrew-English Interlinear Bible.

> *"QUOTE"*
>
> *"And from the tree of the knowledge of good and evil not you shall eat from **him** because on the day of eating you from **him** die die."*

As you can see the tree is not an ordinary tree. This personalization of the tree becomes clearer as we continue. For now I want to concentrate on what the tree is. The tree's name tells us one thing about the tree, and the tree's Creator and planter tells us something else about the tree.

To begin with, the tree's name, the knowledge of good and evil, identifies that this was a tree that possessed special ability. How can a tree's fruit transfer knowledge of anything? I am not aware of any tree known to us today that has the ability to transfer knowledge. Therefore, I think we can assume this is a one-of-a-kind tree. To say it was the apple tree as folklore tells us is to suggest that the tree reproduced and we are still partaking of knowledge when we eat the apple.

There has been a lot said about what the knowledge was that would be transferred when consuming this fruit. Although, if we stay true to its name we already know what the knowledge is of. It is very simply the knowledge of good and the knowledge of evil. I need to mention at this point that many subscribe to Matthew Henry's commentary on this tree where he basically says that the tree was not special, only the command not to partake of it and in the event Adam partakes of it, he will understand through his own disobedience the knowledge of good and evil.

I disagree with this. If the only way to know good and evil is by making an evil choice, then how does God know good and evil? In other words, if the tree is the knowledge of good and evil and it is God's creation, whose knowledge of good and evil does it represent? It would be God's knowledge of good and evil. Remember, God stated in Genesis 3:22 that man had become like God in that he now has the knowledge of good and evil.

Now, if we were traveling to another country and we wanted to find out what that country accepted as good and evil behavior, how would we find this information? Would we not access their laws? There was a time when you reached the age where you were able to get a license to drive an automobile. You were not just given the keys to a car. You were taught the law concerning the operation of a motor vehicle.

That is why I believe this tree of the knowledge of good and evil represented the ways of God, His statutes, His laws. The question is begged at this point, *"Did Adam and Eve receive the law of God when they consumed the fruit and if so, in what form did it take in them?"* I would answer "yes" to the first part of the question and to the second part I would say that it took the form of their **conscience**.

Mysteriously, every human being has a conscience that seems to have the same knowledge on it as other human beings. This is not to say that the conscience cannot be manipulated or altered. What I am saying is that we can observe from culture to culture the existence of certain moral principles. The founding fathers of the United States of America succinctly put it this way in the Declaration of Independence.

> *"We hold these truths to be self-evident, that all men are created equal, that they are endowed by their Creator with certain unalienable Rights, that among these are Life, Liberty and the pursuit of Happiness."*

There is something within us all that we understand to be self-evident. In fact, we are even shocked when others do not seem to exhibit those same traits. Why would we be shocked at the murder of a two-year-old when animals kill their young all the time? Why is it different for us? And why do we know that it is wrong? Where does this information come from and why do the majority of human beings arrange their lives and laws to reflect these ideas? Most importantly, why do we assume that others should have this knowledge as well?

If this knowledge is common knowledge and we were not instructed in it, where did it come from? We gasp when someone does something that is against this common knowledge, but why? Is there an expectation within us that all other human beings have this same knowledge? Is there biblical proof of this common knowledge among humans?

> **Romans 2:14-15** *For when Gentiles who do not have the Law do instinctively the things of the Law, these, not having the Law, are a law to themselves, in that they show the work of* **the Law written in their hearts,** *their* **conscience** *bearing witness and their thoughts alternately accusing or else defending them,*

Those questions can only be answered by understanding that the conscience of man has this information written upon it. What was Adam and Eve's response when they partook of the tree of the knowledge of good and evil? Their eyes were opened to their nakedness and they sought to cover themselves. They were ashamed of their nakedness. Where did that information come from? Why are humans the only species that covers their body?

When God came to the garden to speak to them, they told God they were naked. God's response was, *"Who told you that you were naked?" "Have you eaten from the tree of which I commanded you not to eat?"* Why would God say that unless that information came from the tree? This is an important revelation.

God knew that man could never live according to His ways which are His laws. God knew that in the day Adam and Eve had knowledge of His ways they would be responsible to abide by them perfectly or He, the Righteous Judge, would have to kill them. This means that God never had intentions of mere men having to live at the same standard as God lives. Here we see the ultimate love of God, and we also see the ultimate abhorrence of Satan for both God and mankind.

Think of a newborn baby. Why don't we expect them to use the toilet? Why don't we expect them to feed themselves? We understand that as a newborn they are incapable of living like we do. We understand they do not have the same level of knowledge and ability that we do, therefore, we do not hold them responsible to that knowledge. We do not discipline a baby when they wet their diaper. We are like that newborn baby in comparison with the vast knowledge and ability of our Creator. So it makes sense that God did not want us to have that knowledge, He wanted us to be like the newborn and just enjoy a relationship that would be a great joy between a parent and a child.

Satan knew what he was doing in tricking Adam and Eve. I'll bet he thought he could force God into a position where God would have to kill those He loved. What a sinister, maniacal, and twisted being who would take pleasure from forcing a Father to have to kill His children because of the Father's laws. There would be no recusing Himself from that decision as God alone is the Judge of all His creation.

Nevertheless, God will never be outsmarted by one of His creatures. God was well aware of what man would do in response to Satan. God had already seen the cross with His own Son hanging on it, the only remedy to man's plight. This raises an irritation in me. We see this cultural trend rising in the Church that suggests there are many ways to salvation. They say, *"How dare you say Jesus is the only way to heaven."* Well, how dare you say that He is not the only way!

Who do you think you are! How much of the knowledge of the universe do you have at your disposal whereby you can make such a statement? When one understands the concept of original sin then they can see that yes, Jesus is the only way to heaven!

Since it took eating fruit to bring death upon all of us human beings, we would now have to eat fruit again to bring eternal life.

> ***John 6:53-58*** *So Jesus said to them, "Truly, truly, I say to you, unless you **eat** the flesh of the Son of Man and drink His blood, you have no life in yourselves. He who **eats** My flesh and drinks My blood has eternal life, and I will raise him up on the last day. For My flesh is true food, and My blood is true drink."*
>
> *56 "He who **eats** My flesh and drinks My blood abides in Me, and I in him. As the living Father sent Me, and I live because of the Father, so he who **eats** Me, he also will live because of Me. This is the bread which came down out of heaven; not as the fathers ate and died; he who **eats** this bread will live forever."*

Keep in mind that Jesus is called the Word. As we consume the Word by faith we have eternal life, and we celebrate our faith through the act of communion.

The "Tree of Life," however, has now swallowed up the "Tree of the knowledge of good and evil" just as Moses' rod swallowed up the other serpents that were the rods of the Egyptians. Jesus fulfilled the tree of the knowledge of good and evil by following every law found in it. It was as if there were seeds in that forbidden fruit; with each seed representing a law of the Creator and taking deep root into the heart of man. As a species created in God's image, we have upon us a death sentence. We are all guilty.

God's Son hung on a tree we call the cross. He died and took the punishment for our inability to do all that the tree demands. He nailed the knowledge of good and evil to the cross;

He placed it back onto a tree where it belonged. Then as we partake of the fruit hanging from that bloody cross, as we eat His flesh and drink His blood, we have life! Now we would have to eat from death in order to have life! The only thing the devil had to use against us to cause our eternal death—accusation—has been taken away. Glory to God in the highest!

> ***Colossians 2:13-15** When you were dead in your transgressions and the uncircumcision of your flesh, He made you alive together with Him, having forgiven us all our transgressions, having canceled out the certificate of debt consisting of decrees against us, which was hostile to us; and He has taken it out of the way, having nailed it to the cross.* **When He had disarmed the rulers and authorities, He made a public display of them, having triumphed over them through Him.**

When Paul used the words, *"He made you alive together with Him..."* I wonder if he was thinking back to that moment in the garden where death was brought not only into the human condition, but into all of creation. Although death came to mankind through a tree by disobedience, now life is brought to mankind through a tree (the cross) by obedience. **Yes! Jesus is the only way to the Father! For only by Him do we have forgiveness of sins.**

I want to draw your attention to the last part of that passage. Notice that rulers and authorities were disarmed. I want to explore this for a moment. First, we need to discern whether Paul is speaking of the spiritual world or the human world. It becomes obvious that worldly authorities have not been disarmed so this must refer to the spiritual realm. This begs the question, *"If your enemy has been disarmed, why do you act as if he is holding you hostage?"*

Many of the people I have come in contact with in the Body of Christ act as if they are powerless against the enemy. Their lives reflect a weak Savior and a strong enemy. Is it no wonder that the Bible tells us to magnify God? So much has been said and written that magnifies the power of the enemy when his true state is one of defeat and submission.

If we are ever to become effective in warfare, we need to understand where our enemy is already defeated so we do not waste time and resources fighting an artificial battle. Real warfare must be waged in order to resist the operations of our enemy. Recall that when Jesus was resurrected, life just defeated death!

> *1 Corinthians 15:54-55 But when this perishable will have put on the imperishable, and this mortal will have put on immortality, then will come about the saying that is written, "**Death is swallowed up in victory.** O death, where is your victory? O death, where is your sting?"*

> *2 Corinthians 5:4-5 For indeed while we are in this tent, we groan, being burdened, because we do not want to be unclothed but to be clothed, so that what is mortal will be **swallowed up by life**. Now He who prepared us for this very purpose is God, who gave to us the Spirit as a pledge.*

The tree of the knowledge of good and evil has been swallowed up by the tree of the cross. The fruit of the cross now has the power to set us free from fruit of the tree of the knowledge of good and evil. Jesus is our Tree of Life! The Tree of Life is also a "Him." Whereas the devil was tempting Eve to partake of the fruit of that tree, now he is trying to prevent humanity from partaking of the fruit of the cross. Do not underestimate the power of the "one way!"

As we get back to Genesis, take note that in the following exchange Eve had softened the punishment that God declared in chapter two.

> **Genesis 3:1** *Now the serpent was more crafty than any beast of the field which the Lord God had made. And he said to the woman,* **"Indeed, has God said,** *'You shall not eat from any tree of the garden?'"*

Observe the tactic of the enemy. He immediately seeks to undermine the Word of God. He tries to cast doubt in Eve's mind of the validity of God's statements. This is the great battlefield that is left undiscovered in the Church. *"Indeed, has God said…"* is a phrase that reveals more about the enemy than we may be aware of on the surface.

The word "indeed" is a primitive root word that means "burning." It is the picture of judgment. Judgment demands a just or right verdict in order for the punishment to be just or right. Thus, the word also means to be "right." When the serpent asks the question, he is undermining God's right judgment or righteousness. In other words, he is undermining the character of God. If you will pay attention to your thoughts you will find that same sadistic voice undermining the character of God at every turn in your mind.

We lose our job and we hear that voice, a loved one dies and we hear that voice, someone calls us worthless and we hear that voice always undermining God's character. Consequently, in order to battle this first in our own minds, we must have an understanding of and belief in the character and nature of God. God is always good. God is always just. God is always right. God is always true. Anything that would suggest God is not any one of those is meant to ultimately destroy you!

This is why that beautiful Hebraic culture developed a thing called "block logic." Block logic is a way of protecting the nature of God through interpretation of events. If, for instance, an event takes place that causes one to question God's nature, this system would set the record straight and maintain God's integrity.

Block logic is the compartmentalization of God's absolute nature. God never ceases to be any of the things He attributes to His own nature. When God reveals that He is love, there is no time where we can say God did not love. Even though the action may appear as such, the reality is, God is love. So we judge the circumstance, or event, through the nature of God.

How many people have lost their faith in God because they were unable to interpret their circumstance through God's absolute nature? I am reminded of a man all of you are familiar with; Charles Darwin, who wrote "Origin of the Species." Darwin started out as a half-hearted theologian. But then his daughter died when she was young and he became convinced that God did not exist. He could not reconcile the death of his daughter with the actions of a loving God, ergo, God does not exist.

Can you see the enemy's hand in this? No doubt, as he was doing with Eve, he was doing with Charles. That ploy was to undermine the nature or judgments of God. Pay attention to your own thoughts and you will find the enemy trying relentlessly to undermine what God has said. Following this line of thinking, ponder the following.

> ***Matthew 13:19*** *"When anyone hears the word of the kingdom and does not understand it, the evil one comes and snatches away what has been sown in his heart. This is the one on whom seed was sown beside the road."*

Any time we are faced with a situation that we cannot apply understanding to from the Word of God, like the death of a daughter or son, then the enemy comes and steals the words that were sown. What I am saying is that when we hear God is love and then are faced with a situation where we need to apply that truth to the situation, and we do not understand God's love, the enemy can steal that word from our heart.

Like Darwin, we will begin to doubt even the existence of the Almighty. This is what Satan was doing with Eve. He was trying to undermine God's rightness. Like: Perhaps God is not pure in His dealings. Maybe there is an ulterior motive to God's actions. Maybe He just wants to keep me stupid so I will do what He says. If you have found yourself questioning God, you have been a victim of the enemy's tactic of undermining God's right judgment.

> ***Genesis 3:2-3*** *The woman said to the serpent, "From the fruit of the trees of the garden we may eat; but from the fruit of the tree which is in the middle of the garden, God has said, 'You shall not eat from it or touch it, or you will die.'"*

A couple things need to be commented on with regard to Eve's response to the devil's accusation. First, Eve has added to what God said. God's command concerning the tree did not include not touching the tree. She changed the command. God's words are not to be changed, even if you think you are making his command stronger. Just as important as not taking anything away from God's Word is adding something to it. Yet, Eve not only added to the command of God, but she also took away from it. To see this we need to look again at how the Lexham Hebrew-English Interlinear Bible renders that last sentence.

> *"QUOTE"*
>
> *"And from the fruit of the tree that is in the midst of the garden said God not you shall eat from him and not touch on him lest you die."*

Observe that in the Lexham rendering of Genesis 2:17 where God is giving His command concerning the tree, he said "die" twice. When a word is repeated in Hebrew it is done so to give strength and emphasis to it. This is why in the NASB in 2:17 it is rendered "surely die" and in 3:3 it is rendered just "die." This shows that Eve is already changing the strength of what God said.

Before you become critical of Eve, be aware that Satan could have been the one undermining this in her consciousness before he decided to tempt her with the forbidden fruit. Again, the tactic of the enemy is to undermine the true nature of God to the end that in your mind, God becomes something He is not—repulsive. As we proceed in Genesis, detect the change in boldness from Satan after Eve made her reply.

> **Genesis 3:4-5** *The serpent said to the woman, "You surely will not die! "For God knows that in the day you eat from it your eyes will be opened, and you will be like God, knowing good and evil."*

If this were not so serious it would be laughable. Satan actually quotes God correctly by using the term "die" twice, whereas Eve did not. However, he rebukes the idea that they would die. I can just hear him now. *"How could God kill you if He loved you?"* This is so important to remember. Satan is always deflating God's nature in your mind.

Other than the statement that they would not die, what lie was told to Eve? Surprisingly, it was **not** the words that Satan spoke about becoming like God. Here we can learn another important lesson regarding the tactic of the enemy. He will use a truth and slightly twist its intention which is a nuance often overlooked by Christians. Note the following:

> **Genesis 3:22** *Then the Lord God said, "Behold, the man has become like one of Us, knowing good and evil; and now, he might stretch out his hand, and take also from the tree of life, and eat, and live forever."*

God had not revealed to Adam and Eve this truth about becoming like Him, yet the devil knew it. Moreover, it must be said that Adam and Eve would not become like God, but they would become like God only in that they now have knowledge of good and evil. This supports my thesis that the tree is the Law or nature of God.

For the moment, we need to look at the twist that Satan used. The twist was changing the intent of God for not eating of the tree. Satan will quote God accurately, but he changes God's intent that He put upon His words. This is how the devil has craftily deceived men and women since the beginning of mankind. What was the twist?

Satan accused God of not wanting Adam and Eve to eat of the tree because they would be elevated to God status concerning knowledge. Notice the difference in intent. What is the real reason God did not want them to eat of that tree? Was God afraid of Adam and Eve becoming a god on par with Himself? On the other hand, more likely, was God trying to protect them from being responsible for a standard they could not attain because being made in the image of God, they would be responsible with that knowledge of good and evil?

God's intent for that command was one of protection. God's intent was born out of love and kindness for His creation. God knew that if Adam and Eve did eat they would have to die, and for this reason God did not want them to eat of it. Again, if the tree represents God's laws, then partaking of this information would cause Adam and Eve to become responsible for every action since they would understand what actions are good and what actions are evil. In addition, knowing that these laws are a picture of God's nature, how would God's creation be able to live up to the perfection that can only belong to God?

The enemy, however, had changed God's intent to make God look smug, elitist, and prideful. According to the devil, God did not want His creation eating from this tree because they would become gods as well. See how this subtle change in intent impugns God? Now God looks weak and barely able to hold onto His seat of power. Any minute someone might become like Him and perhaps dethrone Him. How absurd! For someone who is not familiar with God's nature though, it becomes believable to them.

Since we have knowledge of these tactics of the enemy, I want to take a look at his nature. He is busy impugning God's nature while he is hiding his own. *"The lady doth protest too much,"* Shakespeare aptly penned. How typical that the accuser is actually those things he accuses others of.

Serpent

At this point we need to look at one of the terms given for Satan. What is interesting is that God is fully aware at all times of the movement of His enemy. He is never surprised by a tactic or strategy. Satan will never be able to outmaneuver or outsmart God. Satan cannot even spawn a thought without God knowing before he thought it.

The fact that he continues to try speaks of the evil of his nature. I think this has been lost on the Church; that the devil is so evil he cannot stop doing what he is doing even though he knows that ultimately it will not work. His defeat, he is unmistakably aware of. Look at what the demons in the demoniac said just before Jesus extricated them. *"Are you come to torment us before our time?"* Is that not a glaring statement of destiny?

"QUOTE"

Hebrew – Serpent

(naw·khawsh)

נָחָשׁ *m.—(1) a serpent, so called from its hissing (see the root) Gen. 3:1, seq.; Ex. 4:3; 7:15; 2 Ki. 18:4. Used of the constellation of the serpent or dragon in the northern part of the sky,*

ROOT (naw·khash)

TO HISS, TO WHISPER *(zifchen, zifcheln), specially used of the whispering of soothsayers (see* לָחַשׁ *Piel, Psalm 58:6) compare Nasor.* سعر *to whisper (see Cod. Nas. III. p. 88, line 16, 18; II. p. 138, line 9).*

Piel—(1) to practise enchantment, to use sorcery, i.q. Arab. فَنَخَشَ *Lev. 19:26; Deu. 18:10; 2 Ki. 17:17; 21:6. Some understand this of* ὀφιμαντεία, *divination by serpents; as if it were denom. from* נָחָשׁ, *see Bochart, Hieroz. t. i. p. 21.* [1]

Satan whispers to us and casts doubt upon the intent and nature of our God. I found it interesting that this Word mentions a constellation of stars also so named. What of this constellation of the serpent in the northern sky? In light of Kathryn's journey, I am

---

[1] Gesenius

curious to find any evidence to support or refute it. First, I need to get the "north" connection. As I was listening to Kathryn give account of what she saw, I asked her where she was going. Immediately and without pause, she said, *"You know up north."* When she said that, I went in my mind to the Word that states God's throne is in the north.

> ***Job 37:22*** *"Out of the **north** comes golden splendor; Around God is awesome majesty."*

Here we see an allusion to God's throne being in the north. God is outside of space and time. We cannot point to one part of the universe and say, *"There is God's throne."* All the same, God seems to indicate that the entrance to the dimension that begins God's dwelling is in the north.

> ***Isaiah 14:12-14*** *"How you have fallen from heaven, O star of the morning, son of the dawn! You have been cut down to the earth, You who have weakened the nations! But you said in your heart, 'I will ascend to heaven; I will raise my throne above the stars of God, And I will sit on the mount of assembly **In the recesses of the north.** 'I will ascend above the heights of the clouds; I will make myself like the Most High.'"*

This piece of Scripture is attributed to Satan and his rebellion in heaven. Some theologians say that the context suggests this is speaking of an earthly king. I would point out, however, that verse twelve seems to be saying that whoever this is speaking about seems to have had access to heaven. What else can be meant by *"cut down to the earth?"* What I want to point out is that we have mention of the north again with regard to God's throne.

On to the constellation called the twisted serpent. If this is a constellation in the northern sky, is God trying to tell us something? Are there some truths we can learn from this? Does God even want us looking at constellations?

> ***Genesis 1:14*** *Then God said, "Let there be lights in the expanse of the heavens to separate the day from the night, and let them be for signs and for seasons and for days and years."*

Could this mean God has placed signs in the stars and that we can see His creative hand, His imprint, and His signature in their arrangement? I believe God has shown us things in the heavens. Even God speaks of the names of constellations so I think we are free to look. The only caution is that we do not start worshiping or developing extra-biblical doctrines.

> ***Job 26:13*** *"By His breath the heavens are cleared; is hand has pierced the **fleeing serpent**."*

If God's throne is beyond the north of the heavens, and at the gate of that realm we call heaven is a constellation called the twisted serpent, and we know that Satan is called the serpent or dragon, and we also know that Satan was kicked out of heaven, then is this constellation actually a picture of Satan being removed from heaven? If this is so, then the picture that we have of our enemy is that he is running for his life from a holy God.

> ***Luke 10:18*** *And He said to them, "I was watching Satan fall from heaven like lightning."*

Make no mistake, Satan was fleeing! Imagine when God made the stars that He would arrange one constellation to be an everlasting picture for us of the utterly conquered state of the one who fights against us. The devil is defeated and we need to have that truth firmly etched in our hearts.

> ***Isaiah 27:1*** *In that day the Lord will punish Leviathan the **fleeing serpent**,* WITH HIS FIERCE AND

> *GREAT AND MIGHTY SWORD, Even Leviathan the **twisted serpent**; And He will kill the dragon who lives in the sea.*

Satan twists everything God says. He is a twisted serpent. After man was separated from God, Satan could rule over him. That is what the devil wanted all along. It is always about power with him. He wants to rule over man and in order to do that man must be separated from God. The rebellion of Adam accomplished that. Even so, God's plan for us would reunite or reconcile us back to Him. When man was reconnected back to God, we received power over Satan.

> **Luke 10:18-19** *And He said to them, "I was watching Satan fall from heaven like lightning. Behold, I have given you authority to tread on serpents and scorpions, and over all the power of the enemy, and nothing will injure you."*

We are now like Adam and Eve before they fell. We have been reconciled back to God and Satan is powerless to harm us, but he can still deceive us. Having been restored, we need to know how the enemy is attacking us and what kind of warfare we should be engaged in as Christians.

Faith Academics

Chapter Three

Faith seems to be a strange subject when dealing with the area of spiritual warfare. If one is to be engaged in the battle, however, it is crucial. As you understand what faith is and how it is inseparable with regard to warfare, you will want to make sure that you spend the time necessary to get it into your heart.

For the longest time the word "faith" has been misappropriated, misused, misunderstood, and unexplained. The purpose of this chapter is to get a biblical, working knowledge of what faith really is. The Bible says that *"the just shall live by faith."* I think that qualifies it to be an important enough subject to study so that we can better live a life of faith. We are going to define faith, find out where it comes from, and how to increase our faith.

What is Faith?

When asking that question you will get about as many different responses as the number of people you ask. This is indicative of the fact that this important subject has a lot of confusion surrounding it. There is only one right answer to the question, *"What is biblical faith?"* The right answer is always the truth and the truth will always set you free.

Anytime we are incorrectly taught about a subject, whether biblical or otherwise, and we believe that false information, we are in bondage to it. We are in bondage because our actions are then based upon something believed to be true that is not. This is why truth always has the quality that it will set you free.

If I wanted to wallpaper a room in my house, but did not know how to do it, I would seek out someone who could teach me how to apply wallpaper. If that teacher taught me incorrectly and I proceeded to install the wallpaper using the faulty instructions I received, I would be in bondage to a terrible result as a direct consequence of being taught a lie.

If, however, I learn the correct way to apply the wallpaper, the job becomes easier and the finished product looks so much better. Now it results in the comfort of being in a room that looks and feels wonderful.

Let's apply this to biblical teaching and realize that the truth will literally set you free. The Bible has instructions and answers to life issues that we have to deal with everyday. If we can apply truth to each issue, then we are much better prepared to deal with issues in a way that will result in consequences that are in line with both what our Lord wants for our lives and our own expectations. We know Jesus said I came to give you life and to give it more abundantly. But in order to access this life we must walk the path of truth that leads to the abundant life.

What is Biblical Faith?

The word *"faith"* is a word that encompasses many different meanings among believers. This stems from various reasons, namely that the New Testament Christian uses the word extensively and in many different ways. What I would like to do is nail down some fundamental definitions of the word so we may better understand it, and how it can enhance our relationship with God and with our brothers and sisters in Christ.

Definition

faith n. 1. Confident belief in the truth, value, or trustworthiness of a person, an idea, or a thing.

[Middle English, from Anglo-Norman fed, from Latin fides. (From which we get our word "fidelity") See bheidh- means "to abide."][2]

What Biblical Faith is Not

First, let's deal with what biblical faith is not.

(A) Biblical faith is not a denomination. Baptist is not faith, Assembly of God is not faith, Presbyterian is not faith, Methodist is not faith, Lutheran is not faith, and Catholic is not faith. Biblical faith cannot be reduced to the definition of a denomination. To speak of denominations in this way suggests that each denomination has a different faith and this leaves the impression that denominations are completely different in what they accept as truth.

(B) Biblical faith is not belief alone. Belief is necessary for faith to be active and living, but it is not faith by itself. *"The devils also believe in God and tremble."*

(C) Biblical faith is not blind faith. God has given us reason for our faith.

In light of the question that Jesus asks in Luke 18:8 *("...however, when the Son of Man comes, will He find faith on the earth?")*, I think it would be a good idea to find out just what it is that He means. He obviously knew the answer to His own question; therefore, the question is for our benefit, not His.

THE HEBREW WORD "FAITH"

Faith in the Hebrew language carried the idea of firmness, steadfastness, security, and truth.

---

[2] American Heritage Dictionary

אָמַן —*(1) (aman) prop. to prop, to stay, to sustain, to support* [3]

You should recognize this Hebrew word. You end your prayers with it! Although we have come to say "amen," it is derived from this word. What does it mean then when we end our prayers with this word? It means faithful. We pray and then at the end of that prayer we make a declaration of the faithfulness of God. He is faithful to hear and answer my prayer.

The picture that the Hebrew language is trying to draw for you concerning the word *"faith"* is something upon which you can confidently put your full weight. It is something firm. I like to use the analogy of a chair. When we sit in our favorite chair at home, we don't even wonder if it will hold us. We sit down in that chair having faith that it will carry our weight. Why do we have faith in the chair? Because the chair has proven itself faithful.

THE GREEK WORD "FAITH"

The Greek has the following meaning:

31.43 pistis-- that which is completely believable--what can be fully believed, that which is worthy of belief, believable evidence, proof. [4]

Findings

From both the Hebrew and the Greek we have the thought of *faithful* even before we have the thought of *faith*. The reason for this is that God has to first be faithful before we can have faith in

---

[3] Gesenius, W., & Tregelles, S. P. (2003). *Gesenius' Hebrew and Chaldee lexicon to the Old Testament Scriptures.*

[4] *Louw, J. P. & Nida, E. A. (1996, c1989). Greek-English lexicon of the New Testament: Based on semantic domains. New York: United Bible societies.*

what He promises. Faith means that it is reliant upon something or someone that is faithful. Again, when I sit down on a chair, because the chair has proven itself faithful, I have faith that it will hold my weight. God is faithful, and He provides proof of His faithfulness. We can put our full weight upon what He says.

Three Parts of Faith

Now I am going to show you that living faith can be broken down into three distinct parts, and if any one of these parts is absent then that faith is dead.

Part One: Revelation Knowledge

The first element needed for faith is revelation knowledge; without it there is nothing to believe. Revelation knowledge is a truth revealed to you by the Holy Spirit. It can come from what someone else is saying by unction, but it is the action of the Holy Spirit that causes you to understand. It can come from reading the Bible, but it is the Holy Spirit that causes one to understand.

> *1 Corinthians 2:14 (KJV) But the natural man receiveth not the things of the Spirit of God: for they are foolishness unto him: neither can he know them, because they are spiritually discerned.*

You received revelation knowledge when you first believed. When you first believed, God revealed Himself to you. In light of who He is, you saw how inadequate you were. As a result, you believed in the sacrifice that was offered to cleanse you of all your sin. It was the work of the Holy Spirit that made that message alive. You knew that it was truth and you believed; that belief made you righteous because your faith was complete by your confession.

> *1 Corinthians 2:3-5 And I was with you in weakness and in fear and in much trembling. And*

*my message and my preaching were not in persuasive words of wisdom, but in **demonstration** of the Spirit and of power, **that your faith should not rest on the wisdom of men, but on the power of God.***

Some might say that "demonstration" is referring to miracles that Paul performed, but the article of the demonstration of the Spirit is Paul's message and preaching. I heard one Greek scholar say that the Greek word for "demonstration" means "to grasp and hold on to." This would seem to indicate further that Paul was not speaking of the manifestation of miracles, but the miracle of the Spirit acting upon the words spoken by Paul to cause a changed life.

"QUOTE"

DEMONSTRATION

*APODEIXIS (ἀπόδειξις , (585)), lit., a pointing out (apo, forth, deiknumi, to show), **a showing or demonstrating by argument**, is found in 1 Cor. 2:4, where the Apostle speaks of a proof, a showing forth or display, by the operation of the Spirit of God in him, as affecting the hearts and lives of his hearers, in contrast to the attempted methods of proof by rhetorical arts and philosophic arguments.* [5]

---

lit. literally

[5] Vine, W., & Bruce, F. (1981; Published in electronic form by Logos Research Systems, 1996). *Vine's Expository dictionary of Old and New Testament words* (292). Old Tappan NJ: Revell.

We can see by the above verses and definition of the word "demonstration" that Paul relied upon the Holy Spirit to reveal the truth. He was just the spokesman of the words of the Holy Spirit. Without the life-giving work and power of the Spirit those words would have meant nothing. Hence, whether the Holy Spirit speaks revelation knowledge to you directly or you hear it through someone else speaking the words, it is the Holy Spirit that interacts with the hearer and is communicating that truth to their spirit. We also see evidence that we are only the mouth piece in the following text.

> ***1 Corinthians 3:5-8*** *What then is Apollos? And what is Paul? servants through whom you believed, even as the Lord gave opportunity to each one. I planted, Apollos watered, but God was causing the growth. So then neither the one who plants nor the one who waters is anything, but God who causes the growth. Now he who plants and he who waters are one; but each will receive his own reward according to his own labor.*

We derive from this that it is not the minister that is anything; all he does is verbalize the words that he feels God is telling him to speak. It is God that causes the growth, and it is God that reveals those words as truth to the person's spirit! So the next logical step is to look at the association of hearing and faith.

> ***Romans 10:17*** *So faith comes from hearing, and hearing by the word of Christ.*

> ***Galatians 3:2*** *This is the only thing I want to find out from you: did you receive the Spirit by the works of the Law or by* ***hearing with faith****?*

> *Galatians 3:5 Does He then, Who provides you with the Spirit and works miracles among you, do it by the works of the Law or by **hearing with faith**?*

Here is the link between faith and hearing. What are we hearing? We are hearing the Word of God. For faith to become alive it starts with hearing, and that hearing is receiving revelation knowledge of the Word of God.

> *Hebrews 11:7 By faith Noah, **being warned by God** about things not yet seen, in reverence prepared an ark for the salvation of his household, by which he condemned the world, and became an heir of the righteousness which is according to faith.*

Noah **heard** God and received revelation knowledge.

> *Hebrews 11:8 By faith Abraham, **when he was called**, obeyed by going out to a place which he was to receive for an inheritance; and he went out, not knowing where he was going.*

Abraham **heard** God and received revelation knowledge.

We could show many more instances of this, but I think you can see that the first step in faith is hearing and receiving revelation knowledge.

Since faith starts by God revealing something to you, then the initiation or authoring of faith is not something that you can control other then availing yourself to hear. In fact, you are at the complete submission of the Holy Spirit. Although you do control whether you hear it in the first place. If you don't put yourself in a place of reading or hearing the Word, then you will not be able to grow your faith. It is interesting, especially in light of the importance that hearing plays in faith, that the word "obey" in the

Greek means "to hear." If we look up "obey" in the Greek this is what we find:

> *"Quote"*
>
> *5219 [hupakouo /hoop·ak·oo·o/] v. **1a** of one who on the knock at the door comes to listen who it is, (the duty of a porter). **2** to harken to a command. **2a** to obey, be obedient to, submit to.[6]*

At the heart of obedience is the hearing of something to which one is to be obedient.

> **Hebrews 12:2** *fixing our eyes on Jesus, the **author and perfecter of faith**, who for the joy set before Him endured the cross, despising the shame, and has sat down at the right hand of the throne of God.*

Faith is not started by you. You cannot work it up. It has to be given by God. Jesus is its Author and Perfecter in our lives. Therefore, it is out of your hands as far as the initiation of faith. The thing in which you are to believe must be given by God. We can conclude from this, that without God giving revelation knowledge, faith cannot exist in us at all.

What we are responsible to do is hear. How many times does the Word say *"...he who has an ear, hear...?"* It is our decision to hear what God is saying to us. This obviously is not talking about just the ability to hear sound with our ears, but the conscious decision to actually listen and digest the information to which you are listening with the intent of understanding.

---

[6] *Strong, J. (1996). The exhaustive concordance of the Bible: (electronic ed.) (G5219). Ontario: Woodside Bible Fellowship.*

Part Two: Belief

The second part of faith is our part. It is belief or acceptance in the revealed knowledge of God. Let's go through this again. First, God reveals truth to you **(part 1)**; then you believe or accept this information as truth **(part 2)**.

So, because we trust God is faithful, we believe.

***Hebrews 11:8** By faith Abraham, when he was called, **obeyed** by going out to a place which he was to receive for an inheritance; and he went out, not knowing where he was going.*

Again, Abraham believed what God told him to do.

***Romans 4:11** and he received the sign of circumcision, a seal of the righteousness of the faith which he had while uncircumcised, that he might be the father of all who believe without being circumcised, that righteousness might be reckoned to them…*

Paul was trying to convey to the Romans that circumcision was meaningless to them. We are not heirs of circumcision, but we are heirs of faith. This was so because God declared Abraham righteous before he was circumcised. Why? It is because he **believed** God. FAITH COMES ALIVE WHEN WE BELIEVE IT AND APPLY IT AS TRUTH TO OUR LIVES.

***Romans 4:19-22** And without becoming weak in faith he contemplated his own body, now as good as dead since he was about a hundred years old, and the deadness of Sarah's womb; yet, with respect to the promise of God, he did not waver in unbelief, but grew strong in faith, giving glory to God, and being fully assured that what He had promised, He* *was able also to perform. Therefore also it was reckoned to him as righteousness.*

This is exactly what faith is. We are so convinced that God will do what He says that we waver not in believing. Notice also that Abraham's faith grows. This means that we can have different levels of faith. Nevertheless, it should be growing, not shrinking or static. Also, if we can show that one can turn away from faith, then we prove that faith is something we have a part in.

1 Timothy 4:1-2 *But the Spirit explicitly says that in later times some will fall away from the faith, paying attention to deceitful spirits and doctrines of demons, by means of the hypocrisy of liars seared in their own conscience as with a branding iron...*

From this section of Scripture we can deduce the following:

- Some will stop believing the faith.
- Some will stop believing the revealed truth given by God.
- Some will stop believing revelation knowledge.
- By not believing, they make living faith dead. They destroy the work the Holy Spirit wants to do in their life.

1 Timothy 5:8 *But if anyone does not provide for his own, and especially for those of his household, he has denied the faith, and is worse than an unbeliever.*

Again, we see that some can turn from faith. So we know by this that it is our part concerning faith to believe the Holy Spirit as He reveals truth to us. You know that God is absolutely, infinitely trustworthy! There is not a SINGLE FLAW in His character. HE IS PERFECT! HE IS ALL KNOWING! HE IS

LOVE! Since we know this is who God is, then we should have no trouble believing and trusting Him.

Part Three: Action

The last part is a natural result or consequence of the first two parts: (God's part) revealed truth and (man's part) believe that truth. The last part is to act (natural result) upon that belief. Faith is something to be obeyed; therefore, it must be something revealed to us (truth, knowledge, information) that requires obedience.

> *James 2:17 Even so faith, if it has no works, is dead, being by itself.*

We might also conclude that works without faith are dead. Many Christians engage in this practice. They quote or speak what they would like, but have no faith. They do things they think they should do, but they have no faith. The work does not guarantee that one has faith, but the lack of work guarantees that they do not have faith.

The works (step 3) portion of faith is necessary to **qualify** your belief (step 2) in the truth revealed to you (step 1).

> *James 2:21-23 Was not Abraham our father justified by works, when he offered up Isaac his son on the altar? You see that faith was working with his works, and as a result of the works, faith was perfected; and the Scripture was fulfilled which says, "And Abraham believed God, and it was reckoned to him as righteousness," and he was called the friend of God.*

You see how James says that faith and **what was done** worked together? The works are a natural result of the belief. If the deeds were not there, then the faith is dead because it is alone; it was not accompanied by belief. If it were, then the deeds would have proven it. Thus, we have the three steps that are necessary for living faith, they are:

1. REVELATION KNOWLEDGE

2. BELIEF

3. DOING

Revelation knowledge *(God's part)* is necessary to initiate faith.

Belief *(man's part)* is necessary to activate faith.

Doing *(natural result of the partnership)* is necessary to qualify or perfect faith.

What I want you to see is that faith is a partnership between God and man. It is not God alone or man alone, but it is both together. It is God working with man and man working with God.

Hebrews 11:1 (KJV) *Now faith is the substance of things hoped for, the evidence of things not seen.*

This is an interesting verse. It is not so much a definition of faith, but a picture of faith. There are some important truths to grasp here. We have two key words; they are *"substance"* and *"evidence."* Let's consider *"substance"* first.

Sub-stance is an excellent translation from the original Greek. *"Sub"* is a prefix that means *"under."* Submarine literally means under the water. Now *"stance"* means *"to stand."* The true picture is something that is under you and able to carry your weight. We could then say the things hoped for are such that we can put our full weight upon that promise. It will carry our weight; we can really thrust all of our trust upon it.

Evidence would be better translated as *"a proof."* Proof is something whereby we can measure something else. The word in the Bible that is used for this word is *"reproof."* The Word of God is a reproof in that we can measure all things we hear against it. So **our action** is the proof that we believe in those things we have not seen.

Conclusion

We have found that faith is composed of two parts with one qualifier as the third part. We can see this at work in many areas of our lives. Every day we do things that require faith. You see, faith is not something that is just blind; it is based on evidence. Albeit the evidence may not be tangible in the sense that others have the same evidence; nevertheless, it is real to you because you heard, believed, and acted upon it.

For instance, if you have a car that will not run, what do you do? You take it to a mechanic. You take it to a particular mechanic based on your trust level in that mechanic. If that mechanic tells you that you will have to replace the engine, you have received revelation knowledge. This is something that you did not know. This is step one in our model of faith. If you trust this mechanic, you will believe what he says. This is step two in our model. Then based on your belief in the knowledge, you allow the mechanic to put a new engine in your car. This is an action on your part that qualified your belief in the knowledge that the mechanic revealed to you. This is step three in our model of faith.

Now, if you did not believe the mechanic, your action would be different. You would have taken your car to another mechanic to get a second opinion. This is how we can see actions proving what you believe. This is why Jesus said that by their fruits or actions you shall know them.

The connection between faith and spiritual warfare will become clear in the next chapter as we delve into the working of the enemy as we can witness in our own past.

Perception vs Reality

Chapter Four

The purpose of this chapter is to give the reader a clear understanding of how to develop their critical thinking skills; to have the tools to develop a competent, accurate world-view; to give them the tools in which to test information to determine its validity.

Influencing the Masses

A few years ago God laid upon my heart to study Hitler's rise to power. In doing so, a particular character began to emerge as one of the biggest influences in helping to bring Hitler to a place of influence. His name was Joseph Goebbels. His job was to make Hitler palatable to the nation of Germany. To do so, he had to make Hitler a virtual god. The means by which this was accomplished was through the media.

What is required for any person or group to effectively communicate their message in and through any medium is the ability to get the audience to perceive their words as the truth. **For some, it is not even important what the truth is, only that the people hearing or viewing their message perceive their words as truth so that their targeted audience can be manipulated into a particular action.**

If the people perceive their message as truth, they will act upon that information, whether it is a vote for a mad man or the purchase of a burrito. The same tactics that Goebbels used are the same tactics that advertisers use. I was even surprised to hear that Goebbels is studied in journalism as a method of effective communication.

Judging

We live in a world that is full of stimuli that is transported by media to our five senses every day. It is through these senses that we process information. Our senses, of themselves, are incapable of making decisions regarding the information they take in. Their only job is to deliver the information they come in contact with to the mind. Our eyes see, our ears hear, our mouth tastes, our nose smells, and our hands touch. All of the information taken in by these senses is delivered to the mind. Once received, our mind processes the information to determine if it is true.

The mind will use the information of all the senses to discern what is happening. For instance, you might be surprised at how much you rely upon your sight to hear. The next time you are in a conversation, ask yourself why you look at the person who is speaking in the mouth, but when you are speaking it is more natural to look them in the eyes. The reason is that the mind is relying on the sight to help the ears hear by reading the lips.

When all of this information is acquired by the mind, it compares it with data already stored in our memory. What information is stored in our memory is determined by many different variables. One of those variables is how long we have been able to acquire data. What I am saying is that at conception, a baby is a virtual blank slate where it concerns memory. That is not to say he or she is not human or that he or she has any less value. We do not place a greater or lesser value on a human being's life by the measure of knowledge they have retained. As a child progresses, knowledge is being added to the memory and the older the child gets, the more information that is stored. The more information that is stored, the more resources a person has from which to compare new information.

Where is our memory? Science tells us that our brain tissue is where our memory is stored. Recently they have even said that our stomach also has a memory. However, from a nonphysical perspective memory takes on a new idea. If you are a spiritual being, you must also have a spiritual memory. In fact, you have a perfect photographic memory in your spirit. Think about this for a moment. When you die your spirit separates from your body and retains none of the organic matter of the body in its separation.

Therefore, if memory were just organic, one would be in a state of not even knowing who they were at death. Yet, biblically, we can see that we retain our identity when we leave the body, and we know who people are and their relationship to us while on earth. So I would propose to you that your true memory is spiritual and located in your spirit.

> NOTE
>
> *Nearly every culture associates age with wisdom. It is the natural progression of information evaluation that causes this view to be born out. We must, however, note that just because information has been accepted as being true, that does not make it so.*

Children begin assimilating information from their surroundings. As the parents teach the children, the children accept that information as truth and store it in their memory. Then as children get older, other factors come into play. Their field of information increases as they become more cognitively developed and increase their sources of information outside the confines of their home.

It is at this point and time that teachers, friends, and relatives all become part of the information resources. As children's cognitive abilities increase, they may even begin to question some of the information received from their parents as they take in contrary information. Now that we have a good understanding on how we take in information, what do we do with it once it is there?

Programming

When we receive information that we perceive to be true, we store it. We then use that stored information, which has already been accepted as truth, to compare with any new data. We do this to determine the possibility of that new information being reliable and true or being unreliable and false. If the information received is determined to be true, it is stored to become part of our collection of truths. If it is determined to be false, it is discarded with a note to our memory that any other information that is like this is to be immediately discarded.

So we have *"anchored"* information that we perceive as truth and *"tagged"* information that we perceive as false. This is great if what you have already perceived as true actually lines up with what is reality. If the *anchored* information that you have is false, then you are deceived. If the *tagged* information is true, then you are also deceived. Another way of saying it is if what you perceive to be true is a lie and what you perceive to be a lie is true, then you are in a place of deception regarding those things.

There is an old computer programmer's axiom which states, *"Garbage in, garbage out."* That statement means that if I write a software program to be used by a computer and I program in bad code, then the computer can only do what it is programmed to do, and in this case it will operate badly because of bad code.

Deprogramming

When someone is in this state of deception, they need to undergo a system of deprogramming to release those false concepts and ideas if they are to ever receive the truth into the areas they have been deceived. If you have ever had to deal with a person who was raised by their parents in a cultic belief system, you will see the devastation that floods the person upon learning that their parents were not correct. It then becomes a long journey of healing for them as they begin to reprogram their belief system upon truth.

Testing

As we grow up, we begin to test all that we have accepted thus far as true. We use our logical abilities to test for illogical positions. When we find what appears to be an illogical position, we reject it or we test it further, and if it holds to be logical, we modify our belief system. However, not everyone does this. Those that are too comfortable with what they already believe will refuse to test it. This is where we get the connection to spiritual warfare. When we are so sure that we have the truth, we will never be able to hear anything else. How then will you be able to be set free from deception if you are unwilling to even hear?

Something else I have observed with regard to human behavior. When a person has a belief that is illogical or even self refuting, but they are not cognizant that it is illogical, the result is unidentified confusion. You see, the subconscious may understand that the position is illogical. You have therefore set up an illogical construct in your subconscious that will return confusion to your mind. The more dogmatic you become over that illogical position, the more difficult it is to recognize it.

Unidentified confusion based in dogmatic belief will nearly always manifest in a refusal to hear a differing opinion. This can even happen to us as Christians if we are not careful. If we do not understand our faith in which we become dogmatic, we become people that are closed off with regard to hearing and ineffective in presenting our beliefs in a way that makes sense. God is reasonable. You may not see Him physically, but you see Him like the wind. You can see His signature in creation.

Why is it two people can get the same information and one might say it is true and the other may say it is a lie? It is because of the information they have anchored and tagged. What do they consider to be true and what do they consider to be a lie?

Deceiving

In order to get adults to believe information that is NOT based in truth, there has to be a series of truths that validate or qualify the whole of the information. In other words, truth mixed or twisted with lies can deceive. Certain elements of truth are piggybacked with false information so that when the truth is accepted, oftentimes so is the lie. When this method is used the elements of truth have to be so plain and simple that anyone would be a fool not to accept it. However, the lies that ride upon that truth have to be small bits of information that will not counter the plain simple truth, in other words, a twisting of the truth.

All of us are victims of this, we have been fooled into trusting people who were not who we thought they were. Their message started out as sweet, but eventually the actions of the individual belied the words they spoke. This is what Jesus meant when He said, *"By their fruits you shall know them."* Notice He did not say, *"By their words."* **In reality, it is actions that speak louder than words.**

Painting

This is the foundation of true faith. Faith is that which we believe and act upon with our lives. How many times have we seen someone talk about the courage they would have when faced with a certain situation; then upon being faced with that situation react completely different than what their words portrayed?

Sometimes WE speak words that paint a picture of who WE would like to be, or who WE would like people to think WE are. In fact, we often deceive ourselves by conversation out of our own mouths that portrays what we would like to be.

We have to be honest with ourselves if we are going to live in reality. Reality may not be pretty and neat in many situations, but if you are to be sane and sound in your thinking, you will need to face reality and deal with it as it arises. Herein we find another problem. People have found many different ways to escape their reality, which gives rise to isolation or even addictions.

Deceiving the Conscience

I want to get back to Goebbels now and look at some of his techniques. Remember that Satan only comes to kill, steal, and destroy. Although, as a spiritual being without a body, he is limited in his ability to accomplish those things. He needs to convince others to do it for him. This is important to understand. Satan does not go around murdering because he cannot. But what if he can convince you to do it? Then he can murder through you. Goebbels convinced a multitude of people to consider the Jews worth killing. How is it you can get that large a number of people to consider exterminating a particular group of human beings?

In studying this, I notice that there has to be an attack on two fronts. First, convince the masses that Jews are not fully human. This is done to alleviate the natural instinct of moral behavior among humans that tells all of us that killing innocent human beings is wrong. That is the law of God written upon all of our consciences. But if what you are killing is thought to be nothing more than an animal, then it becomes morally permissible. This is a process that I call *"deceiving the conscience."*

Labeling

Let's look at a quote from Goebbels.

> *QUOTE*
>
> *"That is an elementary principle of racial, national and social hygiene. They will never give us rest. If they could, they would drive one nation after another into war against us. Who cares about their difficulties, they who only want to force the world to accept their bloody financial domination?* **The Jews are a parasitic race that feeds like a foul fungus on the cultures of healthy but ignorant peoples.** *There is only one effective measure: cut them out."* [7]

Look at how he words his message. He uses the terms *"parasitic race"* and *"a foul fungus."* These words are designed to **dehumanize** the Jews in the eyes of the German people. Let's look at another one.

> *QUOTE*
>
> *"The fact that the Jew still lives among us is no proof that he belongs among us, just as a* ***flea*** *is not a household pet simply because it lives in a house."* [8]

And again...

---

[7] -Goebbels

[8] -Goebbels

> *QUOTE*
>
> *"Provided one has the power to do so, the Jews must be destroyed once and for all, **like rats**. In Germany we have, thank God, already dealt with the matter fully. I hope that the world will learn an example from it."* [9]

Here the fully-human Jews are portrayed as *"rats"* and *"fleas."* Then Goebbels actually thanks God that the German people have exterminated them. Still, this is not enough to get normal people to the place that they are willing to kill other humans. This leads to the second thing necessary for the deception to be complete.

God's Work

After dehumanizing the ones that he wanted killed, it was time for the other propaganda machine to come into play again. The second front upon which the war for the minds of the German people was waged was that of doing God's work. First, you dehumanize, and then you make the subject think they are doing a moral act by killing the Jew. Look at the following quote.

> *QUOTE*
>
> *"If we Germans have a fateful flaw in our national character, it is forgetfulness. This failing speaks well of our human decency and generosity, but not always for our political wisdom or intelligence. We think everyone else is as good natured as we are."* [10]

---

[9] -Goebbels

[10] -Goebbels

All of this brought to bear the systematic extermination of the Jewish race with the blessings of the masses. First, the conscience must be deceived in order to silence it with regard to morality. Second, convince them that they are morally servicing their fellow man in doing so. If this is a pattern that transcends human behavior and is therefore from the realm of spirits, then we must look for this same method being employed across generations.

Take today for instance. What group of people has been dehumanized in order to justify their killing? Yes, babies. Not only are they dehumanized by being called a part of the mother's body when scientifically that is impossible, but they are also called a blob of tissue, not a human being. Next, the action of killing must be moralized. Thus, the mother hears discouraging comments, such as there is a problem with over population, or because of finances she would not be able to properly care for the child, and so on.

Take some time to think about it and you will see this same pattern employed no matter what time frame you look at. Think of some other groups of people this has happened to. It won't take you long to see the same method being used time and time again.

Warnings

Make no mistake; the German people were warned. Look at the following quote from Gregor Strasser made in 1932.

> QUOTE
>
> *"Whatever happens, mark what I say. From now on Germany is in the hands of an Austrian, who is a congenital liar (Hitler), a former officer who is a pervert (Röhm), and a clubfoot (Goebbels). And*

I tell you the last is the worst of them all. This is Satan in human form." [11]

There were a number of German people who would not be fooled by this regime. They were the heroes of their people. Some of them paid with their life and possessions to bring to light the truth.

How to Keep From Being Deceived

How can we protect ourselves from being deceived? No one wants to be led astray. Are there things we can do that will keep us walking in truth? Yes! God did not leave us defenseless against our enemy, rather He defeated him. So can you!

Conscious Perceiving

If we are to be careful in our walk to make sure that we do not become pawns in Satan's army to fight his fight against God, we must understand that we all live at the level of **perception**. What we perceive as real is what drives our actions. If those perceptions are not based on truth, we act upon lies. We must understand that only God is and knows absolute truth, so knowing our own weaknesses can help us defend against the attack of deception.

The Source of Truth

In order to protect us from entering into deception, we need a source of truth that is absolutely reliable whereby we can compare all information in order to validate it; especially with regard to morality. Jesus said, *"I am the way, the truth, and the life...."* Jesus made the claim that He was reality, that He was

---

[11] - Gregor Strasser, 1932.

absolute truth; therefore, His words are truth. In fact, that is what John said, *"Thy word is truth."*

To sum this up: We have God, Who is absolute truth, and He provided writings that are absolute truth. By reason of this, we must know the truth before the truth can set us free. We have His Word, but if we do not study it we have no foundation for reality.

Trojan Horse Deception

I have heard people say so many times that they only live by the words Jesus said and they deny the rest of the Bible. Many of us are at least guilty of placing more importance on the red letters in our Bibles. When you study the Scriptures, however, you will see that Jesus affirmed much of the Old Testament by quoting from it as truth. If we are to have a standard of absolute truth, we must also accept the Bible's statements no matter how much it may offend us.

It is not the truth that is the problem, it is us. People begin to accept morally corrupt practices when those practices come to their world. Look at the time in which we live. Homosexuality is a practice that many are now calling moral. When a person declares that it is an abomination, they are harangued as the immoral one. We must hold to the truth no matter how painful the consequences. God has provided a model for morality and law. Even if we find that we have broken those standards, we must always acknowledge those standards as right and true.

In our most recent presidential election I paid attention to what seemed to be important to people. I noted that intellectual prowess and the ability to speak well was extremely important qualities when considering the leader of the free world. However, intellectual prowess and verdant speech are not moral qualities. Hitler was considered a great speaker. How is it that we have been fooled into thinking these qualities are the more essential ones.

Morality should be our number one consideration with regard to choosing those who lead this nation.

You see, we are all just the summation of our own **perceived** realities. We all produce a model within ourselves that we build our lives around. This is termed as your worldview. **When that model is based in reality, we mimic Christ.** Yet, many of us have a model that is based partially in truth and partially in a lie. The most dangerous lie is the one that is a Trojan horse disguising itself in truth. This is how Satan has been deceiving mankind from our beginning.

Examples: Twelve Spies

Let's take a journey through the Bible and see if we can find examples of perception versus reality. The first one that comes to mind is the account of the twelve spies as told in the book of Numbers. Moses chose twelve spies, one from each of the twelve tribes of Israel, to go into the Promise Land to check it out. All twelve spies saw the same things, but there were two different reports.

Ten of the spies said there were mighty people in the land and they would not be able to take it. The other two spies said that God will deliver the inhabitants into their hands. They were ready to go take the land. What was the real story or reality? The reality was that God had indeed wanted the people to have faith and take the land as He had instructed.

The difference of the two reports was based in the difference of the level of faith the two groups had. I told you faith was important to spiritual warfare. The group of two had seen God do miracles, mighty acts of power, and deliver His people. They were confident that God would be faithful to deliver the enemy into their hands. The group of ten, even though they had seen God do the same mighty acts, had not applied it as faith in their lives.

They were not driven by the truth of God's protection, and thus, they had a different report. The truth was that God was going to give them the land. The report of the spies, however, was able to convince the masses that they were doomed if they attempted to take the land.

Example: The Temptation of Jesus

> ***Matthew 4:5-7*** *Then the devil took Him into the holy city and had Him stand on the pinnacle of the temple, and said to Him, "If You are the Son of God, throw Yourself down; for it is written, 'He will command His angels concerning You,' and 'On their hands they will bear You up, so that You will not strike Your foot against a stone.'" Jesus said to him, "On the other hand, it is written, 'You shall not put the Lord your God to the test.'"*

I want you to notice again that Satan quoted the Scripture accurately. It was the truth. That begs the question, *"If it was quoted accurately, what was wrong with it?"* It is in the hidden meanings that we find the deception. On the surface the quote was true, but hidden within the quote was a false interpretation of Scripture. **A false intent was applied to a correct text.** This is Satan's modus operandi.

Indeed, the Scripture does tell us that the angels of God would bear up the Messiah so that He would not even dash His foot against a stone. The twist, however, is found in that Satan was asking Jesus to purposely cast Himself off the cliff. The Scripture was worded to protect the Messiah against an accident. Satan quoted it with the hidden meaning of doing a foolish thing on purpose. Jesus identified it as testing God, which we are commanded not to do.

This is why Jesus revealed Satan's false interpretation with another Scripture. This shows us that Satan's interpretation must be at fault. This is a classic Trojan horse deception and is a good model upon which we can understand it.

Evidence

- ***Touching:*** *Have you ever stuck you hand in cold water and thought it was hot at first?*
- ***Hearing:*** *Have you ever heard a sound that you thought was something that it was not?*
- ***Smelling:*** *Have you ever smelled something that was not what you thought it was?*
- ***Tasting:*** *How many times have you eaten something that tasted like something else?*
- ***Seeing:*** *How about your sight, have you ever thought you saw something that turned out to be an illusion?*

Esteem Extremes

What we can rely on is what God says, what He said in the Bible. If we let that be our standard of measure, we can keep ourselves from being deceived. If we look at the problems that people have, we find most often there is a belief that is not founded in truth. This, in reality, the source of their problem. Look at all the self-esteem problems we have, not just low self-esteem, but the egotistical as well. Both extremes are based in lies. The low self-esteem belief is destroyed by the fact that God sent Jesus to die in your place. The egotistical belief is destroyed by the Bible's statement that we all have sinned and come short of the glory of God.

A biblically-balanced viewpoint is what happens when we allow the God of the Bible to define reality for us. It puts us in the place of perfect balance and in His will. **In fact, reality is seeing things the same way that God sees them.** God always sees things the way they really are because He is the Creator of all things. He is the source of reality! You may hate yourself, but God loves you. That is reality.

Reprogramming

As I wrote earlier, the process of programming ourselves with truth is by our belief. Many times we think we believe something, but then our practices prove something else. The Bible gives us some clues on how this is accomplished. We have to look at the seat of the will.

Interestingly, the Bible speaks of a willing mind, a willing heart, and a willing spirit. So there seems to be a seat of will on all three fronts. The heart seems to be a term for the inner man as a whole, which would include both spirit and conscience. The heart is the only part that is talked about as having tablets. In order to understand what I am saying, let's take a look at a particular verse that will help us to get an idea of the difference.

> ***Proverbs 3:3*** *Let not mercy and truth forsake you; bind them around your neck, write them on the tablet of your heart...*

From this we see that man has the ability to write information on the heart. There is a huge difference in information that comes into the mind and knowledge that is written upon the heart. The knowledge that is written upon the heart is information that we have accepted as truth with the mind, information that becomes fixed in us to the point of belief and which will guide our actions for as long as it is accepted as true. Information in the mind is just information that has not yet been accepted as truth.

The problem arises in all of us when some of the knowledge written upon our hearts is not actually true. When we have knowledge written upon the stone tablets of our hearts, and that knowledge is in reality not true, then our life will be guided by a lie and our actions will prove it.

My dad always explained this process of writing truths to the heart as *"swallowing it."* We all know what this is like. We have all experienced the swallowing of certain information as truth and made it a part of our lives, but the chiseling of certain information upon our hearts seems rather final.

According to the letter to the Romans, Paul says that all have the law of God written on the heart. That would constitute our conscience. The word conscience is a compound word: "con" means "with" and "science" means "knowledge." When you put them together it means "with knowledge." A pain of conscience is that prick in our heart that we feel when we do something wrong. The conscience is a powerful component in informing us of our actions regarding morality.

Softening

> ***Ezekiel 36:26-28*** *"I will give you a new heart and put a new spirit within you; I will take the heart of stone out of your flesh and give you a heart of flesh. I will put My Spirit within you and cause you to walk in My statutes, and you will keep My judgments and do them. Then you shall dwell in the land that I gave to your fathers; you shall be My people, and I will be your God."*

This is the act of God's grace upon our lives. He will give us a new heart upon which are written the truths of His reality. That is why we see people's lives change when they receive Jesus. We become a new creation and old things pass away and behold all things are new (2 Cor. 5:17). Our actions are predicated upon the information written upon our hearts. Change the information in the heart and you change the actions. The act of the new birth in which the Spirit of God comes to dwell in the heart of a man causes that man to act differently.

This is why so many people who say they believe in God actually show no evidence of that belief in their life. They only believed with the mind, but never wrote it upon their hearts. This is why Paul said the following:

> **Romans 10:9-10** *"that if you confess with your mouth the Lord Jesus and believe in your heart that God has raised Him from the dead, you will be saved. For with the heart one believes unto righteousness, and with the mouth confession is made unto salvation."*

We have to believe with the heart to be saved, not just our minds. We have to come to the place of swallowing that truth and thereby be converted by the Word Who is Christ. From that point on we will possess certain changes in our behavior that reflect the changes in our heart. That is what faith is; it is information that you have written upon your heart as truth which then becomes knowledge. It is not enough just to believe in God with our minds; it must go to the depths of our hearts in order to bring us to salvation. Believing with the mind is not really belief at all because information in the mind has not been processed as being true or false.

Passion

We cannot mistake passion for truth. How many times have the passionate been wrong? Your passion on any subject is not the proof of its validity. Does your belief upon which you are so passionate agree with the Scriptures? That can be the only standard for truth. **It is upon the words of God that reality dwells, and this is what we must write upon the tablets of our hearts.**

The Bible warns us that, *"There is a way that seems right to a man, but the end thereof is death"* (Prov. 14:12, 16:25). We must go beyond perceiving what truth is, and we must ground ourselves in truth and the reality of the Word of God. We cannot be passionate about something that is against God's moral standard and then claim that we are in truth.

The word *"Christian"* means to be a follower of Christ. How many times do we see people who claim to be a follower of Jesus and yet reject what He says? It happens every two years with our major elections. People who believe they are followers of Christ vote for individuals that support the killing of the unborn and homosexuality. Rather than vote their conscience upon which is written the laws of God, they vote their pocketbook. As Christians we need to get back to morality voting rather than financial voting.

Speech vs. Action

We hear people say, *"I believe in God,"* and then say homosexuality is not a sin. We hear people say, *"I believe in God,"* and then say a woman has the right to kill her unborn baby. We hear people say, *"I believe in God,"* and then justify cheating on their spouse. We hear people say, *"I believe in God,"* and then say the Bible is just myth. We hear people say, *"I believe in God,"* and then say that all religions lead to the same God. That is why Jesus said, *"Why do you call me Lord and do not the things I say?"* (Luke 6:46). **There is an adultery of the heart and mind that states one thing and then does another.** James tells us to be doers of the word, not hearers only (James 1:22). It is in the doing that what is written upon the heart is actually revealed.

Guarding the Truth

It does not mean that after conversion we will not commit sin anymore. We still have the influence of the enemy and the sin that dwells in our body working on our minds, but we also have the power of a changed heart and the help of the Holy Spirit to overcome that sin.

Peace

Let's then understand the peace of God. It is like a closed loop that is self existent as long as we allow it to exist. The best way to understand what peace does is to look at why it is absent, so we can determine why it is there in the first place. The lack of peace is directly tied to two things; willfully diverting your path from the will of God and not believing what the Giver of that peace says. It is our heart's belief that brings us peace, and it is peace that guards our heart's belief. When we believe in the words that our Savior has said, we have peace. We know without a doubt that our destiny is set and sure that nothing can destroy it. When trouble comes, the peace that is produced by that belief will carry us through.

> ***Philippians 4:7*** *"And the peace of God, which surpasses all comprehension, will* ***guard*** *your hearts and your minds in Christ Jesus."*

> ***1 Timothy 6:20-21*** *"O Timothy,* ***guard*** *what has been entrusted to you, avoiding worldly and empty chatter and the opposing arguments of what is falsely called "knowledge"- which some have*

professed and thus gone astray from the faith. Grace be with you."

The Spirit of Truth vs. the Spirit of Error

Going astray from the faith is tied to false knowledge. When we believe something that is false, we live in untruth. It is that untruth that will destroy faith in God. Once we allow precepts that are contrary to the Word of God to be written upon our hearts, our faith begins to take on water and shipwreck is just a short time away. It is the foundation of truth that sustains us, and from this foundation of truth we have peace. It is that foundation whereby we know the spirit of truth and the spirit of error. Make no mistake; false knowledge is widespread in our society today. It is rampant in our government, flourishes in our colleges, lives in our schools, and resides in our churches.

It is not a problem just of this time period, but is traced back to the very Garden of Eden. We must be aware of the Devil's devices and be able to distinguish between truth and error.

> ***1 John 4:4-6 (The Message)*** *"My dear children, you come from God and belong to God. You have already won a big victory over those false teachers, for the Spirit in you is far stronger than anything in the world. These people belong to the Christ-denying world. They talk the world's language and the world eats it up. But we come from God and belong to God. Anyone who knows God, understands us and listens. The person who has nothing to do with God will, of course, not listen to us. This is another test for telling the Spirit of Truth from the spirit of deception."*

Notice that we can tell a spirit of error by the fact that it will not even listen to the truth. This is paramount in understanding truth. If we are not willing to hear an opposing opinion, we are operating in a spirit of error. It is in hearing opposing opinions that actually make the truth in you even stronger. In Acts 17 the Bereans were called a nobler people because they were willing to hear this new gospel and searched the Scriptures to see if it were true. That is the spirit of truth. It searches to prove what is said rather than just outright rejection of it. Those that claim Christians are intolerant are also those that will not tolerate hearing the message of Christ.

Intolerance

When we look at society today we are all too often ready to shout from the housetops that we should accept all other beliefs as valid. This is in conflict with the Scriptures, for Jesus made the ultimate "intolerant" statement (as that word is used in today's society) when He said, *"I am the way, the truth, and the life, and no one comes to the Father but by Me"* (John 14:6). Most people today see that statement as Christianity's ultimate statement of intolerance. Consequently, we have to ask the next question.

Rejection

Why are we so surprised about the world not accepting the Christian message from our mouths? Jesus warned us that the world hated Him and that it would hate you too if you are His follower. How many of our brothers and sisters have gone to their grave because of their belief? Yet, how is it that we want to not upset the world for fear of being called intolerant?

Escaping

We must guard our hearts and minds from accepting anything other than what the truth says. Our perception should be in line with reality. So many try to escape reality because of the situations in which they find themselves. They turn to drugs or alcohol to find escape; they turn to suicide to get out completely, so they think. However, none of these things are a solution.

Drug addicts find they must be on drugs all the time and in doing that, they only produce an even more unhappy reality. It then becomes a self-existing circle of need wherein they find that they cannot free themselves from its power. The drugs help them escape, but the drugs also produce the reality from which they are trying to escape. Suicide only puts the person in the state of eternity where there is a reality that they are faced with due to their death. They now stand before God to give an account. That is not a reality that I would like to be in myself.

Trusting

> *2 Timothy 1:12-14 For this reason I also suffer these things, but I am not ashamed; for I know whom I have believed and I am convinced that He is able to guard what I have entrusted to Him until that day. Retain the standard of sound words which you have heard from me, in the faith and love which are in Christ Jesus. Guard, through the Holy Spirit who dwells in us, the treasure which has been entrusted to you.*

Many people do not like to pray to ask for God's protection over them; they feel it is a lack of faith or a sign of weakness. Well, we are weak; it is time we acknowledge that so God's power can be perfected in our weaknesses. Verse 13 says to *"Retain the standard of sound words...."* This is how we guard our hearts and minds. Verse 14 talks about what God has entrusted to us. The picture we get here is that we are to entrust our lives to God, retain sound words, and guard by the Holy Spirit that which God entrusted to us. God is guarding what we give to Him and He wants us to guard what He gives to us.

Conclusion

> ***2 Peter 3:17*** *"You therefore, beloved, knowing this beforehand, be on your guard lest, being carried away by the error of unprincipled men, you fall from your own steadfastness."*

This verse tells us that it is the error that causes us to fall. God has delivered to us the words from which we are to believe. This belief then causes us to align our perception with reality; producing a lasting peace if we hold to it and act upon it.

If we were only to look at the examples of history, we would see a clear picture of what happens when we choose to live under knowledge that is false. It will produce sorrow and bondage every time. It will hinder our destiny, stifle peace, destroy relationships, and produce error. It can do no good and will produce no good. We must hold to the foundation of reality, that standard of words that are so clearly put forth in our Bibles, and that will lead us to meaningful, peaceful, and productive lives. Anything else is only perception.

The Road To Freedom

Chapter Five

The word "freedom" conjures up many pictures in the minds of us all. For the Christian it has a different meaning than to the non-Christian. Some look at it in the sense of physical freedom, others see it as political freedom, and still others see it as social freedom. But for the Christian, what does it mean and how do we obtain it? Once obtained, how do we keep it?

Jesus said, *"So if the Son makes you free, you will be free indeed."* To understand your freedom you must first understand your bondage. If you do not understand your bondage, you would not know the need to be free. We find that Jesus gave us a picture of both bondage and freedom. We can understand more about both of them by looking at the very thing Jesus told us would set us free.

> ***John 8:32*** *...and you will know the truth, and the truth will make you free.*

If truth is the component that sets us free, conversely, deception must be the component that puts us in bondage. If truth is the tool that Jesus has given us whereby we may set others free, then conversely, a lie or deception is the tool by which the enemy puts people into bondage. This is not a surprising statement, since we can see who the Purveyor of truth is and who the purveyor of lies is. The purpose of a lie is to hide the truth. There is no other logical intention of a lie than to keep its hearer from knowing what is real.

> ***John 8:43-47*** *Why do you not understand what I am saying? It is because you cannot hear My word. "You are of your father the devil, and you want to*

> *do the desires of your father. He was a murderer from the beginning, and does not stand in the truth because there is no truth in him. Whenever he speaks a lie, he speaks from his own nature, for he is a liar and the father of lies. "But because I speak the truth, you do not believe Me. "Which one of you convicts Me of sin? If I speak truth, why do you not believe Me? "He who is of God hears the words of God; for this reason you do not hear them, because you are not of God.*

This is an interesting piece of Scripture and it sets the stage for understanding where our spiritual warfare really takes place. Jesus first asked a question and followed by answering His own question. Obviously, there is no need for Him to answer His own question, unless, He is trying to teach a principle that is important. He gave a very telling answer to His own question. He said, *"It is because you cannot HEAR My word."*

Either your frame of information is based in truth, is based in deception, or it is a mixture of truth and deception. As I pointed out earlier, God seeks to draw us into truth; the devil seeks to draw us into a fantasy of lies. Therefore, if a person is incapable of hearing the truth, the only conclusion is that their frame of reference (which is that which they already believe to be true) is based in deception.

Keep in mind what we learned about the devil from the Garden of Eden experience. Jesus told the Jewish political and religious leaders that they were of their father the devil. Were the leaders of Israel worshiping the devil? No! How then could Jesus make this statement? They apparently had accepted the devil's words as true and this is what kept them from being able to hear the truth from God Himself. That is what made Satan their father or in other words, their leader. This is what Satan has always been after; getting mankind to follow him instead of God. By understanding this passage we learn that this is accomplished through believing the devil's lies.

> ***2 Corinthians 4:4*** *...in whose case the god of this world has **blinded the minds of the unbelieving** so that they might not see the light of the gospel of the glory of Christ, who is the image of God.*

It is not enough to just hear the truth; it must be heard and believed. Once information is rejected, a person will not hear that information again, that is, they will not even accept hearing it. Even though the ears may hear the sounds that produce the words that compose the sentences that convey the ideas, the heart is disengaged and is neither hearing nor willing to do so.

Recall that when information is accepted, it is accepted based upon the belief that the information is accurate and true. Once accepted, this information is used as a filter to determine whether other information heard is true or false. People are unable to hear the truth because they think that what they believe is the truth when in actuality it is not. Think about the simplicity of this. Those that heard the truth with their physical ears were incapable of hearing the truth with their hearts (spiritual ears).

You have heard the statement, *"It's written in stone"* to project the idea that it is unalterable. As we pointed out in the last chapter, the Bible tells us that our hearts have tablets on which things are written.

> ***Proverbs 3:3*** *Do not let kindness and truth leave you; Bind them around your neck, Write them on the tablet of your heart.*

I think this is a parallel to the tablets of stone in which God wrote the law. That is why I believe this is the place where our core beliefs are held. For the sake of clarity I will reiterate this principle. When our minds receive information from our senses, we weigh that information against what we already perceive to be true in our hearts.

Notice I used the word "perceive." This means we possess the ability to write information to the tablet of our heart that is NOT true. Once we have done this, when we hear something that goes against this "perceived truth," we will reject it outright. That is why Jesus told the Jews they could not hear His words because although they could hear with their physical ears, they could not hear with the ears of their heart. This was because they had a core belief system based in information that was gathered from the devil and was false. Moreover, that made the devil their leader whether they were cognizant of it or not.

I recently witnessed one example of this. It was a "Christian" who believed the lie of evolution. He was so convinced of it and even taught that it was in the Bible. When he was confronted with the truth that destroyed that concept, he refused to believe it, and remained in his deception as if he had never even heard the evidence.

When you accept a deception as truth, everything becomes skewed and you create a world for yourself that is no longer real. Thus, you become enslaved to a lie. A false belief will distort reality and that which you think you know to be real is actually not real at all.

Ask anyone around you if what they are afraid of is real to them. If it were not, they would not be afraid. Most fear is actually based in deception. It is the belief in something in the future that is not based in truth, but in an experience in the past. Those suffering from fear have allowed a false concept to be written upon their hearts. Fear can also be measured in risk. That is, some fears are valid based upon the risk factor. Would it be natural to have some fear going into space on the space shuttle?

Truth states that you are the apple of God's eye; He loves you and cares for you and your life is completely in His hands! If you believe otherwise, you have allowed a deception to rule your reality which gives you only a perception of what is real. Often times fear is based on past experiences that were very real, but that is not a determination of the future.

> *Example*
>
> *For instance, if a person's car was struck by a semi truck running a red light, they may have developed a fear of semi trucks. So now their view of semi trucks is such that they believe they will be struck by one. Now, that statement is untrue because it is based in conjecture not fact (fact states that it is possible to be struck by a semi truck, but not certain,) nevertheless, the reality of experience overpowers that which is unknown.*

Herein we find the problem with fear. We often allow past experiences to interpret our future. This is deception. How can we overcome this fear? By knowing that God loves you and your life; that He is in control and by knowing that death is not a cessation of existence. These things the Bible teaches us. So, if we believe the things that God has said to us, then we are able to overcome fears that hinder us.

> **Hebrews 2:15** *and might free those who through* **fear of death** *were subject to* **slavery** *all their lives.*

The Greatest Danger

If I were to ask people, *"What is the most dangerous thing to us as Christians that we should be fighting against more than anything else?"* I would get all kinds of responses. I would probably hear it is the devil or demons. Our greatest danger is the very thing that puts us in bondage. If we look at the actions of most Christians, however, we do not see a battle being waged on this front. What we see is either a disengagement altogether from the battle or we see great battles taking place, but on false fronts.

> ***Matthew 4:8-11*** *Again, the devil took Him to a very high mountain and showed Him all the kingdoms of the world and their glory; and he said to Him, "All these things I will give You, if You fall down and worship me." Then Jesus said to him, "Go, Satan! For it is written, 'YOU SHALL WORSHIP THE LORD YOUR GOD, AND SERVE HIM ONLY.' " Then the devil left Him; and behold, angels came and began to minister to Him.*

God can only act and speak in truth and the devil can only act and speak in lies, each seeking the will and heart of man to accomplish their respective wills. God seeks the heart of man that He might bless him and bring him into His family where He can care for Him; furthermore, so that the man might be used of God to bless others and thus accomplish His will to provide abundant life. Satan seeks the heart of man that he might destroy him and use him to destroy others, thus accomplishing his will.

> ***2 Corinthians 4:3-4*** *And even if our gospel is veiled, it is veiled to those who are perishing, in whose case the god of this world has blinded the minds of the unbelieving so that they might not see the light of the gospel of the glory of Christ, who is the image of God.*

In this we see the result of deception which is able to put its believer in bondage so they cannot hear the truth. Now that we know where the real threat is, let's move into the next logical phase and that is, how do we operate in truth and how do we guard against lies?

> ***John 10:10*** *The thief comes only to steal and kill and destroy; I came that they may have life, and have it abundantly.*

Here we have the two great motives for mankind and each of us must decide whether we will serve God's purposes planned for us, or will we serve the enemy's purposes planned for us. There is no middle ground; either you are accomplishing God's will or the enemy's. There are no positions of neutrality. Even though we all like to think that we are doing good things, if they are not based in obedience to the Spirit of God, they have the capacity to be used by the enemy. Even those things that to the natural man look like acts of compassion, if they are not in obedience to Christ there is no accomplishing of God's will.

> ***Ephesians 5:6 (RSV)*** *Let no one deceive you with **empty** words, for it is because of these things that the wrath of God comes upon the sons of disobedience.*

The word "empty" in that verse is the Greek [kenos /ken·os/] and means to be "devoid of truth." Your enemy the devil seeks to hide the truth with words devoid of truth to the end that you will become deceived and thereby become bound by your actions to do the devil's will. When we believe what God says, that is faith, and it opens a window of opportunity for God to accomplish His will through us. When we believe a lie, that too is faith, and it opens a window of opportunity for the devil to accomplish his will.

The Greatest Safety

We must understand that as humans we are capable only of perception, as previously mentioned. Reality is the quality or state of being actual or true. True is being consistent with fact or reality. By this we know that God is Reality because God is Truth, therefore, knowing reality is seeing everything through His eyes and is the same as knowing the truth.

> ***John 17:17** Sanctify them in the truth; Your word is truth.*

That means if we want to know what is real concerning anything, we need to see it through the mind of God. We do not know all things as God does, but God will let us know what we need to know that we may have a worldview that is based in reality. Recall that Jesus said, *"you shall know the truth and the truth shall set you free?"* Knowing the truth; believing the truth is the act of experiencing reality.

> ***1 Corinthians 2:11-12** For who among men knows the thoughts of a man except the spirit of the man which is in him? Even so the thoughts of God no one knows except the Spirit of God. Now we have received, not the spirit of the world, but the Spirit who is from God, so that we may know the things freely given to us by God,*

Since the believer has the Spirit of God, they are capable of living in reality. This is because the Spirit of God will lead them and guide them into all truth. The un-believer is incapable of living in reality because they do not possess the Spirit of truth. That is why the Scripture goes on to say:

> ***1 Corinthians 2:14** But a natural man does not accept the things of the Spirit of God, for they are*

foolishness to him; and he cannot understand them, because they are spiritually appraised.

The natural man thinks he is living in reality; he cannot see that he is deceived by the enemy. This is because our perceptions are the reality we create for our worldview. As a result, that which we believe to be true becomes our reality. No matter if that which is believed to be true is actually false. If it is false, then that reality is a pseudo-reality.

For instance, there are those who believe God does not exist. Their belief does not change the facts. If they were to die they would certainly know that God does, indeed, exist. Yet, their life is lived based on their own perceptions, and to them their perceptions are real. Consequently, their perceptions define their worldview. Thus, they live their life defining their own morals because they do not believe in God. Of these it is said in 2 Timothy 3:7 that they are *"always learning and never able to come to the knowledge of the truth."*

Not only does the believer have the Spirit of God that leads and guides them into all truth, but they also have certain principles that we know are real. These principles are found in our bibles, and God has given them to us that we might have the tools with which to test our environment to establish that which is true and that which is error.

The world does not accept the doctrines of Christ, but it will accept the doctrines of the devil. Accordingly, when people refuse to listen to the words in the Bible they are destined to operate in error, and we are able to tell what spirit they are operating from. This is just like Jesus' question. *"Why can't you hear what I say?"*

> ***1 Timothy 4:1*** *But the Spirit explicitly says that in later times some will fall away from the faith,*

paying attention to deceitful spirits and doctrines of demons...

Testing

We as Christians can determine what is truth and what is deception. One way to do that is to test what is being offered. I have found that those that are presenting what they believe to be truth accept being tested and even welcome it, but deception rebels against testing.

I have used this principle many times to determine if the person is offering what is true or is trying to deceive. Those that are presenting things that are false get upset when you question them. The reason for this is that they know if tested they cannot defend what they are saying and may even be found out. Those that are presenting what they believe to be truth are happy to discuss it further to enlighten you to it because they believe they can defend it. This does not necessarily tell us what truth is, but does tell us if the person teaching is trying to present the truth or a deception.

Here we need to differentiate between lying and deception. A person who is lying to you is trying to deceive you knowingly. A person who has heard a lie and believed it is deceived. They may repeat that lie to others by presenting it as truth and thereby deceive many without purposely trying to deceive others. This means there are a lot of well meaning folks out there that are deceiving others unknowingly.

We must put to the test everything we hear so that we are able to walk in reality. We also need to test what we already believe to make sure that we walk in truth. We all have a combination of truth and deception that make up our core set of beliefs. **Finding and dismissing deceptions is what brings ever**

greater freedom to your life. Therefore, it should also be your life's quest.

> *1 John 4:1 Beloved, do not believe every spirit, but test the spirits to see whether they are from God, because many false prophets have gone out into the world.*

This is the duty of every Christian. Always test the word you receive to see if it is from God. The first thing we should do is compare it to the written Word of God and ask for the Holy Spirit to enlighten us. If we do these things, we will be assured that we can walk in truth and guard against that which is false.

It is important to understand that we do have a source for absolute truth. Knowing this, we can test information by this standard to determine what is true and therein is your safety. How can we teach what is truth if we are not willing to invest the time to read the only book that has a claim on truth?

There are obstacles in our way that cause us to be unable to receive the mind of Christ. Those obstacles are mindsets.

> *2 Corinthians 10:4-5 (YLT) for the weapons of our warfare are not fleshly, but powerful to God for bringing down of strongholds, reasonings bringing down, and every high thing lifted up against the knowledge of God, and bringing into captivity every thought to the obedience of the Christ...*

Here we find that what we fight directly against are not demons and devils, but rather, we fight against arguments, theories, and reasoning's that are based in false concepts, lies, and deceptions. These false concepts, lies, and deceptions are perpetuated by demons and devils. Wouldn't it be great if Satan was the one that had to say, *"Why can't you hear what I am saying?"* because we have God's truth in our heart and that truth takes captive every thought the enemy plants?

This is where the battle is found and it is also where we find victory. **We do not defeat the devil by just ordering him to leave,** but we do defeat him by believing the Word and quoting it to him. We defeat him when we refuse to believe his lies. Satan seeks to destroy through deception; **therefore, we can destroy his work by knowing the truth**. In order to destroy any of these concepts in your life you must have an open mind to hear the truth.

> ***Acts 17:11 (KJV)*** *These were more noble than those in Thessalonica, in that they received the word with all readiness of mind, and searched the scriptures daily, whether those things were so.*

Here we have a group of people who were ready to hear what others had to say even though it went against what they had already perceived to be true. The pattern laid out for us here we do well to heed. First, they were willing to hear what people had to say, then after hearing them, they searched the scriptures to see if these people were telling the truth.

The result in this case was that these people received the message of the apostles and with gladness received Christ in their hearts. When you **have a closed mind on an issue it means you are incapable of hearing something different that someone is saying.**

This was the problem that Jesus dealt with when trying to teach the truth. We must note here that those He was trying to teach were the religious leaders who were also the teachers of the Law! We must be ready to hear differing opinions and we must be willing to search the scriptures to ferret out that which is true. To do so will make you well able to give a defense for the hope that lies within you.

> ***Mark 16:14** Afterward He appeared to the eleven themselves as they were reclining at the table; and **He reproached them for their unbelief and hardness of heart,** because they had not believed those who had seen Him after He had risen.*

We understand unbelief, but let's consider the meaning of a hard heart as used in this context. It goes back to what I said earlier about information being written to our hearts. A hard heart will not budge from what is written "in stone." But the promise of God toward us is that He will remove our heart of stone and replace it with a heart of flesh. A heart of flesh then is able to adjust to the truth by removing those things that are written upon it that are not true. A heart of stone does not allow this.

Our Armor

When we look at the armor of God we find only two offensive weapons. That is the shield and the sword. One without the other is of little use. Now Paul labels these two weapons as the *"shield of faith"* and the *"sword of the Spirit which is the Word of God."* Let's think on these things for a moment. Remember that faith believes information, converting it to knowledge. So, the Word of God is that information, and faith believes it. Together they set you free!

> ***Ephesians 6:16 (KJV)** Above all, taking the shield of faith, wherewith ye shall be able to quench all the fiery darts of the wicked.*

And there it is. This is the graphic image of the statement, *"bringing into captivity every thought to the obedience of Christ."* When we believe the Word of God we are able to quench or suppress every attack of our enemy, the devil. Truth coupled with belief, which is another way of saying "know the truth," is actually how we are set free. Keep in mind this is a broad theme that must rule our lives for we all have things in us that are pieces of deceptions that have allowed the enemy to access certain recesses of our lives.

Finding and replacing these deceptions with the truth sets us free in that area of our lives. As we use these truths to destroy the strongholds of false concepts in our lives, we find that our lives will become more abundant. The will be filled with life to the full just as Jesus promised us.

> ***Romans 15:13*** *Now may the God of hope fill you with all joy and peace in believing, so that you will abound in hope by the power of the Holy Spirit.*

Faith, the Window to the Spirit Realm

Now the aspect of faith comes fully into the picture. This is needed so that we will have an accurate understanding of the creative power of believing the truth and the destructive power of believing a lie with regard to spiritual warfare.

Faith then becomes a door of access into the spiritual realm. I cannot bring that which is spiritual into a world that is natural unless I do so using faith. **What must be understood though is that this door allows the spirit realm to access me and allows me to access the spirit realm.** When I believe God, I open a door that allows access to God Who is Spirit, and God access to me within the aspect of my faith. This is a spiritual law that governs the whole of the spirit realm.

For instance, I do not have access to salvation unless I first believe. By believing I have access to God for salvation and God has access to me to create a new spirit within me. Let's look at this from another angle.

> ***James 1:5-8*** *But if any of you lacks wisdom, let him ask of God, who gives to all generously and without reproach, and it will be given to him. But he must ask in faith without any doubting, for the one who doubts is like the surf of the sea, driven and tossed by the wind. For that man ought not to expect that he will receive anything from the Lord, being a double-minded man, unstable in all his ways.*

In this example, wisdom is the product, but as with salvation, faith is the currency. If you have no currency, do not expect to receive anything. Why is this important? Because it works the same way with the enemy. However, most people don't willingly have faith in the devil. They must be tricked into it. How are they tricked? By deception! The enemy says something and that is the revelation part of faith, if you believe it you will act upon it and it is that action that the devil is after.

What would it look like to have faith in something the enemy says? Keep in mind, the enemy is powerless with regard to you as a Christian. The only way he can gain power is by trickery. He has to get the Christian to believe, and it is this faith that unleashes the enemy to plunder the Christian's life.

What works with God Who is Spirit also works with the enemy who is a spirit. Both God and Satan are vying for your will. Since you have free will you can do things that are against God's will. Therefore, when we believe God, we are aligning our wills with His. That will provide the atmosphere where God will empower our lives concerning what we believe. Consider this carefully because as I said it works for the whole of the spiritual realm. Recall that faith is really a partnership. It takes a speaker and a believing listener. When we hear a truth and believe it, that is faith.

Hence, if God is the Creator of truth, believing Him opens a door whereby He is able to do miracles in your life. Similarly, if Satan is the creator of lies, believing him opens a door whereby he is able to destroy you. God accomplishes His will through human beings. Satan also accomplishes his will through human beings.

If you believe a deception by Satan, you are aligning your will with Satan and allowing him to use your life. It matters not to him whether you are doing so willfully or through deceit. **The problem is, when people think of spiritual warfare they often do not think of faith, truth, or the Word of God**. But those are the weapons that God has given us to defeat the enemy.

Satan's only weapon against you is deception. If he can get you to believe that he is powerful, then he can be powerful in your life. For instance, if he can get you to believe that you are cursed, then he can curse you. On the other hand, if you believe the words of Jesus when He said that He has given us all power over the enemy, then we close that door of deceptive faith and cease the operations of the enemy in our lives.

This is how it works. First, there must be information that is false. Second, there must be a willing listener. Third, the listener must believe the lie. The result is they open a door to the spirit realm that brings the enemy into their lives.

Hosea 4:6 *My people are destroyed for lack of knowledge….*

It is critically imperative that we put no faith in the things set before us by the enemy. I have heard of so many Christians that have even sought the words of fortunetellers for direction in their lives. Likewise, I have seen Christians afraid of being cursed by Satanist or witches. By believing that those curses have power, they open a door of faith for them to work. If, however, the Christian would believe that these things (curses) have no power over the Christian because of who their God is, then they (curses) would not have power because they place their faith in God.

If we are being transformed into the image of Christ through growing our faith, what does having faith in the enemy do to us? Could it be that that door of faith opened to the enemy causes us to undergo a transformation as well? Only this transformation takes on the nature of the enemy. Could this be the source of anger, bitterness, depression, and on and on? If it is, oh how easy it will be to get them out of our lives by simply coming out of agreement with the devil.

Conclusion

It is my desire that from this you would get understanding. First, the enemy has no power over you where you are walking in truth. When ministers teach that the enemy is totally defeated and powerless against the life that is anchored in truth, then people are free.

Second, understanding that we all have areas that cause us problems in our lives. By finding the principle or belief associated with that problem you are able to get free from it. We must understand that abundant life, as promised by Jesus, is contingent on us believing the words that He spoke.

We cannot access anything from God without faith in God. This is proved out when the disciple asked Jesus the question, *"What must we do to work the works of God?"* That is a very pertinent and important question. You may be surprised by the answer that Jesus gave though. Let's take a look.

> ***John 6:28-29 (KJV)*** *Then said they unto him, What shall we do, that we might work the works of God? Jesus answered and said unto them, This is the work of God, that ye believe on him whom he hath sent.*

In order to do the work of God, we must believe. Indeed, Jesus even said that believing is the work of God. Believing is the key to accessing the things of God. It is the key to working miracles, to raising the dead, to healing the sick, to preaching the gospel! Too often we focus on the actions of a person rather than the thought processes that are behind those actions.

When we look at the foundation framework of a person's belief structure, we can shine the light of the glorious gospel of truth and dispel a thought process that causes them to be in bondage! Do you want to be free? Your road to freedom is paved with truth. By believing and accepting the truth, you dispel lies; you empower God in your life and at the same time you prohibit the enemy! Read and listen to the Word of God and set yourself free completely!

Rules of Engagement

Chapter Six

Many Christians have the wrong idea when it comes to spiritual warfare. The purpose of this chapter is to give the reader an understanding of spiritual warfare, what it is, and what it is not; to prepare the reader to do correct warfare so they might know how to set at liberty first themselves and then others; to properly engage the enemy in the ways taught us by the Master and our King, Jesus.

Who Or What Are We At War With?

> ***Ephesians 6:12*** *For our struggle is not against flesh and blood, but against the rulers, against the powers, against the world forces of this darkness, against the spiritual forces of wickedness in the heavenly places.*

We must keep at the forefront of our minds the idea that we are not at war with people. We are at war with spiritual entities. But we must also be aware of the fact that human beings are the pawns being used to accomplish the devil's will. Understanding this, we must also understand how physical beings can be at war with spiritual beings. After all, I cannot see these spirits and I cannot hit what I cannot see. If that is the case, how do we battle against these invisible beings? What would that battle look like? How do I fight spiritual beings when they do their bidding through humans beings? We have identified our enemy; therefore, to understand the battle, we must understand what the enemy is attacking and how he fights. Since we know who our enemy is, we need to look at his character to better understand what we are facing.

The Names of Satan

The best way to get a good understanding of the enemy is to look at his numerous names. Names are used to bring understanding about the one named. God has several names applied to Him so that people can understand His nature. The same can be applied to the enemy.

- He is called the *"adversary."*
- He is called "Abaddon" in Hebrew which means "destruction" and "Appolyon" in the Greek with means "destroyer."
- He is called the "accuser of the brethren."
- He is called "Beelzebub" which means "lord of the house."
- He is also called "Belial" which means "worthless or wicked."
- He is called "the devil" which in the Greek is "diablos" which is a compound word that means "to strike repeatedly" and it also means "a slanderer or false accuser."
- He is called "a liar" and "the father of lies."
- He is called "the deceiver."
- He is called "a murderer."

With all of these titles in mind he also appears as "an angel of light." This last title should cause us to be very careful with the experiences that people have. Everything must be tested by the Scriptures. We should never have an experience in search of evidence to support it.

We have an idea of the nature of our enemy by the number of titles he is given. By understanding that nature we can also understand some of the methods that he uses to do battle against us. He is an accuser, he accuses us day and night, but he is also a liar so his accusations cannot be trusted. He is a destroyer, so he seeks to destroy with his lies. Now let's take a look at how he wars against humanity.

How Satan Wars Against God & Humanity

> ***2 Corinthians 4:3-4*** *And even if our gospel is veiled, it is veiled to those who are perishing, in whose case the god of this world has blinded the minds of the unbelieving so that they might not see the light of the gospel of the glory of Christ, who is the image of God.*

The devil is constantly blinding the humanity of this world to keep the gospel hidden from them. How does the devil blind mankind? If we look at verse six, we can get the answer to that question.

> ***2 Corinthians 4:6*** *For God, who said, "Light shall shine out of darkness," is the One who has shone in our hearts to give the Light of the knowledge of the glory of God in the face of Christ.*

Physical blindness creates a physical darkness. Spiritual blindness creates a spiritual darkness. Mental blindness creates a **philosophical darkness**. Paul likens the knowledge of God with the light of creation. If the knowledge of God is truth, reality, or what is really real, then blindness or darkness must represent a lack of knowledge or truth and that which is really false or deception. In the place of light, truth, or reality there is only ignorance, lies, and deceptions.

Since the place of blindness is the mind and the spirit, it is either the mind and spirit that is lightened with the truth of God, or the mind and spirit that is darkened with the deception of the enemy. If this is correct, it stands to reason that we should see plenty of evidence in the Bible to back up this idea.

> ***Acts 26:16-18*** *But get up and stand on your feet; for this purpose I have appeared to you, to appoint you a minister and a witness not only to the things which you have seen, but also to the things in which I will appear to you; rescuing you from the Jewish people and from the Gentiles, to whom I am sending you,* **to open their eyes so that they may turn from darkness to light and from the dominion of Satan to God***, that they may receive forgiveness of sins and an inheritance among those who have been sanctified by faith in Me.*

Here is the idea that blindness or darkness represents the dominion of Satan and light represents the dominion of God. Opening the eyes denotes that a person is going from a position of darkness to a position of light, from blindness to seeing, and from deception or ignorance to truth. Ignorance simply does **not** know something. Deception is different in that you have been convinced to believe a different report. Darkness always hides reality, but light will always exposes reality.

> ***Ephesians 5:6-9*** *Let no one deceive you with empty words, for because of these things the wrath of God comes upon the sons of disobedience. Therefore do not be partakers with them; for you were formerly darkness, but now you are Light in the Lord; walk as children of Light (for the fruit of the Light consists in all goodness and righteousness and truth),*

Here again, deception is likened to darkness and light is likened to truth.

> ***Isaiah 5:20 (KJV)*** *Woe unto them that call evil good, and good evil; that put darkness for light, and*

light for darkness; that put bitter for sweet, and sweet for bitter!

Isaiah 42:16 (KJV) *And I will bring the blind by a way that they knew not; I will lead them in paths that they have not known: I will make darkness light before them, and crooked things straight. These things will I do unto them, and not forsake them.*

This presents us with a good example of both ideas of deception and ignorance equaling darkness. Calling good evil is deception, but following a path in darkness denotes ignorance.

It is important to draw these conclusions in order to understand what is meant by spiritual warfare. There are all kinds of ideas of what spiritual warfare consists of. Some believe that they are literally physically fighting demonic spirits. Others believe that casting out spirits is spiritual warfare. What we must do, however, is to allow the Word to define what spiritual warfare is.

Review

Satan wars against us by using blindness and God sets us free by using light. Blindness or darkness is associated with lies and deceptions. Light is associated with truth and reality. We should be able to conclude from this that Satan's primary weapon is **deception** and God's primary weapon to defeat the enemy is **truth**. Darkness is not a thing, it is the absence of something. Deception is not a thing, it is the absence of something. Whereas darkness is a state that is defined by the absence of light, deception is a state defined by the absence of truth. This is why your Bible calls it "empty words." Again, if this idea is true there should be plenty of evidence in the Word to back it up.

The Battle

The Battle Type

If the devil is a roaring lion seeking whom he may devour, how do we reconcile his only weapon as deception? If Satan could take a person's life, do you think there would be any life left on this planet? How then does the devil murder? Murder must be done by another human. Why? Spiritual entities cannot just take human life by themselves unless given permission by God, as in the case of angels killing human armies.

For the most part they need a human being to commit the murder for them. In other words, a human being becomes the physical entity to manifest the desire of a spirit being. Why do you think the Scripture declares that Satan is seeking whom he **may** devour? In the book of Job we find that Satan was allowed to afflict Job, but God said you cannot kill him. Later, we also find that Jesus has the keys of death and hell.

> ***Revelation 1:18*** *...and the living One; and I was dead, and behold, I am alive forevermore, and I have the keys of death and of Hades.*

This is further evidence that Satan cannot just kill a human being. He must convince another human being to do the act for him. This is what has been going on for ages. Satan has possessed or deceived human beings to wreak havoc on the rest of the earth. From the first murderer Cain, to the likes of evil filled people in today's world, it has not changed. Satan blinds a person's heart to the truth and then deceives them into doing the things he wants them to do. This is where the idea of faith comes into play again. When Satan convinces us of something we act upon it because we believe it. That is faith. Can we have faith in someone other than God? YES!

This is the fight that is being waged in the earth. God is sharing truth with the world to the end that people would act upon His Word and do it. Satan is sharing lies with the world to the end that people would act upon his word and do it. When we believe those things that God says and we do them, God's will is being accomplished in the earth as it is in heaven. When we believe those things that Satan says and we do them, Satan's will is being accomplished in the earth.

God's will is marked by light, truth, love, and peace. *(Ephesians 5:9 for the fruit of the Light consists in all goodness and righteousness and truth).* Satan's will is marked by darkness, deception, hate, destruction, evil, chaos, and so on. There you have a big picture view of the warfare being waged in the earth. All humans are engaged in that warfare whether they understand it or not. Either we serve God or we are serving the devil. When Jesus taught His disciples how to pray, He used the phrase, *"Your will be done on earth as it is in heaven."* How is God's will done on earth? It is done when people hear His Word, believe His Word, and do His Word.

Why is There a Battle?

Why is warfare waged in this way? Why doesn't God just intervene and do things Himself? You must understand that God is an absolute God. He cannot lie because He cannot sin. He cannot make a mistake either or else He would not be perfect. Therefore, when God says something it stands forever and is unchangeable. When God created man, what did He say about man?

He said *"Let him have dominion over . . ."* Since man was given dominion over the earth, if anything is to be accomplished in the earth it will be done through those that have dominion on the earth. What quality must be possessed to have dominion on the earth? You must be human. What does being human mean? You must possess a body and be a spirit.

Satan may be a spirit but he does not possess a body, therefore, he does not have dominion. God is spirit and did not possess a body therefore has removed Himself from taking dominion. Hence, both beings are actively engaged in convincing humans of their respective words. Satan is a liar and cannot tell the truth, whereas God is honest and cannot tell a lie. Whomever you listen to and believe is for whom you are working. God is able to intervene. He is not powerless, but as long as He gives man that position of having dominion, He will allow man to accomplish His will. This is also only a portion of God's will.

Let's consider some evidence. First, *"Who named Adam?"* God! *"Who named all the creatures of the earth?"* Adam! When someone names something they are demonstrating their right of dominion over that thing. You would not think of going to your neighbor's house to name their newborn child. Thus, right from the beginning we see that God is backing up His Word by having Adam name all the creatures, thereby showing Adam's dominion over them. Next, if Satan is the god of this world, how did he arrive at that position?

Form of the Battle

God demonstrated His authority over Adam by naming him. However, God also created Adam in such a way that he was not enslaved to serve God. Adam possessed a free will. When Adam listened to what God said, he served God, and thus, God's will was done in earth. Consequently, God's dominion over earth was demonstrated through man. But when Adam rebelled against God and listened and obeyed the words of Satan, Adam gave Satan dominion by being obedient to him. **So, the dominion of God or Satan is reliant upon man believing and obeying their respective words. In other words, whoever is to be god of this world is made so by the faith of humanity.**

Is it any wonder then that Satan is called the god of this world? That title was apprehended by deceiving the masses to believe in him. This is substantiated by the devil offering the kingdoms of this world to Jesus. Jesus did not contend with his possession of those kingdoms.

Since we have developed a principle here, it bears repeating so that you will see clearly what kind of battle you are in and how you can engage the enemy and on what front that fight takes place. If it is faith that brought Satan to dominance over the earth through people believing and following his lies, then to diminish his authority all we need do is bring those same souls into the light where they can see the truth.

This means that as you contend for the faith that is in you, you are making others aware of the darkness or deception that they are in. By doing this we reduce the influence of the devil in the earth. Also, if it is by faith that Satan has the kingdoms of this world, then demonic authorities also set up over regions of the earth. This is supported by the Book of Daniel who talks about a demonic authority called the prince of Persia.

It is my belief that demonic and angelic authorities establish their position of power through the leadership. If the leadership is serving darkness through deception, that sets up a demonic authority over that sphere of governing authority. If the leadership is serving the light through truth, that sets up an angelic authority over that sphere of governing authority. This is why we see the prince of Persia ruling over that region and we see Michael the Arch Angel ruling over Israel.

I say all of this to substantiate the following. As Christians we cannot unseat demonic authorities over regions. There are groups of Christians that try to do warfare in the heavenly by rebuking regional authorities and I think they are endangering their own lives and those under their care. These authorities have right to that position. Did Jesus contend with Satan over his right of the kingdoms he was offering Him? If you want to unseat a demonic authority over a region then you must unseat that human authority.

By disengaging from the process whereby this can take place, the Christian hands those kingdoms to the devil through their apathy and ignorance. Jesus' brand of warfare is correct. How did He tell us to fight? "Go into all the world and make disciples (students) of every nation." Why we don't take those words more serious is, I think, a picture of how successful Satan has been in blinding the Church.

Before you begin to think that God is between a rock and a hard place, let me remind you of Noah. The whole world was willing to serve the devil except for one family. What happened? God destroyed them and protected His own. A whole city was willing to serve the devil except for one family. What happened? Sodom and Gomorrah was destroyed, but that one family is saved. Do you not thing God will do it again?

To the degree humanity follows the words of God, God's will is getting done in the earth and to the degree that humanity follows the words of Satan, Satan's will is getting done in the earth. Recall, when Jesus went into the wilderness to be tempted of the devil and the devil showed Jesus all of his kingdoms, Jesus never disputed Satan's right to those kingdoms. This shows that God respects authority where authority is established. This leads us to another scripture where it becomes clearer.

> ***Matthew 13:18-23*** *"Hear then the parable of the sower. "When anyone hears the word of the kingdom and does not understand it, the evil one comes and snatches away what has been sown in his heart. This is the one on whom seed was sown beside the road."*

20 "The one on whom seed was sown on the rocky places, this is the man who hears the word and immediately receives it with joy; 21 yet he has no firm root in himself, but is only temporary, and when affliction or persecution arises because of the word, immediately he falls away".

22 "And the one on whom seed was sown among the thorns, this is the man who hears the word, and the worry of the world and the deceitfulness of wealth choke the word, and it becomes unfruitful."

23" And the one on whom seed was sown on the good soil, this is the man who hears the word and understands it; who indeed bears fruit and brings forth, some a hundredfold, some sixty, and some thirty."

Here we have four types of hearers. The first one hears, but has no understanding. He cannot grasp what is being said, which allows that word to be easily stolen by the enemy. How does the enemy steal a word that is not understood? It is through deceiving the hearer to believe something contrary and often in advance of hearing that truth.

The second hearer understands the word, but this person has no root in himself. What does that mean? It means that one does not have a foundation upon which to test information. This causes one to hear, but with time it is lost because it is not fully tested and believed. For something to take root, it must begin to drive its roots from the mind deep into the heart. We cannot believe from the mind, only from the heart.

The third hearer is one who hears, but he is deceived in the pursuit of wealth and that consumes his time so he is not a doer of God's Word. This one is worried about provision and so he seeks to develop a great surplus in order to allay his fears. If he had put his faith in the words of God, he would know that he need not worry about his sustenance. This is because his loving Father would make sure that he has what he needs, as long as his pursuit is the kingdom of God and its righteousness.

The fourth hearer is one who hears, understands, believes and does. The fruit that is produced by the seed (word) is the doing. Now in this parable we find that we are faced with the importance of doing God's words. This agrees with the idea of doing warfare that we have acknowledged earlier. Now we will take a look at some more evidence of this warfare.

> ***John 8:42-47*** *Jesus said to them, "If God were your Father, you would love Me, for I proceeded forth and have come from God, for I have not even come on My own initiative, but He sent Me. Why do you not understand what I am saying? It is because you cannot hear My word. You **are of** your father the devil, and you want to do the desires of your father. He was a murderer from the beginning, and does not stand in the truth because there is no truth in him. Whenever he speaks a lie, he speaks from his own nature, for he is a liar and the father of lies."*
>
> *45 "But because I speak the truth, you do not believe Me. Which one of you convicts Me of sin? If I speak truth, why do you not believe Me? He who is of God hears the words of God; for this reason you do not hear them, because you **are not of** God."*

Here is a very telling scripture. Jesus asks them why they cannot understand what He is saying. Then He answers His own question by saying that they cannot hear Him. Jesus finally reveals the problem. They are of their father the devil and they want to do the desires of their father. Jesus additionally reveals that the devil is a liar and there is no truth in him, thus, the problem.

Let's simplify this. If your favorite weather man said that it was going to rain today, you would not hear me if I were to tell you that it is not going to rain. In fact, what I said even sounds foolish to you because you have believed something different. This is what Jesus was saying. They were so convinced they were walking in the truth that they did not recognize the truth when it was standing right in front of them.

In fact, they thought they were of God. They thought what they believed was from God. They did not willfully serve the devil and listen to him. They were deceived or blinded by the devil; they were walking in darkness and could not see the light. The *"they"* are actually the Pharisees. These were the religious teachers of the time. They really thought they were of God, but they were deceived.

> ***Matthew 6:22-23*** *"The eye is the lamp of the body; so then if your eye is clear, your whole body will be full of light. But if your eye is bad, your whole body will be full of darkness. If then the light that is in you is darkness, how great is the darkness!"*

If we continue the definitions of light and darkness as truth and deception, then this scripture begins to make a lot of sense. The line that I want to draw your attention to is the one that says, *"If then the light that is in you is darkness, how great is the darkness."*

Here we have three states revealed. First is the state of truth. When we walk in the truth, our whole being is in light. The second state is walking against the truth. I know what the truth is; I just do not like it so I rebel against it. When I rebel against the truth, I walk in darkness. But the third state is the most dangerous.

If what I believe to be light is actually darkness, how great is the darkness! In other words, when I believe a lie to be the truth, I am truly deceived and walking in darkness because I actually believe it to be the light.

> *Luke 6:47-49 "Everyone who comes to Me and hears My words and acts on them, I will show you whom he is like: he is like a man building a house, who dug deep and laid a foundation on the rock; and when a flood occurred, the torrent burst against that house and could not shake it, because it had been well built. But the one who has heard and has not acted accordingly, is like a man who built a house on the ground without any foundation; and the torrent burst against it and immediately it collapsed, and the ruin of that house was great."*

In light of what we have already learned, this scripture needs little explanation. Jesus shows us how to arrange our lives in such a way that we cannot be moved. It is by believing Him and doing what He has said. In his first letter, John (1 John 5:4) said, ". . . this is the victory that has overcome the world–our faith." Your beliefs are what cause you either to overcome if you are walking in truth, or to be overcome if you do not believe or are deceived. Notice the language. Victory and overcoming sound a lot like warfare. The victory of the battle is directly tied to faith.

> *John 18:37 ...For this I have been born, and for this I have come into the world, to testify to the truth. Everyone who is of the truth hears My voice."*

To sum up this section, it really comes down to whom you choose to listen. Jesus says that if you are of the truth, you will hear His voice. We can conversely also say that whoever is not of the truth does not hear His voice. We have from this the idea that the battle that is being waged is **the battle for your will.**

If Satan can get you to believe him, you will to do his will whether you do so with knowledge or by deception. Jesus wants us to walk in truth and by doing so we are solidifying our ability to stand in the midst of trouble. Now let's go on to see the battle as it truly is and how we are to wage war against our enemy.

How to Fight the Battle

We can find out how to wage this war by reading of the accounts in the Bible that describe the battle. Another help is to look at the armor and the weapons that are given to us to wage this war. When Jesus was taken into the wilderness to be tempted by the devil, He did not do hand to hand combat with him.

There were no swords clanging with sparks flying as they met in battle. This was an epic battle of truth vs. lies. The account of this is found in both Matthew 4 and Luke 4. First, let's clear up some misconceptions. Jesus did not fast 40 days and then was tempted. No, he fasted 40 days and was tempted 40 days. We are not privy to all that took place. What we do know is enough to set the stage for understanding true spiritual warfare.

We are only given a glimpse of the end of these 40 days of temptation. The first one recorded is a temptation for self preservation. Satan tempts Jesus to make the stones into bread. Observe the presumptuous statement; *"If you be the Son of God ..."* Satan was also tempting Jesus to operate on his terms of disclosure. But notice how Jesus did battle. **He quoted the Scriptures!** What does that tell you about the Old Testament scriptures? It tells us they are really the Words of God and are adequate in doing warfare. What a shame that many Christians avoid the Old Testament text. This first temptation was playing on the weakness Jesus was experiencing in His body by fasting.

The next temptation was against Jesus' mind. The mind is the seat of your will. Satan tried to tempt Jesus to prove that He was who He said He was. Notice that Satan is attacking Jesus' identity. *"If you be the Son of God..."* was an attack against His physical identity. Remember that God is Jesus' true Father.

When you think this through what Satan was doing was calling Jesus a liar. He was questioning Jesus' identity. He tempts Jesus to prove who He is by forcefully fulfilling a prophecy. Again, Jesus responds by quoting the Word of God.

The last temptation was against His spirit. Jesus came to win back what Adam had lost in the Garden of Eden. Satan was trying to tempt Jesus to take a short cut. He was willing to give up the kingdoms of this world if Jesus would just worship him. Jesus responded again by quoting the Word of God. We worship in spirit and so this temptation was a spiritual temptation.

In all three encounters Jesus responded with the same method. **Is Jesus trying to tell us something here?** Is He trying to show us that spiritual warfare is in the realm of ideas? Indeed, we can back this idea up further with other scriptures.

> ***2 Corinthians 10:3-6*** *For though we walk in the flesh, we do not war according to the flesh, for the weapons of our warfare are not of the flesh, but divinely powerful for the destruction of fortresses. We are destroying speculations and every lofty thing raised up against the knowledge of God, and we are taking every thought captive to the obedience of Christ, and we are ready to punish all disobedience, whenever your obedience is complete.*

"For though we walk in the flesh, we do not war according to the flesh" This statement shows us that our battle is not a physical one. We are not doing a physical battle, but rather we are doing a mental and philosophical battle; a battle of ideas and

reasoning, of truth and lies. Paul's next statement is one meant to prove the first one.

"For the weapons of our warfare are not of the flesh . . ." Paul is really saying that if our battle was physical we would be using physical weapons. Since we are not using physical weapons then our battle cannot be physical.

". . .but divinely powerful for the destruction of fortresses." Paul describes our weapons as divinely powerful, therefore, it is reasoned that these weapons are empowered by, and/or come from God. In other words, we are not waging a war that is physical because the weapons that are given us to wage war are not physical, but they are divinely powerful in destroying fortresses.

Okay, that should be clear. Now the next question must be, *"What is a fortress (that which we are fighting against) and what are we fighting to protect?"* Many just think they are doing spiritual warfare to protect themselves, but that is never true in any real war. Every war fought is for a common goal, not an individualistic goal. Although survival is a goal, it is not *the* goal. We find that some people even willfully give their lives for the acquirement of the goal. We are not fighting just for our own survival, after all the battle is not physical. We may ask, what is that common goal that we are trying to reach?

"~~We are~~ destroying speculations and every lofty thing raised up against the knowledge of God" I have *"we are"* struck out because it is not in the original Greek and it does change the meaning in a sense. It shifts the action of destruction from the weapons to the people. This takes away from the power of these divine weapons and so the strength of the text is actually focused on the weapon, not the person. This statement, however, reveals what we are fighting against and what we are defending.

We are defending the knowledge of God; we are fighting anything that comes against that knowledge. Let's break this down a bit. What is the knowledge of God? What is knowledge? **Knowledge is information that is accepted as true and right.** This is not just information. Information has yet to be judged so at this point it is only information. Knowledge is information that has been judged and decided upon.

We, therefore, are defending information about God that is true and right, and we are fighting against information about God that is **not** true and right. In this statement we also find the definition of a fortress. If our weapons destroy fortresses and they destroy false speculations about God, what destroys a lie? Since **a fortress is anything believed about God that is not true,** then that which is true about God is the only thing that will destroy it. Thus, the weapon that is divinely powerful must be the knowledge of God, or the truth.

"and ~~we are~~ *taking every thought captive to the obedience of Christ"* Notice that again I have struck out *"we are."* The reason is that the translators put that in to bring clarity in their estimation. If we leave it out though, we find that a different meaning arises. Instead of *"we are"* taking every thought captive, the divinely powerful weapons are taking every thought captive. What a difference! I have had Christians tell me they are trying to take every thought captive to the obedience of Christ. When I revealed to them that they are not capable of doing such a thing and that only the divinely powerful weapon can do it, then they are set free. Now they know how to win the battle by getting more of the Word of God in them.

So, it is not *"we are"* that are destroying speculations, it is not *"we are"* that are taking every thought captive, rather, it is divinely powerful weapons that destroy speculations and take every thought captive. If you don't equip yourself with the weapons, you will not survive the battle. Your job then is to equip yourself with the weapons and get training in the use of those weapons.

"and we are ready to punish all disobedience, whenever your obedience is complete." Here we have a real *"we are"* in the text. This seems to be a bit confusing in light of the subject, but if we look to the original Greek, it makes sense. The word disobedience in the Greek is:

"QUOTE"

***3876 ðáñáêoÞ** [\parakoe /par·ak·o·ay/. **1** a hearing amiss. **2** disobedience.* [12]

That was Strong's definition; let's take a look at another. The Intermediate Greek-English Lexicon states that word as *"unwillingness to hear."* Now it starts to make sense. Paul is saying that He is ready to correct anyone who is unwilling to hear once they have heard all of the truth that Jesus taught. Again, we are talking about concepts and this fits with the context of this section. Next, we will look at the weapons themselves.

Our Battle Equipment

We started this chapter with Ephesians 6:12. It would be prudent to read on from there to gain an understanding of our struggle.

> ***Ephesians 6:12-17** For our struggle is not against flesh and blood, but against the rulers, against the powers, against the world forces of this darkness, against the spiritual forces of wickedness in the heavenly places. **Therefore**, take up the full armor*

---

[12] -Strong's Concordance

> *of God, so that you will be able to resist in the evil day, and having done everything, to stand firm. Stand firm therefore, having girded your loins with truth, and having put on the breastplate of righteousness, and having shod your feet with the preparation of the gospel of peace; in addition to all, taking up the shield of faith with which you will be able to extinguish all the flaming arrows of the evil one. And take the helmet of salvation, and the sword of the Spirit, which is the Word of God.*

Verse 13 says *"Therefore . . ."* This is in response to verse twelve. We are in a spiritual struggle. Therefore, make sure you arm yourself with the armor and weapons that God has provided. The first item mentioned is the belt of truth. Paul was using a model of the Roman soldier's battle armor to draw a picture for what we have available to us. The Roman model of armor used the belt to literally attach all the other pieces of armor. If that soldier did not have a belt, he could not attach the rest of his armor. Without truth there is no other armor to put on.

Upon truth, we are enabled to live a righteous life. Truth is the knowledge of God, and the knowledge of God will enable you to live righteous. (Colossians 1:9-10) Your feet are to be covered with the preparation of the gospel of peace. It is not the gospel of peace that protects the feet, but it is the preparation of it. It is the application of oneself to the understanding of the gospel. It is filling oneself with the knowledge of God. It is applying oneself to learning the things in the Word of God.

The next item is the shield of faith. This shield is able to extinguish every arrow that the devil throws at you. Faith is revelation knowledge of God that is believed and acted upon. When you believe truth, the devil is unable to deceive you in that area.

The next item is the helmet of salvation. Without salvation having been applied to your life, you would not be able to understand the gospel of Christ. The Word of God says that the gospel is foolishness to the unbeliever. One cannot understand the words of God because they are spiritually discerned. It takes the indwelling Holy Spirit to illuminate our minds to understand God's Word. That is why this item is on your head. If you are not saved, you do not have the Spirit of God. If you do not have the Spirit of God, you are unable to understand the words of God. If you are unable to understand the words of God, you are unable to put on the armor of God.

The last item is the sword of the Spirit which is the Word of God. This offensive (vs. defensive) weapon is the Word of God. The power of the Word of God is all that is needed to defeat the devil in combat. Jesus used it in His struggle; He authorizes us to use it as well. When we have put on the armor of God and we have done all to stand, we can stand firm because that weaponry will win the battle if we apply it. We will deal with the armor in greater detail in another chapter.

Conclusion

Spiritual warfare is not yelling at the devil, it is not hand to hand combat with the devil, and it is not casting the devil out. However, casting the devil out is a result of doing spiritual warfare. Just as the disciples were unable to cast out a demon and when they asked Jesus why they could not cast it out, Jesus replied that it was because of the littleness of their faith. Had they done the faith building that is spiritual warfare, the result would be the ability to cast out the demon.

Remember when Jesus gave His disciples' power and sent them out to minister? When they came back they were all excited by the fact that the demons were subject to them as they cast them out. Jesus' response was not to rejoice over that, but rejoice because your names are written in the Lamb's book of life.

Spiritual warfare is destroying lies and protecting the truth. In order to protect the truth, you have to know it. Knowing the truth gives you the knowledge of God. Having the knowledge of God allows you to do battle against the enemy.

The more of the knowledge of God that you have, the harder it is for the enemy to deceive you. The more of the knowledge of God that you have, the greater the threat you are to Satan's kingdom. The more knowledge of God that you have, the more you will be destroying those fortresses of deception in your life and in the lives of others.

You are now a bearer of light and you bring freedom to those who have been captivated to do the devil's will in the earth. Take your position and destroy the darkness!

Building A Philosophy For Life

Chapter Seven

People come and go, but their ideas can last much longer. There are ideas and concepts that are presented to an attentive public that can span generations and have long lasting effects of which even the perpetrator of that idea did not expect. There are even seasons and times in which an idea is formulated and presented, but is subsequently rejected by the current social opinion. Because this idea was put into print, however, it is picked up later by a different generation and lauded as the latest fanciful belief. Ideas are able to outlive their proponents or creators. Case in point, only eleven people came to Carl Marx's funeral, yet his ideas shaped the thinking of many leaders since then.

Here in America we are flirting with Marxist ideals in society and government. Have we learned nothing in the last century? Marxist ideas are responsible for nearly 170 million deaths in the twentieth century. Why is it that a culture will not allow a bad idea to die? It is because those ideas are not human ideas. They are demonic. How can I say these ideas are demonic? Because of the fruit these ideas have produced. If Satan comes only to steal, kill, and destroy, then if we look at the fruit of communism what do we see? Do we see benevolence for the common man as it espouses, or do we see fields of murder, cities of destitution, and citizens with rations. This is the great utopia of so-called human thought?

In studying the evolution of thought, one is tempted to dismiss the effect of a thesis upon a culture. Yet, if we are careful in our exploration, we will realize that one can find a principle or idea behind every atrocity committed against mankind. Thus, the danger of thinking that our ideas are weighty and powerful without a moral standard to measure them by is a coldhearted empty deception. A thesis can only be as powerful as the number of people who come to believe it along with the influence these people have upon the culture.

What I am trying to say is what God says is weighty and powerful, and what man says apart from God is foolish. It is therefore necessary if a society is to remain healthy that it needs to have a moral conscience. The moral conscience of any society is revealed by its religious structure and for America that conscience has been the Body of Christ or the Church—that is until recently. When the moral conscience of a society becomes corrupted, expect that society to become corrupted as well.

What we are going to do is trace some ideas (philosophical concepts) and show how they have shaped the society of which we find ourselves a part. Ravi Zacharias wrote a book called *"Deliver Us From Evil."* This is an excellent book and I recommend everyone add it to your library.

The word *"philosophy"* is from a compound Greek word. The Greek word *"Phileo"* means *"love"* and *"sophia"* means *"wisdom."* Its meaning then is love of wisdom. This word can cover a multitude of fields.

When considering the evil actions of leaders in the twentieth century, we see that it is the habit of media in their reporting to hone in on the action of those atrocities committed by leaders without actually concentrating upon the reasons or ideas that are behind them.

"QUOTE"

"Behind an act is a thought or belief, and those thoughts unleashed in antisocial behavior make

> *the headlines. Yet seldom are these thoughts and beliefs scrutinized."* [13]

So even though we find the reporting of evil, we seem to never actually be able to discern why the evil took place. I am reminded of the Columbine shooting. When the event occurred we were all wondering what could have brought these two young men to do this terrible act of murder and suicide. The media were throwing out all sorts of possibilities. They were asking questions like, *"What kind of parents did they have? – What kind of friends did they have? – What do their friends say about them? – Where did they hang out?"*

The one thing they never addressed were the philosophies that these two had accepted as true and consequently drove their actions. Could it be that the philosophy of these two teens was a little too close to that of the elite media moguls? For instance, the media never reported that before these two killers murdered a person, they asked if their victims were a Christian. If the victim said yes, they were killed. Is that not important enough to report? Do you think if these two asked if the person were homosexual before they killed them that it would have been plastered on every news outlet?

The media never told us they wore tee shirts that had the words *"Natural Selection"* emblazoned on them. What does this have to do with anything? It shows an underlying philosophy that paves the way for wickedness to take place. Natural selection is the idea of survival of the fittest. That philosophy has been used many times to justify the killing of those deemed weak; thus, the question of being a Christian. It was found that they believed Christians to be weak and if allowed to reproduce that weakness

---

[13] – Ravi Zacharias "Deliver us From Evil"

would be passed on and wind up polluting the gene pool. Where did they get these ideas? Could the seeds of their philosophy have been planted in their hearts right there in that public high school? Is that why this important evidence was to be hushed?

Ravi Zacharias reveals two important questions that must be asked.

"Quote"

1. *"Can an individual or society live with complete disregard for a moral and spiritual center and not suffer from the wounds of wickedness?"*

2. *"Can the soul of a people who have lived without restraint be left unravaged?"* [14]

Even though America has made great gains in the area of intellect, we are all the more plagued by the weakness of our hearts. Consequently, all we wind up with are smarter sinners, or intelligent barbarians. We are left with immoral people that are ever better able to justify their acts of immorality.

"Quote"

"The cultural revolt that was spawned in educated minds proved that the mind can be well fed while the spirit is starved and that people are more than ideas." [15]

Humanity is so much more than a coalescence of ideas. We are the glory of an absolute Creator who defines reality and loves His own with an intensity that can only be measured in the cross of

---

[14] – Ravi Zacharias "Deliver us From Evil"

[15] – Ravi Zacharias "Deliver us From Evil"

His Son! We must be able to see clearly into the mirror of the Word of God so that we will be able to see our self as God sees us. If we do not, then we will not become what God created us to become. This is the insidious nature of the beliefs that this nation has embraced.

From here we will look at the long road to moral decay. We will take a brief look at different philosophers and their contribution to moral decay. America did not get to this place over night and if we are to turn the tide, it will take our repentance and God's power.

The History of Philosophy

There are three major streams of philosophy.

1. Western Philosophy
    a. Ancient
    b. Medieval
    c. Modern
    d. Contemporary or Post Modern
2. Eastern Philosophy
    a. Indian
    b. Persian
    c. Chinese
    d. Buddhist
3. Abrahamic and African Philosophy
    a. Jewish
    b. Islamic
    c. African

We are only concerned at this point with western philosophy. Note the difference between the divisions of western philosophy with that of the other two. Western philosophy is divided along a time line, whereas the others are divided along cultural lines. What has impacted America the most is obviously western philosophy.

Ancient Philosophy

Although it can become tedious to trace philosophical thought through history to the present, doing so will give you a real sense of the battle against unseen forces of evil.

Thales of Miletus

624-546 BC

He is the first of the western philosophers. He postulates that all is water. Thales recognizes a transcendental God, who has neither beginning nor end. He believes that God is just and expects men to behave justly. Neither men being unjust nor thinking injustice escape the notice of the gods. In this form of polytheism the transcendental god expresses himself through gods so that a man can say and mean God.

Even though he recognizes a transcendent God, he interjects the idea of multiple gods. This is a significant shift from the one true God. Although it may seem like tripe, the importance of this shift is found in the subtlety of it. Satan does not blow up the mountain, he erodes it. The erosion is so insignificant that each generation is unaware that the mountain is shrinking. Until finally we get to a generation that is not even aware of a mountain ever being there.

> *"That for which we blame others, let us not do ourselves"*

His idea of justice was an eye for an eye and a tooth for a tooth, although he also believed that men were greater than women.

Anaximander

610-546 BC

He is the first to use the Greek word for limitless or infinite. According to Anaximander, the Universe originates in the separation of opposites in the primordial matter. It embraces the opposites of hot and cold, wet and dry, and directs the movement of things; an entire host of shapes and differences then grow that are found in "all the worlds" (for he believed there were many).

He begins the move away from the idea of all things originating from one or more of the four basic elements of air, earth, fire, or water.

> *"QUOTE"*
>
> *"Anaximander of Miletus considered that from warmed up water and earth emerged either fish or entirely fishlike animals. Inside these animals, men took form and embryos were held prisoners until puberty; only then, after these animals burst open, could men and women come out, now able to feed themselves."* [16]

And you thought Darwin was responsible for the idea of evolution. In that quote we have the birthing of an evolution philosophy. We also have a denial of the Genesis account.

---

[16] De Die Natali, IV, 7

Heraclitus

535-475 BC

"This universe, which is the same for all, has not been made by any god or man, but it always has been, is, and will be an ever-living fire, kindling itself by regular measures and going out by regular measures."

Here we have the elimination of God for a view that falls along the lines of naturalism. Nevertheless, when Heraclitus wrote his book, he dedicated it to the temple of the god Artemis who was the daughter of Zeus in Greek mythology.

The idea of the *logos* is also credited to him, as he proclaims that everything originates out of the logos. Further, Heraclitus said *"I am as I am not"*, and *"He who hears not me but the logos will say: All is one."*

This is an interesting statement considering John 1:1.

Socrates

470-399 BC

If anything in general can be said about the philosophical beliefs of Socrates, it is that he was morally, intellectually, and politically at odds with his fellow Athenians. When he is on trial for heresy and corrupting the young, he uses his method of *elenchos* to demonstrate to the jurors that their moral values are wrong-headed. He tells them that they are concerned with their families, careers, and political responsibilities when they ought to be worried about the *"welfare of their souls."* This belief in an immortal soul only brought ridicule to Socrates. Even though he believed in an immortal soul, he also believed that the gods had called him to be their ambassador.

Socrates believed that the best way for people to live was to focus on self-development rather than the pursuit of material wealth. (Gross 2) He always invited others to try to concentrate more on friendships and a sense of true community, for Socrates felt this was the best way for people to grow together as a populace. His actions lived up to this. In the end, Socrates accepted his death sentence when most thought he would simply leave Athens. Socrates had a reputation for valor on the battlefield that was without reproach, and he felt he could not run away from or go against the will of his community.

The idea that humans possessed certain virtues formed a common thread in Socrates' teachings. These virtues represented the most important qualities for a person to have, foremost of which were the philosophical or intellectual virtues. Socrates stressed that, *"...virtue was the most valuable of all possessions; the ideal life was spent in search of the Good. Truth lies beneath the shadows of existence, and that it is the job of the philosopher to show the rest how little they really know."* (Solomon 44)

Ultimately, virtue relates to the form of the Good; to truly be good and not just act with "right opinion" one must come to know the unchanging Good in itself. In the *Republic*, he describes the "divided line", a continuum of ignorance to knowledge with the Good on top of it all; only at the top of this line do we find true good and the knowledge of such.

Socrates is an admirable man. He believed in the public debate of morality; something that our own society cannot abide. He may not have known God personally, but he acknowledged Him publically. His ideas were not always biblically correct, but that is to be expected without the knowledge of God. Like many believers of God, Socrates gave his life for his beliefs. He saw himself as called to that city and he remained faithful to it unto death.

Plato

428-348 BC

Plato is widely believed to have been a student of Socrates and to have been deeply influenced by his teacher's unjust death. Plato's brilliance as a writer and thinker can be witnessed by reading his Socratic dialogues.

"QUOTE"

> *"Until philosophers rule as kings or those who are now called kings and leading men genuinely and adequately philosophise, that is, until political power and philosophy entirely coincide, while the many natures who at present pursue either one exclusively are forcibly prevented from doing so, cities will have no rest from evils,... nor, I think, will the human race."* [17]

Plato describes these *"philosopher kings"* as *"those who love the sight of truth"*[18] and supports the idea with the analogy of a captain and his ship or a doctor and his medicine. Sailing and health are not things that everyone is qualified to practice by nature. A large part of the *Republic* addresses how the educational system should be set up to produce these philosopher kings.

According to Plato, a state, which is made up of different kinds of souls, will overall decline from an *aristocracy* (rule by the

---

[17] Republic 473c-d

[18] Republic 475c

best) to a *timocracy* (rule by the honorable), then to an *oligarchy* (rule by the few), then to a *democracy* (rule by the people), and finally to *tyranny* (rule by one person, rule by a tyrant). What is interesting is that without knowledge of God, these two men, Socrates and Plato, are left with defining good or morality through either themselves or through the populous. Without God's law man is left to do what is right in his own eyes and this can change on a whim.

Aristotle

384-322 BC

Aristotle identified the common highest good as *"happiness."* Aristotle points out that almost everyone in all times and places give the same answer. Therefore, he sees no objection, and accepts this premise.

Aristotle then points out that the term happiness needs to be refined because popular opinion as to what happiness is was divided, even though the divisions were small in number. They were able to classify happiness into four major categories.

1. Happiness is *pleasure*.
2. Happiness is *honor*.
3. Happiness is *virtue*, or excellence.
4. Happiness is *bodily and external goods*, such as health and wealth.

The question must be asked, *"If happiness is the highest goal of the majority, what if the majority would be made happier if they did not have to provide for the handicapped?"* This is always the problem. There is nothing inherently moral or immoral about happiness. Happiness is a state of being and one could derive happiness from torturing another. Without a moral standard guiding all decisions, the pursuit of happiness could create the environment where the end justifies the means by which it is acquired.

Medieval Philosophy

Justin Martyr

100-165 AD

The scene starts with Justin Martyr who had long been a student of philosophy. After becoming a Christian he continued to wear the pallium (the philosopher's cloak). He stated that, *"The only reliable and profitable philosophy"* was the Christian faith. Martyr contended that the Divine Logos had enlightened Socrates to see the error of paganism.

In writing a defense for Christians who were being arrested simply for being Christians, Martyr said the following: *"For from a name neither praise nor punishment could reasonably spring, unless something excellent or base in action be proved."* [19]

What Martyr was saying was that one cannot be judged based upon the name of their belief. What must be judged is a person's action, and so to arrest Christians simply because they call themselves Christians was an unjust act. In his writings he shows how Plato, through deduction, taught the Christian God without any source of knowledge about Him.

---

[19] The First Apology of Justin, chapter four

Anselm

1033-1109 AD

Fast forward now to the eleventh century and we find Anselm having the greatest effect upon thinking for this time period. Anselm is known for the ontological argument. Ontology is a branch of philosophy that deals with *"being."* The *ontological argument* itself though is known in philosophical circles as meaning an argument for the necessity of God's being. Anselm describes God as, *"That than which no greater can be thought."*

Anselm attempts to deduce God through the idea of the *perfect being.* He postulates that since all human beings have an idea about a perfect being, how could that idea be there unless the Perfect Being placed it there? Gaunilo of Marmoutiers, France, wrote a reply to Anselm titled, *On Behalf of the Fool.* He stated that he could imagine the most perfect islands, but that did not mean they existed. This caused Anselm to reply, and the debate continues even today among philosophers.

Saint Thomas Aquinas

1225-1274 AD

One hundred years later Thomas Aquinas appears. While Anselm had few writings, Aquinas had volumes of writings. There are two doctrines that Aquinas had the most influence in. One is the proof of the existence of God and the other is the doctrine of analogy. The proofs for the existence of God are called the *Five Ways.*

Anselm and Aquinas represented two different arguments to prove the existence of God. Whereas Aquinas believed that the existence of God could be proved to any rational man if they would take a close look at creation, Anselm believed that faith and commitment were a prior condition to knowing the existence of God.

Modern Philosophy

Erasmus

1466-1536 AD

"QUOTE"

". . . After the lawyers come the philosophers, who are reverenced for their beards and the fur on their gowns. They announce that they alone are wise and that the rest of men are only passing shadows. . . . The fact that they can never explain why they constantly disagree with each other is sufficient proof that they do not know the truth about anything. They know nothing at all, yet profess to know everything. They are ignorant even of themselves, and are often too absent-minded or near-sighted to see the ditch or stone in front of them. . . ." [20]

The previous quote is a snapshot of Erasmus' consideration of philosophers. In his mind they elevate themselves to a place they should not make claim. All the same, Erasmus believed that man had to play a part in his salvation because he had free will. This caused a split between Martin Luther and himself. Although Erasmus agreed with much of the reason behind the reformation, he rejected it in the end simply because he saw it as causing division within the Body of Christ.

---

[20] Desiderius Erasmus from his book In Praise of Folly. (1509)

I am not aware of the complete argument with regard to man playing a part in salvation, but I will offer the following thought. If by "a part" he means that man must decide to accept or reject the message of the cross then I wholly agree. If by "a part" he means some righteous work that man must do, then I disagree.

It is these small changes to salvation that can result in an inoculation to the Word of God. Erasmus, I think, had a point with regard to division. However, what is one to do with a corrupt church? This will likely be fodder for debate for generations to come.

Martin Luther

1483-1546 AD

Martin Luther despised the philosopher. He called philosophy *"the Great Whore."* He also referred to Aristotle as a *"destroyer of pious doctrine,"* a *"mere sophist and quibbler,"* an *"inventor of fables,"* *"the stinking philosopher,"* a *"billy goat,"* and a *"blind pagan."* Luther complained, *"When I was a monk they used to despise the bible. Nobody understood the Psalter. They used to believe that the Epistle to the Romans contained some controversies about matters of Paul's day and was of no use to our age. Scotus, Thomas, Aristotle were the ones to read."*

This complaint is not unlike our situation today in our modern universities. Some of our so-called Christian universities put more emphasis on the works of intellectual men and criticize the Bible as a book of mere fables.

Rene Descartes

1596-1650 AD

Rene Descartes was the first of the rational philosophers. Descartes saw truth as he saw mathematics, as a chain of elements that led to a sure outcome. He refused to accept anything as truth that could not be derived at in this manner.

My problem with this is how does one know that they have all of the elements involved in the equation? As in mathematics, if one part of the equation is missing or worse yet skewed, one can be led to the wrong conclusion. Descartes believed in God, but not in a personal sense. He believed that by seeing himself as a finite being it necessitated an infinite being. Descartes is credited with the well-known axiom, *"I think, therefore I am."* How he came across this idea is rarely known.

A Muslim philosopher, Iba Sina Abdullah postulated a theory that came to be known as Sina's "Suspended in Space" theory.

"Quote"

> *"If a person were created in a perfect state, but blind and suspended in the air but unable to perceive anything through his senses, would he be able to affirm the existence of his self? Suspended in such a state, he cannot affirm the existence of his body because he is not empirically aware of it, thus the argument may be seen as affirming the independence of the soul from the body, a form of dualism. But in that state he cannot doubt that his self exists because there is a subject that is thinking, thus the argument*

can be seen as an affirmation of the self-awareness of the soul and its substantiality."[21]

This is what influenced Descartes to utter, *"I think, therefore, I am."* Pope John Paul in his book *"Memory and Identity"* gives a good refutation to that statement. The Pope contends that the phraseology is backward and that it should read, *"I am, therefore I think."* The Pope believed this is the more accurate response. We cannot think unless we first are. Being comes before thinking.

Benedictus de Spinoza

1632-1677 AD

Benedictus de Spinoza was a Jew who was expelled from the synagogue because of his free thought. His idea of God was that of pantheism. Spinoza believed that substance was God as the following statement reveals. *"God is the indwelling and not the transient cause of all things."* In the summer of 1656, he was issued the writ of *cherem* (Hebrew: חרם, similar to excommunication) from the Jewish community for the apostasy of how he conceived God.

> *"QUOTE"*
>
> *"...the notion that God took upon Himself the nature of man seemed as self-contradictory as would be the statement that 'the circle has taken on the nature of the square.'"*[22]

---

[21] The Internet Encyclopedia of Philosophy

[22] The Jewish Encyclopedia

Spinoza was deeply impacted by the philosophy of Rene Descartes. His Jewish upbringing was abandoned and he was excommunicated at the age of just twenty three.

G. W. Leibniz

1646-1716 AD

G. W. Leibniz was a protestant philosopher. He was and is considered a genius. He discovered infinitesimal calculus with Newton, invented a calculating machine, created the Prussian Society, and corresponded with and met many of the most prominent minds in Europe. He was an eminent diplomat as well as a philosopher. Leibniz's philosophy concerning God was *deus ex machina* (god from the machinery). He believed that the universe was composed of monads that are the smallest indivisible parts. These monads form an ascending series from lowest which is next to nothing and the highest which is God.

In his own words he says that God is, *"the original simple substance, from which all monads, created and derived, are produced."* Colin Brown in "Philosophy & the Christian Faith" rightly describes the mindset of these rationalists when he says, *"The God of the rationalists was a hypothetical abstraction, a 'dues ex machina,' invoked to make the system work, but not one who was encountered personally in history and present experience."*

Leibniz also struggled with the concept of free will. His thinking is that if God knows something is going to happen then that knowing is the causation of it. Because freedom can only exist in the unpredictable, if something is predictable it is no longer free.

Here is the problem with this line of thinking. God was not predicting what would happen as a scientist puts all the facts together and predicts an outcome. No, God was seeing what was taking place. Seeing what is taking place in the future is not predetermining the future, it is only recording it. The decisions people make are thus revealed and the outcome is as God said it would be.

God was not the machinery nor was He operating a machine. God created time. Since He created time, He cannot be bound by His own creation. This is to say that God must be outside time and being outside time He can see all of time all at once. Being able to see all of time all at once He is able to record the history of time from beginning to end. Thus, He sees the decision but does not cause it.

John Locke

1634-1704 AD

John Locke was read by the founding fathers of this country; his treatise on government being their interest. He was a brilliant mind who understood also the limits of human reason. Whereas other philosophers have elevated reason above faith, Locke explained that they are completely different.

Locke drew a distinction between faith and reason. I think it important to include what he said. Locke said, *"the discovery of the certainty or probability of such propositions or truths, which the mind arrives at by deduction made from such ideas, which it has got by the use of its natural faculties, viz. by sensation or reflection. Faith on the other side, is the assent to any proposition not thus made out by the deductions of reason, but upon the credit of the proposer, as coming from God, in some extraordinary way of communication. This way of discovering truths to men we call Revelation."*

This idea leaves all at the level of perception. When our perception is aligned with the mind of Christ, it is then experiencing reality. At least to Locke, faith is a viable position. This is something that has been lost in modern philosophy. George Berkeley added a twist to Locke's idea. He argued that perception was necessary for a thing to exist. Not that something ceased to exist if one did not perceive it, for it is always perceived by God.

Locke had a knack for simplifying the complicated. In one short statement, the next quote deals with slavery, abortion, tyranny, and a multitude of other sins.

> *"...by his [God] order and about his business, they [humans] are his property whose workmanship they are, made to last during his, not one another's pleasure: and being furnished with like faculties, sharing all in one community of nature, there cannot be supposed any subordination among us, that may authorize us to destroy one another, as if we were made for one another's uses, as the inferior ranks of creatures are for our's."*

Lord Herbert of Cherbury

1583-1648 AD

Lord Herbert of Cherbury is credited for creating deism. Deism had a different look early on than what arose later. Lord Herbert argued basically that certain common notions were imprinted upon the mind of man. These are:

- that there exists one supreme God,
- who is chiefly to be worshipped;
- that the principal part of such worship consists in piety and virtue;

- that we must repent of our sins and that, if we do so, God will pardon us;
- that there are rewards for good men and punishments for evil men both here and hereafter.

At this point a group of others known as the Cambridge Platonists began to state that reason was a gift of God and that to be a good Christian one could not go against reason. This led to the excursion of philosophical thought away from the idea of a transcendent being called God. It is postulated that the reformers could have had a big effect upon philosophy, but did not bother themselves with it. This gave birth to moral relativism.

Once you create a god that is not involved in the supernatural, that is no longer personal, that has not given particular laws to be obeyed, then what is left is a god that can be shaped into a personal deity. A personal deity will allow for those things important to the person. This is how moral relativism was able to arise. God had been reduced enough that He could now be reformed.

Rousseau

1712-1778 AD

Rousseau published his work called *"The Social Contract."* This set out his theory of the state. In it the laws of the state were not a matter of divine appointment, but simply the will of the people. Colin Brown in *"Philosophy & the Christian Faith"* states, *"They (laws) were not to be based upon divine law but upon the will of the people. The only valid basis for a society is for its members to agree to a social pact which will combine freedom with just government in the interest of the majority."*

As a result, the substructure for moral relativism to prosper is born. Whether or not these men realize it, they were giving sanction to the majority. If the majority agrees that slavery is beneficial to that society, then slavery becomes a moral tenant of that culture. If the majority feel that taking the life of retarded people were desirable to society, to do so would be an act of morality and kindness. I wonder if these men would hold to this idea of moral relativism if society suddenly felt that the elimination of philosophers was needed for a healthy community.

Gotthold Ephraim Lessing

1729-1781 AD

Gotthold Ephraim Lessing said, *"Accidental truths of history can never become the proof of necessary truths of reason."* Lessing was basically saying that one cannot give the same level of authenticity to historical accounts as to reasonable deductions. Of course, there is some validity to this as we can define certain truths with reason as in two plus two equals four. Moreover, historical accounts are only as good as the validity of the author of those accounts.

What is not taken into account, however, is that the Author of the Bible is God and therefore His words are valid. These men just can't get past the idea that a human author could actually speak the Words of God on paper. Lessing believed that the value of any religion depends on its capacity to transform life through love. This idea may seem quite credible to some, however, if we inspect what Lessing is saying, he is giving credibility to any religion that practices love. There is nothing about salvation or the need to be cleansed of unrighteousness. This is important because if we look at where we are today, we can still see this idea flourishing in liberal theology.

Immanuel Kant

1724-1804 AD

Immanuel Kant believed that inevitably the mind conditions everything that it encounters; therefore, the mind cannot attain to rational knowledge of anything beyond its immediate experience of the world. This supports the ideas that Lessing posited.

Kant is known for his theory that there is a single moral obligation, which he called the *"Categorical Imperative"*, and is derived from the concept of **duty**. It is from the Categorical Imperative that all other moral obligations are generated, and by which all moral obligations can be tested. He believed that the moral law is a principle of reason itself and is not based on contingent facts about the world such as what would make us happy; but to act upon the moral law which has no other motive than *"worthiness of being happy."* Accordingly, he believed that moral obligation applies to all and only rational agents.

Friedrich Daniel Ernst Schleiermacher

1768-1834 AD

Friedrich Daniel Ernst Schleiermacher was sent to a Moravian seminary by his father in hopes of instilling a pietistic leaning. His father curiously advised his son to read Kant hoping it to be an antidote to modern liberalism. Schleiermacher did read Kant, but he had a different reaction.

He simply defined all of our relationships to God in the term of dependence. He thought Jesus was just a man with a God-consciousness and that He was showing us how to be dependent on

God. This preconceived idea was then applied to all of Scripture and anything that did not fit in with it was discarded. His worldview skewed his attempt to find what was true.

J. G. Fichte

1762-1814 AD

At this point a new title was being given to Berkley's immaterialism and it was called *"idealism."* J. G. Fichte agreed with Kant as well. In short, he believed that our physical universe is the outworking of the spiritual ego. In his famous work *Foundations of Natural Right* (1796), Fichte argued that self-consciousness was a social phenomenon (normative). A necessary condition of any subjects' self-awareness, he argued, is the existence of other rational subjects. Because of this necessity to have relations with other rational beings in order to achieve consciousness, Fichte writes that there must be a *'relation of right,'* in which there is a mutual recognition of rationality by both parties.

Fichte also developed a theory of the state based on the idea of self-sufficiency. In his mind, the state should control international relations, the value of money, and remain an autarky (closed economy). This gives rise to the ideas of communism and social conditioned morality or social relative morality.

Georg Wilhelm Friedrich Hegel

1770-1831 AD

Georg Wilhelm Friedrich Hegel took idealism to prove God's existence and sought to make Christianity palatable to the philosopher. The problem is that idealism cannot be proved. Hence, idealism was superseded by existentialism.

There was a "right" Hegelism and there was a "left" Hegelism. People interpreted his writings in extremely different ways. The right Hegel's advocated Protestant theology and political conservatism. The left Hegel's advocated atheism and liberal democracy.

Perhaps the main reason that so much writing about Hegel emerges from the so-called Left-Hegelians is that the Left-Hegelians spawned Marxism, which inspired a global movement lasting more than 150 years. The movement encompassed the Russian Revolution, the Chinese Revolution, and even more national-liberation movements of the 20th century; although these movements are not any direct result of Hegel's philosophy.

20th century interpretations of Hegel were mostly shaped by one-sided schools of thought: British Idealism, logical positivism, Marxism, Fascism, and postmodernism. Since the fall of the USSR, however, a new wave of Hegel scholarship arose in the West, without the preconceptions of the prior schools of thought.

Soren Aaby Kierkegaard

1813-1855 AD

Kierkegaard stated, *"The thing is to understand myself, to see what God really wishes me to do; the thing is to find a truth which is true for me, to find the idea for which I can live and die."*

Much of his work deals with religious problems such as the nature of faith, the institution of the Christian Church, Christian ethics and theology, and the emotions and feelings of individuals when faced with life choices. His early work was written under various pseudonyms who present their own distinctive viewpoints in a complex dialogue. Kierkegaard left the task of discovering the meaning of the works to the reader, because *"the task must be made difficult, for only the difficult inspires the noble-hearted"*.

Subsequently, many have interpreted Kierkegaard as an existentialist, neo-orthodoxist, postmodernist, humanist, individualist, and so on. Crossing the boundaries of philosophy, theology, psychology, and literature, Kierkegaard came to be regarded as a highly significant and influential figure in contemporary thought.

Ludwig Andreas Feuerbach

1804-1872 AD

Feuerbach graduated at the University of Heidelberg with the intention of pursuing a career in the Church. Through the influence of Prof. Karl Daub he was led to an interest in the then predominant philosophy of Hegel, but in spite of his father's opposition, went to Berlin to study under the master himself. After two years' discipleship, the Hegelian influence began to slacken. Feuerbach became associated with a group known as the Young Hegelians, who synthesized a radical offshoot of Hegelian philosophy.

"Theology," he wrote to a friend, *"I can bring myself to study no more. I long to take nature to my heart, that nature before whose depth the faint-hearted theologian shrinks back; and with nature man, man in his entire quality."* These words are a key to Feuerbach's development. He completed his education at Erlangen at the Friedrich-Alexander-University, Erlangen-Nuremberg, with the study of natural science.

Feuerbach delineated God to mere nature. (Pantheism) He took the idea of absolute dependence and submitted the following. *"That on which man depends and feels himself dependant is none other than nature...theology is nothing else than anthropology–the knowledge of God is nothing else than a knowledge of man!"*

John Stuart Mill

1806-1873 AD

Another movement this important century had to offer was that of Utilitarianism. In its simplest form, Utilitarianism teaches that the right action is the one that promotes (or at least tries to promote) the greatest happiness of the greatest number. It was John Stuart Mill who popularized and laid out its doctrine. The attractiveness of this doctrine had a lot to do with the other philosophical movements of the time. Brown says it best when he says, *"To argue on the grounds of **expediency** seems easier than arguing on grounds of **principle** in a society where objective standards are called into question."*

One argument that Mill develops further than any previous philosopher is the harm principle. The harm principle holds that each individual has the right to act as he wants, so long as these actions do not harm others. If the action is self-regarding, that is, if it only directly affects the person undertaking the action, then society has no right to intervene, even if it feels the actor is harming himself.

Mill excuses those who are *"incapable of self-government"* from this principle, such as young children or those living in *"backward states of society"*. It is important to emphasize that Mill did not consider giving offence to constitute *"harm"*; an action could not be restricted because it violated the conventions or morals of a given society. In other words, the end justifies the means; thus, another reason behind moral relativism. This idea of do no harm must be based upon the complete knowledge of harm. For instance, a parent who is a drug addict might say that they are not hurting anyone else, however, what psychological damage is being done to the child of that parent. Harm comes in many forms and manifests itself in even more shapes.

Charles Darwin

1809-1882 AD

The inclusion of Charles Darwin might seem strange when we are talking about philosophers rather than scientists. However, just as some of the philosophers influenced scientists, so some scientists have influenced philosophers. Such is the case of Charles Darwin. There is no other man that did more to remove God from the consciousness of man than **Charles Darwin**. *"The Origin of the Species"* was the proof that the other nineteenth century philosophers needed. What many are unaware of is the complete title of that book is now missing in modern publications. The full title was:

The Origin of Species
by Means of Natural Selection,
or
The Preservation of Favoured Races in the Struggle for Life

Darwin saw the need for the elimination of certain races of people because they were deemed savage. Yes, this worshiped scientist was also racist. In fact, Hitler used the premises of this book as a reason to eliminate the Jew.

Karl Marx read it and stated, *"Darwin's book is very important and serves me as a basis in natural science for the struggle in history."* Marx even asked if he could dedicate his work *"Capitol"* to Darwin, but he was refused. Still, as Colin Brown in *"Philosophy & the Christian Faith"* states, *"Nevertheless, evolution came to fulfill the role in Communist doctrine that Marx cast for it."*

Though Charles Darwin's family background was nonconformist, and his father, grandfather, and brother were Freethinkers, at first he did not doubt the literal truth of the Bible. He attended a Church of England school and then at Cambridge studied Anglican theology to become a clergyman. He was convinced by William Paley's teleological argument that design in nature proved the existence of God, but during the *Beagle* voyage he questioned, for example, why beautiful deep-ocean creatures had been created where no one could see them (which is a ridiculous argument for he was there seeing them), or how the ichneumon wasp paralyzing caterpillars as live food for its eggs could be reconciled with Paley's vision of beneficent design. He was still quite orthodox and would quote the Bible as an authority on morality, but did not trust the history in the Old Testament.

The 1851 death of Darwin's daughter, Annie, was the final step in pushing an already doubting Darwin away from the idea of a beneficent God. How often it is in history that a man or woman's circumstances served to drive them away from God and to godless thinking.

Karl Marx

1818-1883 AD

Karl Marx credited Feuerbach with founding genuine materialism and positive science. Marx's words are disturbing indeed.

"QUOTE"

"Man makes religion, religion does not make man. Religion is indeed man's self-consciousness and self-awareness as long as he has not found his feet in the universe. But man is not an abstract being, squatting outside the world. Man is the world of men, the State, and society.

This State, this society, produce religion which is an inverted world consciousness, because they are an inverted world...Religious suffering is at the same time an expression of real suffering and a protest against real suffering. Religion is the sigh of the oppressed creature, the sentiment of a heartless world, and the soul of soulless conditions. It is the opium of the people. The abolition of religion, as the illusory happiness of men, is a demand for their real happiness." [23]

T. H. Huxley

1825-1895 AD

The word agnosticism was coined by **T. H. Huxley**, a scientist and friend of **Charles Darwin**. In fact he was known as *"Darwin's bulldog."* He coined the phrase to express his own state of mind. Science was beginning to eliminate God from its framework. This point is underlined by a conversation between Napoleon and the French astronomer, Pierre Simon Laplace. Napoleon remarked that Laplace had eliminated God from his astronomy. To which Laplace said, *"Sire, I have no need for that*

---

[23] *Critique of Hegel's Philosophy of Right.* Introduction

hypothesis." Consequently, God was no longer a term that science has an explanation for.

Friedrich Nietzsche

1844-1900 AD

Friedrich Nietzsche stated, *"The most important of more recent events–that 'god is dead', that the belief in the Christian God has become unworthy of belief–already begins to cast its first shadows over Europe...In fact, we philosophers and 'free spirits' feel ourselves irradiated as by a new dawn by the report that the 'old God is dead'; our hearts overflow with gratitude, astonishment, presentiment and expectation. At last the horizon seems open once more, granting even that it is not bright; our ships can at last put out to sea in face of every danger; every hazard is again permitted to the discerner; the sea, our sea, again lies open before us; perhaps never before did such an 'open sea' exist."*

Thus was born the *"God is dead"* movement. I have to ask though, why was there such a sense of relief? It can only be thought that perhaps that with the death of God in their minds there was also a death of conscience. A death of conscience would indeed be a relief to the atheist.

Nietzsche is credited with the idea of the superman. The superman in their thinking is the man who realizes the human predicament, who creates his own values, and who fashions his life accordingly. He himself is no stranger to anguish, but he triumphs over weakness and despises it in others. Having traced the thinking of those that were well respected in their times it is not hard to see how the Nazi party came to power in Germany.

We cannot complete our brief overview without mentioning that Nietzsche lost his father and brother at an early age. He came from a strong Lutheran family. No doubt the tragedy that surrounded his early life shaped his ideas about God.

During this period theology was being stripped of the miraculous and supernatural elements found in the Bible. The historicity of the Bible was also being called into question. Kant's legacy is the liberalization of the Christian faith. He turned the redemptive Savior into just a moral man. Emphasis then is upon morals rather than a need to be cleansed from sin. The Catholic Church did see the threat of secularism and liberal ideas; although their plan of attack was one that put the church first rather than the existence of God and the authority of the Scriptures.

What we can see, to be sure, is the progression of thought and ideas postulated and subsequently reshaped and manipulated until it ends in the death of Christianity in the mind of the philosopher.

    Descartes—Hume – Kant—Feuerbach and Darwin— Marx

That line of influence culminated in socialism/communism; the legacy which is one of theft, death, and destruction. All of the fruit of Satan's nature is in clear display throughout the twentieth century which has been called the bloodiest century known to mankind. With such dismal failure of systems of thought one would think we would have abandoned these ideas. No, our universities are bursting at the seams with professors who espouse these deadly ideas.

Contemporary or Post Modern Philosophy

The Twentieth Century

The first quarter of the twentieth century was filled with logical positivism. The primary weapon of the Logical Positives was the Verification Principle. This was a way of determining a statement to be true or false. They claim that a statement can only be verified by a scientific process of verification. Can the claim be observed? If not, it is dismissed as false.

A. J. Ayer

1910-1989 AD

A. J. Ayer stated, *"We say that a sentence is factually significant to any given person, if, and only if, he knows how to verify the proposition which it purports to express–that is, if he knows what observations would lead him, under certain conditions, to accept the proposition as being true, or reject it as being false. If, on the other hand, putative proposition is of such a character that the assumption of its truth, or falsehood, is consistent with any assumption whatsoever concerning the nature of his future experience, then, as far as he is concerned, it is, if not a tautology, a mere pseudo-proposition. The sentence expressing it may be emotionally significant to him; but not literally significant."* This idea reduced the Word of God to mere myth.

From Logical Positivism we move to Existentialism. Existentialism flourished in Germany after the First World War and it flourished in France after the Second World War. Colin Brown in *"Philosophy & the Christian Faith"* notes that Existentialism has found its way into some theologians' writings, but more notably it produced a *"militant atheistic progeny."* One of these is:

Jean-Paul Sartre

1905-1980 AD

Feodor Dostoievsky, the Russian novelist, once wrote: *"If God did not exist, everything would be permitted."* Sartre insists that this is the starting point of Existentialism. He insists that humans are just dumped into this world and each person must work out their own values.

As a traveler, Sartre spent much of the rest of his life attempting to reconcile his existentialist ideas about free will with communist principles, which taught that socio-economic forces beyond our immediate individual control play a critical role in shaping our lives. His major defining work of this period, the *Critique de la raison dialectique* (*Critique of Dialectical Reason*), appeared in 1960.

Sartre's emphasis on the humanist values in the early works of Marx led to a dispute with the leading Communist intellectual in France in the 1960s, Louis Althusser, who claimed that the ideas of the young Marx were decisively superseded by the *"scientific"* system of the later Marx. Sartre went to Cuba in the 60's to meet Fidel Castro and Ernesto *"Che"* Guevara. After Guevara's death he said that Guevara was the most complete human being of his age. This is actually noted in the trailers for the film *The Motorcycle Diaries,* which documents Guevara's travels around South America as a young man.

It is amazing that Che is now touted as a hero. This was a cold blooded killer who murdered political opponents. He was a coward that is now idolized by a class of people that are moral relativists.

Add to the existential movement *"radicalism"* and we have the 1960's. The Nietzschian cry that *"God is dead"* was now being resurrected. There were a number of atheist authors working on separate works that were raising the same cry. It came to be known as the creed. It states that God is dead and Jesus is his son. During this time humanism was being raised to a place of religion. Their battle cry being that there are no absolute moral values.

Part II – The Condition of the Church

All of this causes me to reflect upon where we are today as the Church. It becomes obvious to me that there is a desperate need for Christian apologetics, not only for the Church to consume, but also a presentation must be made to the world. The world now has so many reasons to believe that God does not exist, or that if He does, He does not care. We must provide them with real reasons for why we believe what we do.

Much of post-Old Testament philosophy held a presupposition of the existence of God. Yet, as the envelope was pushed in each generation, the next generation was always provided with ideas upon which the erosion of Christianity could progress. The philosophies that started in the first century and have made their way to the twenty first century have produced a society with a worldview that is anti-biblical at its very core.

Indeed, even within the hallowed halls of the organized churches today we find they are fraught with humanistic radical existential thinking. Colin Brown in *"Philosophy & the Christian Faith"* writes, *"The task of Christian apologetics is not to try to discover some neutral, common ground on which the believer and the unbeliever may stand . . . The task is to force him to face up to this (his responsibility before God) and to show that there are no legitimate escape routes."*

In looking at how we have arrived to our present condition, there are some lessons to be learned. The first lesson is that the enemy always starts with subtle changes in Christian doctrine and then builds on the change from generation to generation until the doctrine is completely unrecognizable. We cannot take any change in doctrine lightly. There must be a watchman attitude in the Church to keep pure that which was delivered to us by Jesus and the apostolic writers.

2 Timothy 1:14 *Guard, through the Holy Spirit who dwells in us, the treasure which has been entrusted to you.*

The second lesson is that pride played a huge part in bringing us a society that believes in satisfying self as being pre-eminent to all other endeavors. I ask this question of all and any that would purport to believe that they believe in God, but not a personal Christ. If you believe in God, what makes you think that you have the ability or the power to define God in any way; whether it is how much God interacts with His creation, or whether it be a moral law? If you believe in a God that is transcendent to creation, would it not make sense that this kind of power is not definable by the thing created?

This should have been the starting point with the early Christian philosophers, but they allowed their pride to tell them that they were powerful enough to make changes to biblical principle simply because to them it was reasonable. The Church saw its own existence as superior to the Word of God. As a result, they were willing to surrender the Word of God since they thought this tactic was necessary in order to keep the Church.

What makes a thing created think it can rationalize its Creator to its own understanding? This was the folly that many Christian philosophers engaged in. Thinking they could somehow be exalted enough to describe with human reason the God that created them; they rationalized themselves right into agnosticism and atheism. How foolish, for one would have to have all of the knowledge of the universe to make that kind of rationalization. This happens among Christians all the time. I am baffled by this. If we are created, the One who created us would be far advanced above us. My understanding then of the Creator would be reliant upon His revelation of Himself only.

Progression of the Deconstruction of God

We have six primary progressions to the deconstruction of God in society.

1. We have gone from believing in a God who is personal and a Jesus who is personal and that did miracles, to believing in a God and a Jesus that did not do miracles but who were still personal.
2. We went from believing in a God and a Jesus that was personal but did not do miracles, to believing in just a God who was personal.
3. Then we went from believing in a God who was personal, to believing in a God that is detached from His creation and unknowable. (deism)
4. We went from believing that God is detached from His creation and unknowable, to believing that God is creation or nature and is knowable through natural causes only. (pantheism)
5. We went from believing God is nature, to believing God is dead. If God is dead, all things are permitted. If all things are permitted, then no one can judge another's behavior as right or wrong.

6. We went from believing that God is dead, to believing man is god. (humanism)

This is where we find society today. This is why America is so clearly divided. It is also why America is in a cultural civil war. The Christian is pitted against the secularist and the secularist is pitted against the Christian. In civil government there is a desperate grab for control. For whoever is at the control of government is able to define the direction our society takes. For Christians to ignore civil government is for Christians to eventually sign their own death warrant. At some point, if the secularist wins this war, reading from the Bible will be a hate crime. Churches will be forced to accept homosexuality within them. Crimes against Christians will become socially acceptable.

This may sound apocalyptic to some, however, if we look at what has and is happening in societies around the world, it is not an unfathomable thought. This cultural civil war is not a war where one side takes physical ground from the other side. This war is fought on a different front, where progression of one's army is found in the moral tenants of our laws. If you want to judge the moral health of any society you can do so by looking at the evolution of law in that civilization. When you see the judicial component of a culture begin to liberalize laws through interpretation, it is a barometer of that society.

When our laws begin to disintegrate and disagree with the law of God, the secularists are winning that battle. When our laws have no defined interpretation and they are used only to substantiate the political leanings of a judge, then the secularists are winning the battle.

This shows us a broad overview of how something that starts out small and subtle can wind up changing how people even respect life. It may have taken us two thousand years to get here, but we cannot dismiss the idea that the enemy has had a plan and he is continuing to implement that plan. The words of a wise man once said, *"All evil needs to succeed are that good men do nothing."*

Good men sat by while prayer was taken out of our schools, good men did nothing as the Ten Commandments were taken out of our schools. Now you cannot even say a prayer at a sporting event put on by a school. The Ten Commandments are being removed from court houses. Now the secularists are trying to take "under God" out of the pledge of allegiance. They are trying to remove "In God We Trust" from our currency. How long will good men do nothing to resist this takeover of their religious freedoms?

Immersion Causes Desensitization

According to Ravi Zacharias there is an old eastern proverb that says, *"If you want to know what water is, don't ask the fish."* The idea behind this proverb is that as a society we are surrounded by the things that make us what we are and we cannot see them because they are always there. In other words, immersion causes desensitization. We have been slowly but methodically inundated with various streams of thought through various forms of media.

When it started it was subtle, and only a few saw it for what it was and complained. But as we got used to that idea, another one was presented. We have become so completely immersed in moral relativism that we scarcely know what it is nor are we able to recognize it. According to Barna Research Group, only 46% of born again Christians believe in absolute moral truths.

This condition reminds me of the old adage about the frog that will scramble to escape to save its life after being thrust into a pan of boiling water. But if that frog is put into a pan of cold water and then heated gradually, it is impervious to the fact that its environment is getting to the point of being dangerous. Our gradual change as a society and a Church has gone unnoticed, except for a few perceptive individuals. How long do we have before the boiling begins, because when it starts, the battle is lost.

"QUOTE"

> *"The ideas and personalities that the media thrusts upon our imaginations subtly condition our consciousness in ways that even political totalitarianism cannot accomplish. We are unavoidably beguiled, in this so-called postmodern world, to an unprecedented degree. The constant bombardment of images shapes the perceptions of a whole generation and results in altered beliefs and lifestyles that make even the abhorrent seem normal."* [24]

I found it interesting when I watched the opening scenes of the movie *"The Flags of our Fathers,"* as an aged soldier contemplates the raising of the flag over Iwo Jima in World War II. He made the statement that a war can be won or lost by a single picture. He then asked the question, *"What picture do you remember from World War II?"* The answer was the raising of the Iwo Jima flag in victory. He then asks the question, *"What picture do you remember from the Viet Nam war?"* The answer was a helpless South Vietnamese man being shot through the head by a communist North Vietnamese soldier. Which war did we win and which war did we lose?

The perceptions of the masses are what drive the three major components of any society. The economy, government, and religion of a people are a picture of the belief structure of that

---

[24] – *Ravi Zacharias "Deliver us From Evil"*

culture. Sway the perceptions of the masses and you can secure a certain outcome. Since the problems run so deep, the solutions must run just as deep.

The secularists have done a masterful job of inoculating a whole society from hearing an alternate worldview. They have so successfully labeled the supernatural as absurd that those proponents of the supernatural are seen as snake oil salesmen. The very source of healing for this society has been successfully branded as absurd and irrelevant. This has prevented society from looking in the direction of the Church for solutions to its many problems.

To put this in perspective consider the following. There is a panel of experts discussing a volatile moral issue on prime time television. The panel is comprised of an educator, a philosopher, a civil libertarian, a politician, a lawyer, a journalist, and a minister. Zacharias then asks this question. *"Who would be considered by the listening audience as the most biased or "irrelevant" on the subject and therefore the least credible?"* The obvious answer is the minister. The next step then is to figure out why we think the way we do.

The Three Moods

Ravi Zacharias reveals three things that happened to get us to where we are today. He calls them the "Three Moods." They are secularization, pluralization, and privatization of religion.

Secularization

The relativism of the philosophers has made its way into our culture. How did this happen? Why do we have so many people that believe there is no such thing as an absolute moral? Why did it get a foothold in this country now and why did it not earlier?

The only resistance to moral relativism is the Christian Church. She has stood at the ready to defeat all arguments that have exalted themselves against the knowledge of God. She buttressed the truth and contended for the faith. There is only one place where the fault lies. It lies squarely at the feet of the theologian.

This defection of ministry set the stage for moral relativism to be accepted in America. Ministers turned over their congregations to the wolves. The wolves came in and ravaged the flock. The flock had no way of defending themselves. Failure of leadership is the worst kind of failure for its fruit is measured in many lost souls.

The media outlets already being secularized would only allow those ministers who were secularized to have a voice over their medium. This caused those who were genuine ministers to hunker down in their own little corner and let the world go to hell. This was known as the evangelical movement; named such because they had withdrawn from the political arena to only concentrate on the winning of souls.

Once the Church defects from any arena it by default turns that area over to the enemy. The enemy will then use the power of that arena to cause further damage to the Church. By Christians pulling out of politics, evil men and women were able to grab the reins of power and use those reins to suppress the truth of Christianity. With no public opposition to the secularists it became more difficult to win souls.

What we learn from this is that we must continue to contend for the faith no matter how small or few in number we are. We must be vocal about what we believe. The portrayal of ministers that had no faith leads to a public disdain for Christianity and for ministers. Even the unbeliever has no respect for a person that is unwilling to stand up for what they believe. Because of this, there arose a disdain for every minister. This leads to the next mood.

Pluralization

Pluralization is simply the existence and availability of a number of worldviews, each competing for the minds of the masses. With so many different people from different cultures, each with their own religious ideas coming to this nation, and with the disgust felt toward Christian ministers that defected from their call, people now felt free to dabble in other ways of thinking.

Ravi Zacharias suggests there are two sides to pluralism. There is both a strength and weakness. *"The strength is that pluralism demands that we measure the truthfulness of our own beliefs against competing ideas. The weakness of pluralism is the faulty deduction that all beliefs can be equally true. This weakness has paved the way for the absence of reason in the contemplation of life's most important questions."* [25]

This death of reason is found in the justification of abortion. The rationale behind abortion is that since we do not know when life begins, you may abort at will. How absurd this position is! The death of reason has resulted in the loss of the sanctity of life. Plurality has bred irrationality which Zacharias says is the steppingstone to the unconscionable.

Privatization of Religion

The third mood is the privatization of religion. With the ministry infiltrated and marginalized, now it is time to silence what is left of the sheep. This is the insidious nature of secular humanism; one can pull out a morality out of the air. This is what the secularist did. They made it evil for Christianity to be vocalized

---

[25] Ravi Zacharias "Deliver us From Evil"

in public. If I were to say to this nation 60 years ago that America would no longer discuss religious things publically, I would be brushed off as an object of absurdity.

Nevertheless, here we are. If you don't think this tactic of the enemy was successful, why is it that when Christians start to talk about Jesus they look around and lower their voice to a mere whisper so that no one will hear them? This tactic has been so successful that good, honest, and strong Christians have been fooled by it as well.

What makes Christianity so powerful is that we are able to hear other points of view and engage in a dialogue on them without fear that others who hear would be misled. However, as Zacharias reveals, this strength also becomes a weakness. Look around at all of the other religious beliefs. How many of them are tolerant of a different point of view. Only Christianity allows a freedom of thought and voice without restraint or demeaning those voices of opposition.

Are we to believe that religious ideas are so offensive that they must be relegated to the private realm of one's home? If Christianity is so offensive, what is the definition of that offense? Don't tell me that it is because we say that this or that lifestyle is wrong because if that is offensive to you, you are engaging in the same behavior by saying that we should not vocalize our belief. Consider the following:

> *"QUOTE"*
>
> *"How ironic that sexuality and nudity which are meant to be private are now fare for public consumption while spiritual convictions, which*

are meant to strengthen public polity, are now for private expression only." [26]

Zacharias sums up the problem.

"QUOTE"

"Secularization left society void of shame with no point of reference for decency. Pluralization left society void of reason with no point of reference for rationality. Privatization has left society void of meaning and with no point of reference for life's congruity." [27]

Therefore, we no longer know who we are as a people. We think we know who we are as individuals, but we have lost our national purpose which causes so many to be just about their own life without concern for national survival.

It does not make sense to entrust those who are immoral in their private lives with the power to determine the nation's moral issues. Regardless, this is the trend that we see. We continually see the inclination toward a disregard for the necessity of character in our leaders. This can only produce a harvest of leaders that are morally bankrupt which will only foster more immoral decisions concerning our nation.

When we look at examples from history we can find the same tactics being employed in 400 BC are taking place in 2010 AD. Our enemy has not changed much in the tactics he uses. As a Church we have been duped to think that our fight is within the four walls of a church rather than a vocal high profile debate in the public square. As a result, we have lost our validity in the public

---

[26] – *Ravi Zacharias "Deliver us From Evil"*

[27] – *Ravi Zacharias "Deliver us From Evil"*

square since those so-called Christian voices that do get public air do not have the backbone to stand up and say, *"Yes, Jesus is the only way and this is why."*

Manasseh took Judah from a godly state and plundered her into the depths of sin and in doing so we see a pattern. Hezekiah was the king of Judah before his son Manasseh took the seat of power. Ravi Zacharias alleges there are three things that Manasseh did to bring Judah to the place of destruction. *"The first and most radical decision he made was to lead a reaction against his father's spiritual reforms."* [28]

Manasseh made it his life's work to destroy the one thing that has done more to govern man as an individual and societies than anything else—the law of God. Remove God's law and you remove all restraint against evil behavior. The reason God's law is such a powerful force in governance is that every man and every woman has a conscience that informs them with regard to God's law. The enemy knows that if he can hide God's law from public view then he can skew those laws to be what he wants.

As Americans we have gone from speaking out against the immoral choices committed in this nation to being eerily silent in the face of immorality. We have been pressured by a political move to be silent concerning immorality. We are now called upon by the media elite to celebrate these immoral choices. If we happen to speak out against evil behavior we are called bigots and intolerant. The law of God has already been systematically removed from American society. This can and does have the effect of opening the floodgates of a plethora of unrestrained lusts and every kind of evil work.

---

[28] Ravi Zacharias "Deliver us From Evil"

First, it was prayer being taken out of schools, then it was the Bible, then it was the Ten Commandments, then it was prayer at school events, then it was Christian holidays, then it was the pledge of allegiance. What was put in its place? Making first graders aware of sexuality, planting ideas of sexual orientation in their heads, asking them to choose if they are straight or homosexual. Evolution replaced the Creator. As a result, hope has been replaced with despair, happiness with depression; our children are cutting themselves, they are committing suicide, they are killing one another, they are stealing, they are abusing drugs, they are engaging in fornication, and they are involved in pornography. Yeah, things sure are better since we kicked God out our public schools.

The next step that Manasseh took was a predictable one. Having stripped the land of God's law, Manasseh now led the people into heathenism. He set the example of this behavior by sacrificing his own child upon the altar of the false god Moloch. Can we imagine the effect of a nation's leader taking his own child for all to see, and place that child in the fire? The screams of babies could be heard by the people as one by one they would offer their own to the fire. What effect could this have on the conscience of a nation?

Are we any different? Is there really a difference between forceps or fire? Have we not destroyed the conscience of a nation by sacrificing our children at the altar of self indulgence? While the Church is singing hymns within their four walls, children are being ripped from wombs limb by limb. Does that offend you? It should! It is meant to! You have a voice and if you allow the enemy to continue to silence that voice you will have to give an account as you stand before your Savior.

The third step Manasseh took was to silence those voices that were crying out against his actions. Manasseh had the prophet

Isaiah killed to silence him. We are beginning to see this same pattern in America. There is an all out assault on the voices of reason that are crying against the lawless behavior in this country. The secularists who have removed the law of God and substituted moral relativism, and who have celebrated sexual perversion and the killing of the unborn, are now trying to silence the prophetic voices who cry out against such behavior.

The whole point of state controlled education is so the government can write their doctrines on the young minds of the millions. By doing so, they can develop the conscience of the next generation and thereby control them. This is why there was such an outcry against school vouchers back in the 80's. If school vouchers were used it would empower the parent to seek education along the lines of their own moral convictions. As a result, the government would lose the ability to indoctrinate young minds. They would be unable to produce a generation who would carry forth their secularist beliefs. They so demonized that program in the main stream media that anyone who was for the system was labeled as a fool and an idiot.

To think that any person holding that kind of power will take a position of neutrality is simply willful naiveté. From the halls of academia come the ravaging teeth of a lion who seeks to devour the young of this nation. By passing on their warped images and ideas to our progeny, they are securing for themselves a movement that will outlive them and this is what they are seeking.

Manasseh finally did repent, but it was too late for those he had infected with his doctrines of demons. A whole generation lay lost. He was able to lead the people down the road to destruction, but now he is unable to stop them. By removing the boundaries of God's law, he allowed evil to pour in unabated. Today we find this same spirit debunking the idea of absolute morals. There is only one thing that can come of it. Evil will again come in like a flood and influence our children to live lives of debauchery. So we see the same three moods at work. (Secularization, Pluralism, and Privatization of Religion)

Manasseh left a nation in ruin. They were now morally bankrupt, spiritually sick, and rationally stupid. His predecessor would have to rebuild. Have you noticed that it is always harder to rebuild than it is to destroy? So it is with nations. Corrupt them from within and it is nearly impossible to turn them around.

Josiah would replace Manasseh as king. He sought to bring Judah back to the place his grandfather Hezekiah had left it. The first step that Josiah took was to restore the spiritual leaders and then the law of God. This must be our first step in returning this nation to God. We must restore the spiritual leadership! We must have leaders again who have access to the ears of a nation to hold to the absolutes of the Scriptures and be able to give a defense for their faith. They must be able to point out the logical fallacy of moral relativism and reeducate a people to the law of God. We were warned of this by Daniel Webster in 1823.

> *"Quote"*
>
> *"If truth be not diffused, error will be; if God and His Word are not known and received, the devil and his works will gain the ascendancy; if the evangelical volume does not reach every hamlet, the pages of a corrupt and licentious literature will; if the power of the Gospel is not felt throughout the length and breadth of the land, anarchy and misrule, degradation and misery,*

> *corruption and darkness will reign without mitigation or end."* [29]

Secularism seeks to develop a society outside the temple. To do this they must make those things inside the temple look like they are depraved. Why do you think that every time you see a minister in a movie, he is either a sexual deviant or a bumbling fool. Do you think that a society that is continuously bombarded with these images is not affected by them?

This is how the secularist has been successful in invalidating what takes place inside the temple. It is the justification of sin that is at the heart of these movements. Manasseh wanted to live a life unrestrained by God's laws and God's spokesmen. In a selfish desire to live the way he wanted to without opposition, he destroyed an entire nation. The young were ravaged, the aged invalidated, and its people led to the brink of self destruction. The secularist tells us that we need to respect one another's beliefs. What does that mean?

Does respect mean that I give you audience to voice your opinion without opposing it? That is what they would have you believe while they, using their own definition of that word, disrespect Christianity and its beliefs. Jesus teaches us to treat all with respect, but not to justify sin. There is a difference in tolerating a person and tolerating an idea.

The secularists have opened a door, but what they do not realize is that it will ultimately result in their own doom as well. Anarchy knows no leaders! Even today we have those that call themselves anarchists that march in our streets. Their signature is lawlessness. Our only hope is to bring the law of God back to the

---

[29] – Daniel Webster

forefront of the consciences of those who are still reachable in order to stem the tide of evil that threatens this country.

> *"QUOTE"*
>
> *"If you were stranded on a lonely road in Los Angeles in the dead of night with your head under the hood of your car, and suddenly you heard the sound of footsteps and turned to see ten burly men walking toward you, would it or would it not make a difference to you if you knew they were coming out of a Bible study?"* [30]

Thomas Merton said, *"Man is not at peace with his fellow man because man is not at peace with himself. He is not at peace with himself because he is not at peace with God."* Peace—what a slippery virtue to get a hold of—or is it. Peace cannot be manufactured. It exists without regard to those who access it. In other words, it is there whether you believe it is or not. Peace is a by-product of relationship with God. God offers it, but will we enter in to take it. The author of Hebrews alludes to this when he penned, *"There remains a rest for the people of God."* It is there to be had, but not everyone is entering into that rest.

Secularism gives homage to only one thing—the senses. This causes them to ignore any consequence involved in their behavior. But when we love the law of God, we go beyond the immediate and see that there is a consequence to our action, which has the capacity to cause us to do the right and moral thing. Consequently, we have spawned the *"Me Generation"* who thinks only of the present moment satisfaction of the senses.

---

[30] – *Jewish Philosopher Dennis Prager*

- In 1991 sixty-seven percent of the U.S. population did not believe in absolute truth.
- In 1994 that figure rose to seventy-five percent. That is a startling statistic!
- If that were not bad enough, in 1991 fifty-two percent of evangelicals did not believe in absolute truth.
- In 1994 that figure rose to sixty-two percent.
- It is now at seventy-eight percent, even after the 9-11 attack on America.
- It is now at sixty-eight percent among evangelicals.

This is where the battle must be fought! I am convinced after studying this subject that we cannot make any gains until we restore the idea that there **ARE** absolute truths. We must learn to frame our arguments in such a way that it causes the average person to reconsider their position. We as ministers have got to begin to address this among our congregants. First, we need to make sure they believe in absolute truths. Second, we need to teach them how to defend those truths. What is at stake is the very fabric of our nation. If we want our children to have the blessings of our forefathers, we must turn this around.

How was it that God brought nations to their knees in the past? It is through hardship and calamity. I do not want that for this nation, and I certainly do not want it for our future generations. Oh, I pray that God puts this message upon the hearts of all pastors so that we can begin to turn the tide in this cultural war! At present, we are losing it!

Relativism

Next, I want to simplistically reveal to you the idea of relativism. Here again, there is a wonderful book that I would suggest you get for your library. This is one you will mark up and dog ear frequently. The name of the book is *"Relativism: Feet*

Firmly Planted in Mid-Air." It is authored by Francis Beckwith and Gregory Koukl.

Relativism is the belief that there are no moral absolutes and that all morals are simply relative to the individual or community. An example of moral relativism would be a community that defines what is acceptable and what is not. That is, that morality is not transcendent to the human experience. There is no set standard that we can appeal to for testing all human actions.

This leaves an individual or a society in the position of defining for themselves their own morality. This is why they also are so offended at the notion of a set of moral rules that measures all human behavior. Moral relativism is not new.

> **Proverbs 12:15** *The way of a fool is **right in his own eyes**, But a wise man is he who listens to counsel.*
>
> **Proverbs 21:2** *Every man's way is **right in his own eyes**, But the LORD weighs the hearts.*
>
> **Judges 17:5-6** *And the man Micah had a shrine and he made an ephod and household idols and consecrated one of his sons, that he might become his priest. In those days there was no king in Israel; **every man did what was right in his own eyes**.*

Moral relativism is simply that—doing what is right in your own eyes. The problem raised is that without a moral standard from which to test things, who is to say my morals or your morals are not right? Because the Bible has been invalidated by the secularist, its information with regard to morality is no longer relevant to humanity. This drives the idea that morality must be derived from the individual or the majority.

If someone comes along and says, *"That's not right."* There is usually the response, *"Who are you to say?"* If on the lowest level of authority (person to person) we are unable to discern moral standards, what happens when this goes to higher levels of authority? What happens when the lawmaker is unable to discern a moral standard? Will not the laws become confusing and even incoherent? What happens when this makes its way to the judges in a land? Will that not make their decisions confusing and incoherent? To one murderer the judge may give a short sentence and to another he may give the death penalty.

Our founding fathers understood the importance of a moral standard that transcends mankind. That is, a standard of behavior that comes from One higher than humanity. Without this standard, no society will be able to function in a way that protects its members. This is what they meant by the term, "inalienable rights." The word "inalienable" means absolute. Imagine that! It stands to reason then that an absolute right is one that cannot be surrendered, transferred, or alienated from the individual. Our fathers saw these rights as coming from their Creator. For only God, Who is absolute, could endow man with absolute rights.

This information is hated by the secularist. They do not have fond thoughts of our founding fathers. To dismiss this they became revisionists of history. They have changed what is taught with regard to our founding to our children. Our nation is in real danger because as a Church we have been tricked into silence. We have been told that our battlefield is simply prayer and rebuking demonic authorities over this land.

Demonic authorities are in authority because of the men and women who believe in what they say coming to power in government! Remove those that do not serve God and you remove that demonic authority over that person's sphere of power. We are rebuking demons while the demons are secretly whispering damnable heresies to human beings, who in turn are espousing these ideas without opposition from those who are doing the rebuking.

It has come to the place where the word *"truth"* only means *"what is truth for me."* This statement presupposes that truth is fluid and changeable, not static and absolute. For many, truth is defined by them based upon what is important to them.

Since *"truth for me"* is, for all intents and purposes, the death of reality, all of the constructs of ethics fall with it. It leaves an environment of anything-goes-if-that-is-your-opinion in its place. Virtue is no longer understood by *"What is good"* but by *"What feels good."*

> *"QUOTE"*
>
> *"If there is no truth, nothing has transcendent value, including human beings. The death of morality reduces people to the status of mere creatures. When persons are viewed as things, they begin to be treated as things."*[31]

The authors state that there are two wrongs and two rights. There is rational morality and there is ethical morality. We deal differently with each one. For instance, we do not punish someone for getting an arithmetic problem wrong. That is rational morality. On the other hand, we do punish people for abusing children because that is an unethical behavior.

Those that believe in absolutes believe that moral truths are self evident just as rational truths are self evident. One can discover that $2 + 2 = 4$ and they can discover that deceiving is wrong. Ergo, we do not invent morality.

---

[31] – Relativism

"QUOTE"

Justice Harry Blackburn on Roe vs. Wade decision wrote, "We need not resolve the difficult question of when life begins. When those trained in the respective disciplines of medicine, philosophy, and theology are unable to arrive at any consensus, the judiciary, at this point in the development of man's knowledge, is not in a position to speculate."

Upon that statement the justice justifies the action of abortion. Let's examine this reasoning. If we are not sure when life begins, would we not exercise intuitive prudence and protect that person in case it is a life? For instance, what if you were driving down the highway and ahead of you, you see a pile of clothing in your lane. Not being able to tell of it is just a pile of clothing or a human with clothes on; would you run over the pile or swerve to miss it? Does not the intuitive knowledge of morality dictate that you swerve to miss it in case it is a person? Did not Justice Blackburn show a lack of judgment with this decision?

If we have cheapened life to the point that if we cannot determine with complete confidence that something is a life, that we kill it, we are all in danger. What is the next step, those that do not have all of their mental faculties? It is indeed a slippery slope to presume as Justice Blackburn did, that if life cannot be defined, then it must be considered non-life.

Koukl states a very important observation when dealing with the subject of moral relativism. He states, *"People can talk this way but they cannot live this way."* This is important because when we understand this we will find contradiction in the moral relativist's language very quickly.

Alvin Plantinga of the University Of Notre Dame states, *"If relativists try to use certain objections against moralists, they get stuck on their own objections."* This is where they get stuck. In their objections. They violate their own golden rule of not projecting one's morals upon another.

At the heart of their argument is use of the term "tolerance." The American Heritage Dictionary says that tolerance is, *The capacity for or the practice of recognizing and respecting the beliefs or practices of others.* The way this word is used today is in contention with its actual definition. If you simply voice a disagreement with a relativist, you are usually called intolerant. This idea of tolerance is simply not possible. If voicing an opinion that is different than yours is the definition of intolerant, then your opinion has just become intolerant as well.

Also, if my determination of another's idea is wrong is being intolerant, how can I ever be tolerant since I must think that person's idea is wrong in order to be tolerant? We are to tolerate behavior only as long as it remains moral and civil. We are to tolerate beliefs only as long as they are sound and true.

Conclusion

The following quote is, I think, the best worded, most important, and of the greatest value of anything in the book. It gets right to the point of the question, *"Why moral relativism?"*

> *"QUOTE"*
>
> *"People are drowning in a sea of moral relativism. **Relativism destroys the conscience.** It produces people without scruples, because it provides no moral impulse to improve. This is why we don't teach relativism to our children. In fact, we labor to teach them just the opposite.*

> *Ultimately relativism is self-centered and egoistic. 'Doing your own thing' is fine for us, but we don't want others to be relativists. We expect them to treat us decently. Relativism is also dangerous. At Auschwitz, Hitler declared, 'I freed Germany from the stupid and degrading fallacies of conscience and morality . . . We will train young people before whom the world will tremble.'"* [32]

This is exactly our enemy's strategy. If Satan can present a philosophy to mankind that silences the conscience, he has effectively inoculated them from ever hearing the gospel. Why? It is the conscience that causes a person to understand his or her own sickness. Without the conscience one is justified in any behavior they desire to engage in.

There is never a reason for a moral relativist to seek forgiveness or redemption. To even suggest that they need forgiveness is to offend them. Satan is effectively convincing morally sick and diseased people that they are healthy and the consequence is that they will never seek a cure. The purpose of God's law is to cause a person to see that they are sinners.

Paul states that God's law was given so that we would see ourselves as exceedingly sinful. In seeing ourselves in this condition we would then seek a cure to this problem; ultimately finding that cure in Jesus. King David says, *"the law is perfect, able to convert the soul."* We absolutely need God's standard of laws in order to convince people that they are in need of salvation.

The item at risk in this argument is a person's worldview. This competition of worldviews has put our own nation in a

---

[32] – Relativism

cultural war. We have those that have a secular worldview and believe in a so-called tolerance where anything goes concerning human behavior, and we have those with a biblical worldview who believe that there are absolute moral principles that inform human behavior.

I do not mean this to say that all people fall into one of these two groups, but I would argue that the majority of this nation's populace does. What is at stake in this cultural war is not just a way of life or a way of governance; at stake are the very souls of human beings and the very existence of this nation. As this nation continues to pour into the ground the blood of thousands of innocent babies on a daily basis, that blood continues to call louder and louder to a Holy God. How can the Church escape judgment when it too has been lulled into silence on these important issues?

We are no longer to be a people blown about by every wind of doctrine. We are to stand for those principles that will reveal that humanity has an eternal terminal disease called *"sin"* and that God has provided an eternal cure in His Son, Jesus.

Can a Christian be Possessed?

Chapter Eight

This question has been posed to me so many times that I could scarcely come up with a number that reflects it accurately. Suffice it to say that it is on the hearts and minds of many Christians today. If we are to get any solid answers we will have to posit the arguments of those that believe a Christian can be possessed. Another question that usually is subservient to the question in the title is, *"Can a Christian who is possessed go to heaven?"*

To be fair, I want to state at the outset that I do not believe Christians can be possessed. The reason is simply holding to the Bible and what it says makes it impossible to believe. One of the things I have observed that mark those who do believe in believer possession is reliance upon experiences over and above Scripture. Since they have known people who by their fruit are Christians and then see the manifestation of demons in an exorcism, they conclude that Christians can be possessed. Then they seek proof of Scripture to back up the experience.

Before I get into the Scriptures used to support the idea that Christians can be possessed, I would like to address the Greek word for demon possession. Some who do believe in believer possession also make the point that there is no such word in the Greek for it. That the word translated to demon possession simply means to be demonized. They do this to get away from the word "possession" because possession denotes ownership, and this is a difficulty especially in light of the Scripture that states we are the possession of Jesus. The word is used thirteen times in the Bible and by looking at these we can get an idea of what it is.

Matthew 4:24—Here it mentions that those that are ill came to be healed of Jesus and then it lists the ailments. Of those ailments, demoniac was one of them. We cannot infer from this that this word simply means to be sick. But we can infer that a demoniac is a suffering. In fact if we look up the word for "ill" we find that it is composed of two Greek words, one of which is "to have" and the other is "suffering." It simply means "to have suffering." Obviously this could refer to physical, emotional, or spiritual suffering. In fact, the word "ill" as it is used in this passage is broken down into two categories. The first one is disease and the second one is rendered "pains." Upon closer inspection, the word pains actually means torments or tortures. This would agree then to demoniac in the list of illnesses.

Matthew 8:16—In this passage we also have use of the word "ill," however, after seeing that it can be speaking of being demonized there is no case to believe it is talking about sickness in a physical sense. Notice the need to "cast out." This suggests that something is in the person that needs to be cast out.

Matthew 8:28—Now we have a two men who are extremely violent. In this case the demons using the men's voice speak in the first person saying, "If you cast us out, send us into that herd of swine." Again being cast out is imperative.

Matthew 8:33—See above.

Matthew 9:32—Here there is the man who is mute that needs a demon cast out.

Matthew 12:22—*In this case, a man was both blind and mute. Note that this is where Jesus is accused of casting out demons by Beelzebub the prince of demons. Jesus corrects them by saying that a house divided against itself cannot stand. How then can Satan cast out Satan? This is also a proof that demonic spirits are fallen angels as Satan is.*

Matthew 15:22—*A mother who has a daughter who is demonized comes to Jesus for healing. By the way healing is used to include both being set free from demons and with regard to disease just as the first time the term is used reveals to us. This does not suggest any relationship between the two other than being in a state of suffering.*

Mark 1:32—*Now we have a distinction between being ill and being demonized. Mark separates them where as Matthew combines them. There is no contradiction here. It is probably a matter of style. In fact that they are mentioned together shows their agreement.*

Mark 5:15—*This is the parallel passage to Matthew 8:28*

Mark 5:16—*See above.*

Mark 5:18—*See above.*

Luke 8:36—*This also is a parallel account of Matthew 8:28*

John 10:21—*In this last passage Jesus is accused of having a demon. Others countered that this could not be the words of a demonized person.*

What did we learn from the thirteen instances where this word for demon possession is used? We learned that these demonic possessions were accompanied with the demonic entities speaking by using the human's voice. We learned that these entities had taken up residence inside of a human and needed to be cast out. Consequently, we can conclude that demon possession is an acceptable term with regard to being demonized since these spirits have the ability to take control of one's vocal cords and inhabit the individual as well. This should put to rest any argument over the Greek word used that is translated demon possessed.

This should not be confused with those who simply come into agreement with what the devil is saying in their mind and then speak it in agreement. This is not, nor can be, demon possession. There is no violation of free will and there is not a taking control of anything. It is no different than me repeating something someone told me that is a deception.

The belief that Christians can be possessed is accompanied with a rise of what is known as "Deliverance Ministries." If we look at history, why is the frequency and number of exorcisms needed directly proportionate with the rise of deliverance ministries? I want to make it clear that I am not treating these ministries as cults because they are also preaching Jesus as other churches do. They just specialize in exorcisms, if you will.

When looking at the doctrines behind Deliverance Ministries keep in mind that it can really run the gamut. One underlying theme, however, is that these demons gain access through sins of one kind or another. It is not easy to define some of their beliefs and I assure you I am not trying to find the most outlandish ones. I actually endeavored to find some serious doctrine on the issue and after hours of research found that not much is out there with regard to serious exegetic work. Every single work I looked at used experience as their primary evidence for this doctrine.

To the question, "Can Christians have a demon?" one response was the following:

> *"In a simple answer, yes, Christians can have demons and at times need to have them cast out. <u>There is no real Biblical basis to claim that Christians cannot have demons.</u> Actually, the Bible shows us clearly that deliverance is geared towards God's children. Jesus actually referred to it as children's bread, and said it was not fit to cast before dogs."*

The "children's bread" statement is based upon the story found in Matthew 15 and Mark 7. In this story a Canaanite woman had a daughter that needed to be set free from demon possession. The comment was made that it is not right to give the children's (Israel) bread to dogs (Gentiles). What is meant by this? As a Canaanite she had no covenant with God. The "children" in that statement is Israel who is under covenant with God. That means there are certain benefits or rights to a person under covenant that is not extended to those who are not. One of those rights is to be delivered. Anyone could become a Jew; it was not an exclusive club. God had set out laws to guide those who wanted to serve Him and come under covenant if they so desired.

Now the question becomes, *"If the children's bread represents deliverance from demons, does that not prove that God's covenant children will need deliverance from demon spirits and thus we can infer that Christians who are also covenant people will also need this deliverance?"*

First of all, I don't disagree that people under covenant are not necessarily protected from demons unless that is a stated benefit. If we look at the Old Covenant we find that one could be under a curse or under a blessing based upon whether they chose to acknowledge and follow God's laws. However, that does not infer that the New Testament Covenant is the same. Let's look at a Scriptural example.

King Saul was an Israelite from the tribe of Benjamin. Saul also had the Holy Spirit of God in him as many times the kings and prophets experienced. Nevertheless, after rebellion and a refusal to repent things changed for Saul. By unction of the Holy Spirit, the prophet Samuel was sent to the house of Jesse to anoint a new king. The Scriptures tell us that as soon as David was anointed king, the Spirit of God left Saul and went into David, and an evil spirit went into Saul. Observe that the Holy Spirit left before a demonic spirit was able to come in.

Now, to appeal to the children's bread story, it can only work if the New Covenant is under the same benefits as the Old Covenant. Also, if there are different benefits in the New Covenant, then discovery of them could produce a beneficial freedom from demonic possession by reason of the Covenant.

Hebrews 8:6 declares that we have a covenant with better promises. Consequently, we need to discover those different promises in order to understand what we have access to. Whereas the Old Covenant was action based (if you do these things), the New Covenant is faith based (whosoever believes).

Also, under the Old Covenant the people were always asking for deliverance, whereas under the New Covenant deliverance is inferred and past tense. So, we cannot appeal to the story of the "children's bread" to support the teaching that Christians can be possessed. Here is another statement.

> *"If Christians couldn't have demons, then somehow they would have to automatically shed them the moment they accept Jesus."*

This statement presupposes that everyone prior to salvation is demonized and second, if that is true, then the Son of God is somehow either unwilling or incapable of setting the captive free at the moment of their salvation. I assume you can see the absurdity of this position. If not, I think you will after I lay out my case against it.

> **Demons return when they are cast out of unbelievers:** *Jesus clearly warned us that if we cast demons out of unbelievers, they are bound to return, each spirit bringing 7 even worse spirits with it (Matthew 12:43-45).*

The argument here is actually stating that we should not cast demons out of unbelievers because of the danger of that demon returning with seven worse spirits. The inference is because of this, demons should be cast out of the believer only. Here is the problem with this argument.

How is the unbeliever ever to come to faith in Christ if they are demonized? In all of the cases where demons were cast out, the person was not in their right mind so they would be unable to ever come to faith in Jesus in that state. To suggest that we refuse deliverance to the unbeliever is to damn them to hell! If we take a careful look at the text it makes reference to these demons coming back and finding the house from which they came swept, clean, and empty. Clue in on the empty part. That actually supports my claim that we cannot be possessed because the inference is that if the house was occupied these spirits would not be able to enter.

This is in agreement with the King Saul episode where the evil spirit was only able to come in after the Holy Spirit left. When an unbeliever is delivered from demons, they are then able to make a decision to fill their temple with God through faith in Jesus or not. Hence, to refuse them deliverance is nonsensical.

> *As for the argument the Holy Spirit will not dwell with a devil in the same body, we ask, **why not?** There is no verse we know of that even suggests this is impossible. Furthermore, the **Holy Spirit dwells in the same body the Christian dwells in,** and the old nature of a Christian **is as wicked as the devil if not more so.** Have you not read, **"The heart is deceitful ABOVE ALL THINGS, and desperately wicked: who can know it"** (Jer. 17:9)?*[33]

We do have Scripture that suggests this is impossible. An example would be of Saul where the Holy Spirit left before an evil spirit entered. Another is that the very presence of God cleanses the temple. According to Matthew 15, the temple is sanctified by Him who dwells in it. The perverse and the unclean will not dwell in God's temple. You are the temple of the Holy Spirit! As to people being evil and the Holy Spirit dwelling in them, have they not read that we are clean because of the word of faith? Have they not read that anything born of God cannot sin? The whole point of the New Covenant is the conversion of the spirit into a new creation.

> *In 2 Cor 11:3-4 Paul makes a rather revealing statement about Christians and other spirits, "But I fear, lest by any means, as the serpent beguiled Eve through his subtlety, so your minds should be corrupted from the simplicity that is in Christ. For if he that cometh preacheth another Jesus, whom we*

---

[33] Article-"Christians and Demon Possession" by Timothy S. Morton

have not preached, or if ye receive another spirit, which ye have not received, or another gospel, which ye have not accepted, ye might well bear with him.

By saying, "if ye receive ANOTHER SPIRIT, which ye have NOT received" Paul is indicating that a Christian who already has the Holy Spirit can receive another spirit besides! Some may argue Paul is speaking to lost people in the Corinthian church, but that doesn't hold up. First, Paul is concerned their minds have been corrupted by Satan (through a false teacher) from the simplicity of receiving and resting in Christ for salvation. He said in verse 2 he was "jealous over [them] with a godly jealously: for I have espoused you to one husband..." that is, Christ. Paul wouldn't espouse lost people to Christ. Furthermore, he says they could receive "ANOTHER spirit" which they did not receive previously (when he was with them). The Spirit they received when he presented them the gospel was the Holy Spirit! He also said they could receive another (false) gospel which they "have not [previously] accepted." This indicates they accepted the true gospel while Paul was with them because the "another gospel" was not preached by him. I know this passage is somewhat confusing, but read it carefully with prayer and the Lord will help us understand. [34]

The mistake here is inferring that "another spirit" is a possession of a demonic spirit. Consider the following.

---

[34] Article-"Christians and Demon Possession" by Timothy S. Morton

> ***1 John 4:1*** *Beloved, do not believe every spirit, but test the spirits to see whether they are from God, because many false prophets have gone out into the world.*

The above passage reveals that we can indeed entertain the words of demonic spirits whether they are coming from human sources or are thoughts that come into your mind. The term "receive a spirit" does not have to infer possession. If I listen to and believe a demonic spirit I have in essence received that spirit. Not that I have taken it inside me to possess me, but I have entertained those statements that spirit made and have believed them and received those thoughts. Besides, this is an obscure text that is not clear with regard to its statements. For the proponent to rely upon this text for proof of Christians being possessed is dubious at best.

Finally, I will take a look at the teachings of probably the most popular proponent of this doctrine, Bob Larson.

> *I realized that those pastors and Bible teachers who had repeatedly reinforced the "Christians can't have a demon" outlook had very little practical experience with the phenomenon. I concluded that, while doctrine is not based on experience, the lack of experiential testimony about such a crucial area of spiritual deliverance was a glaring weakness.*[35]

Right from the beginning we have an appeal to experience again. This is a sure sign of weakness with regard to the existence of doctrine to support it. This is something you will see throughout spiritual warfare subjects. I am not sure what Larson means by *"a lack of experiential testimony."* Does he think that those who do

---

[35] Article-"Can a Christian Have a Demon" by Bob Larson

not believe in Christians being possessed do not have the experiences to support that truth? If so, the lack of demons in Christians is an experiential testimony.

> *In Acts chapter 5, Ananias and Sapphira, members of the early church, lied to the apostle Peter. They had sold some possessions to give to the church, and then had second thoughts and conspired to keep back a portion for themselves. When Peter asked them what amount they had received for the sale, Ananias and Sapphira lied. What was the source of that lie? The apostle Peter said, "Satan filled your heart to lie to the Holy Spirit" (verse 3). In judgment, God struck them dead. If we accept the assumption that Ananias and Sapphira experienced the new birth in Christ, then how can we explain away the fact that their hearts were filled by Satan to such an extent that they were capable of committing a sin worthy of such abrupt and severe divine judgment?* [36]

Earlier in the article (not quoted here), Larson states that the born again spirit of man is off limits to demonic spirits. Now he is using the case of Ananias and Sapphira as a proof that the devil can possess the heart, which is synonymous with the spirit of man, to fill it. Could it be the Scripture is bearing witness of hearts that get filled with lies from the devil? Wasn't basically the same thing said to Judas to whom Jesus said, *"Do what Satan has put in your heart to do."* When we entertain the voices of demonic spirits we become pawns of their destructive desires. When we believe the thoughts they are presenting in our minds we become doers of their words.

---

[36] Article-"Can a Christian Have a Demon" by Bob Larson

> *Satan can, in some instances, take over a Christian's mind and speak through his lips. Demons are in certain instances able to place Christians in a trance state so that the unclean spirit controls psychomotor functions and conscious mental processes. I have dealt with scores of cases with people who were undeniably followers of Christ and yet demons spoke through them and even violently attacked me. It is disingenuous to suggest that they somehow lost their salvation long enough to let a demon in and then thereafter resumed their Christian walk. If Satan can control our speech when we are disobedient and fill our hearts with evil when we are rebellious, he may be able to do a lot more to Christians than we would like to admit. What scriptural lessons can we learn from this startling information?* [37]

Observe that he used the term "unclean spirit." Again, all of this is based upon his experience. If the Word states that I am unable to judge a person's heart whether he is saved or not, how is it suddenly possible to know without a doubt that these people have a demon and are also Christian? What evidence do we have that Peter was controlled by Satan? That he spoke what Satan wanted him to say is not empirical evidence of control. Peter was apparently in agreement with what Satan is saying.

Just as a few verses before that, Peter stated, *"Thou art the Christ, the Son of the living God."* To which Jesus said to Peter that statement did not come from him, but from the Father in Heaven. This begs the question, did the Father control Peter and

---

[37] Article-"Can a Christian Have a Demon" by Bob Larson

force him to say that, or was Peter in agreement with the Father as the Father revealed that revelation to him?

Peter was demonstrating how easy it is for the rest of us to be used of God one moment by listening and coming into agreement with God and the next moment being used of the devil by coming into agreement with what he is saying. This is in agreement with many Scriptures that talk about watching over and guarding our minds.

> *A Christian can be born again and have spiritual victory over the original Adamic sin that eternally separates mankind from God and still have besetting sins (Hebrews 12:1). Uncontrolled thoughts, resentment, anger, and bitterness are some examples. Salvation must not be confused with sanctification. The Holy Spirit's continuing work of grace is a progressive act of God's desire to draw us closer to Him. Those who, yet saved, resist this scriptural plea (1 Thessalonians 4:3) may find they have harbored demonic pockets of activity from their pre-conversion lives. This message needs a greater emphasis in our churches so that we may set free any of our brothers and sisters in Christ who are suffering the "hangover" of Satan's influence from their former lives of sin.* [38]

We have this idea again presented that when we were saved we were not totally delivered. That somehow some demons sneaked by the blood of Jesus and we find ourselves in a state of bondage after receiving the blessed Holy Spirit. The words *"...he who the Son sets free is free indeed"* apparently need not be

---

[38] Article-"Can a Christian Have a Demon" by Bob Larson

employed here. We must search for hidden demons in our lives. These are the kinds of doctrines that actually put people in bondage rather than set them free. They will always think they are unworthy and incapable, that others are always somehow better than they. Nonsense!

What does a person act like who believes they are worthless? What does a person act like who believes they are worthy? What does a person act like who believes they are demon possessed? What does a person act like who believes they have been made free by the power of the Son of God?

The devil has deceived so many into thinking he is in control and that he is incredibly powerful; that the cross can only set a part of me free, but not all of me. In essence they are saying that Jesus did a halfway job; He didn't actually set me free—completely. I now have to go find a deliverance ministry for freedom. Not only that, but every time we exhibit a weakness in our flesh we are left with the assumption that we suddenly have a demon again and we have to find a deliverer again.

The shamefulness of this doctrine is found in the idea that Jesus came to destroy the works of the devil and failed. It literally puffs up the enemy while making Jesus look like a powerless Deliverer who couldn't quite get us completely free. The evolution of this doctrine is also something to behold as they shift the arguments on a regular basis. This is evidence that there is weakness in their interpretation of Scripture.

> *As kindly as I can say it, those who underestimate what Christians can suffer at the hand of Satan are doing a disservice to the body of Christ. They are consigning sincere Christians to a life of continued*

> *demonic influence and causing needless suffering in the lives of those whom the Lord wants to set free.* [39]

I beg to differ. If your doctrine is the one that sets people free, why is it that these people have to continually come back over and over again for deliverance. In my ministry I can appeal to experience with what I feel is greater evidence. That is people who thought they were possessed and had gone from one deliverance ministry to another and finally found true freedom by accepting the immutable fact that Jesus already set them free and that the devil is a defeated foe that only has trickery as his weapon. An amazing thing happens, the torment stops and it stops for good. The one consigning Christians to a life of continual demonic influence is the one passing on a doctrine of demons.

"Who the Lord wants to set free?" Does this not presuppose that the Christian is not set free by Jesus at salvation? Did not the Son set us free already? How then do we place freedom in the Christian's future? I will agree that many have underestimated the suffering that Christians have at the hand of the enemy. Even so, that suffering is tied directly to the belief in the lies that were spoken to them and then reinforced by the enemy with a consistency that resembles Chinese water torture.

Yes, there can be much suffering, but that does not diminish the fact that Jesus set them free from the molestation of their enemy. If they are still believing the lies, that is not the fault of Jesus. All they need for freedom is to come out of agreement with those demonic spirits that are seeking to keep them in bondage.

> *Let no one misunderstand me. A Christian cannot be demonized if by "possession" you mean*

---

[39] Article-"Can a Christian Have a Demon" by Bob Larson

"ownership." The child of God is owned by the Lord. But I will testify that a Christian can be severely influenced by demons and even be inhabited by them. I will also do all that I can in Jesus' name to see that those who are "heirs of God and joint heirs with Christ" (Romans 8:17) will experience the hope of freedom from demonic bondage. [40]

How is it that according to you, Mr. Larson, this demon can take control of a Christian's vocal cords if they are not possessed? This is doublespeak at best. Either a Christian can be possessed or they cannot. This article suggests that demons can take control and then ends with the statement that they cannot do that to Christians—that is only if you "mean" that possession is ownership. Does that mean if I don't consider possession to be ownership then I can call it possession? This is not correct exegetic treatment of the Word of God.

An Argument For Freedom

I have presented some of the most used and popular arguments for a Christian being possessed. Now I want to share my argument why I cannot accept this doctrine of believer possession. I must admit that I am passionate about this subject and I am angry because of the bondage I have seen in people that have come into my own group that reveals the inadequacy of believing this way. It leaves a person angry with their Creator! He did not deliver them as He promised!

---

[40] Article-"Can a Christian Have a Demon" by Bob Larson

What Did Jesus Come to Do About Satan?

> ***Hebrews 2:14*** *Therefore, since the children share in flesh and blood, He Himself likewise also partook of the same, that through death He might **render powerless** him who had the power of death, that is, the devil, and might free those who through fear of death were subject to slavery all their lives.*

We need to address a few things from this passage. We want to first understand what is meant by *"…him who had the power of death?"* If Satan had the power to just inflict death upon anyone he wanted, do you actually think there would be any human life left? In what form then did he have that power? Satan had the power of death through tempting man to sin. The soul that sins shall die.

If the devil cannot take a person's life without using God's Law and its impending judgment, then we already see a powerless foe. He may be able to put unbelievers in fear of death, but the believer is uniquely free from this fear because of the death of Christ. We are dealing with an entity that is limited in his power. Understand that we are looking at two different kingdoms; the kingdom of God and the kingdom of Satan. We will deal with this in more detail later.

How then does the death of Christ render powerless the power of death the devil had? The death of Christ provides a judgment of death—not yours, but His—upon the sins of anyone who would become a believer in Jesus and receive His gift of eternal life. What can the devil do to the Christian with regard to death if the Christian has been crucified with Christ already? Absolutely nothing! My death for my sins is in Jesus. What does this have to do with spiritual warfare?

It has to do with a systematic destruction of Satan's power and kingdom by Jesus through His life, death, resurrection, and ascension. The problem I have with the idea of Christians being possessed is that it inflates the power of the devil while putting believers in bondage and reducing our Lord Jesus to just a nice try. This doctrine, on a perception basis, strengthens demonic power and diminishes the power of the Cross and our Savior and God.

Verse 15 reveals that Christ freed those who by reason of the fear of death were subject to slavery all their lives. If we are slaves of anything as Christians, we are slaves of Christ. The redemption of my Savior bought my freedom from the slavery of sin and the slavery of death.

> *1 John 3:8-10 the one who **practices sin is of the devil**; for the devil has sinned from the beginning. The Son of God appeared for this purpose, to destroy the works of the devil. No one who is born of God practices sin, because His seed abides in him; and he cannot sin, because he is born of God. **By this the children of God and the children of the devil are obvious**: anyone who does not practice righteousness is not of God, nor the one who does not love his brother.*

When one reads this passage they are faced with a separation of the children of God and the children of the devil. You cannot have the children of God acting like the children of the devil and you cannot have the children of the devil acting like the children of God. If you are of God, you are not of the devil. This means you cannot be possessed of a demonic entity and still be a child of God.

> *Mark 16:17 "These signs will accompany those who have believed: in My name they will cast out demons, they will speak with new tongues."*

Here lies an interesting problem. If the Christian can be possessed he also possesses the power to cast it out. This is very illogical. This borders on a house divided against itself. If the Christian has the power to cast demons out, how is it that they can be possessed in the first place?

> ***John 8:36*** *"So if the Son makes you free, you will be free indeed."*

Are we set free by the Son? If so, is not demon possession a form of bondage? Are we not called to walk as free men? Why then would we believe we can be indwelled by the devil if we are freed by the Son?

> ***Luke 10:18-19*** *And He said to them, "I was watching Satan fall from heaven like lightning. Behold, I have given you authority to tread on serpents and scorpions, and over all the power of the enemy, and* **nothing will injure you.**"

Nothing will injure you? That does not sound like the believer can be possessed to me, does it to you? We have authority over him; he does not have authority over us. We are free. The devil has nothing in which to injure you. He is defeated to the Christian.

> ***1 John 5:18-19*** *We know that no one who is born of God sins; but He who was born of God keeps him, and* ***the evil one does not touch him****. We know that we are of God, and that the whole world lies in the power of the evil one.*

The evil one does not touch him. It is the world, the unbeliever, who is under the power of the devil. As Christians, the devil is subject to us. He is the one in bondage to us. How can we be Christian and still be able to be demon possessed? Do we need more evidence?

> ***Colossians 2:14-15*** *having canceled out the certificate of debt consisting of decrees against us, which was hostile to us; and He has taken it out of the way, having nailed it to the cross.* ***When He had disarmed the rulers and authorities, He made a public display of them, having triumphed over them through Him.***

If this is the victory that Christ won on the cross, how is it that we would still be susceptible to demonic infiltration? Jesus thoroughly trounced the devil; He thoroughly stripped him of authority. The Greek word for "disarm" means "to strip one of their garments." Since garments have been a way of showing levels of authority, to strip one of their garment has always been a way of showing that they have been stripped of their authority. This is also a military term.

> "Q*UOTE*"
>
> *After **triumphing over** their enemies and **stripping** them **of their power**, it was customary for Roman victors to lead their captives in a procession and make a **public spectacle of them**; the same imagery is used at 2C 2:14. **Triumphing over them by means of the stake**.*[41]

> ***Colossians 2:10*** *and in Him you have been made complete, and He is the head over all rule and authority.*

If you are in Him, and He is Head over all rule and authority, how is it that He would allow you to be possessed?

---

[41] Stern, D. H. (1992). *Jewish New Testament commentary : A companion volume to the Jewish New Testament*. Includes index. (1st ed.) (Col 2:15). Clarksville, Md.: Jewish New Testament Publications.

> ***Colossians 1:13*** *For He rescued us from the domain of darkness, and transferred us to the kingdom of His beloved Son...*

Wait a minute, He rescued us?! From what did He rescue us if we can still be plundered by the enemy? What are we rescued from if upon conversion to Christ we still have demonic possession?

> ***Acts 26:18*** *to open their eyes so that they may turn from darkness to light and from the dominion of Satan to God, that they may receive forgiveness of sins and an inheritance among those who have been sanctified by faith in Me.*

If Satan's kingdom is called a kingdom of darkness and we see that we go from darkness to light through the born again event, then we should be able to say with confidence that we are free from that kingdom of darkness. Also, if we are free from that kingdom, we are free from the minions of that kingdom.

> ***Ephesians 5:6-8*** *Let no one deceive you with empty words, for because of these things the wrath of God comes upon the sons of disobedience. Therefore do not be partakers with them; for you were formerly darkness, but now you are Light in the Lord; walk as children of Light.*

> ***1 Thessalonians 5:4-5*** *But you, brethren, are not in darkness, that the day would overtake you like a thief; for you are all sons of light and sons of day. We are not of night nor of darkness.*

I have included all of these Scriptures to show there is ample evidence that you belong to the light. You are not of darkness. Therefore, the minions of darkness can have no part of you as a believer. Now let's consider the kingdom aspect deeper than we already have.

Before we look in the Bible I want you to understand what a kingdom is. Kingdom is a word that means the state of the king. The state of the king is the geographical sphere of dominion the king is able to maintain under his control. If a king could not protect the citizens of that kingdom, the king would lose that portion of his kingdom to the plunderer.

In talking about kingdoms there is one significant difference and that is we are speaking of spiritual kingdoms. When Jesus was questioned by Pilate He stated that His kingdom was not of this world and shortly thereafter He said it was not of this realm. This forces the question, *"How then is this kingdom measured?"*

As a spiritual kingdom it is measured in spirits; those spirits being both human and angelic. As Lord of Hosts, the hosts are the angelic beings that are under the influence and control of the Lord. The human spirits are where the kingdoms are growing or shrinking.

A kingdom has citizens. You cannot have dual citizenship. You are either a citizen of the kingdom of God or you are a citizen of the kingdom of Satan. Those who are of the kingdom of Satan are unbelievers. Those who belong to the kingdom of God are believers. One cannot be a believer and be a part of the kingdom of Satan.

> ***Matthew 13:37-38*** *And He said, "The one who sows the good seed is the Son of Man, and the field is the world; and as for the good seed, these are the sons of the kingdom; and the tares are the sons of the evil one."*

There is no instance of the spirit of God inhabiting a son of the kingdom of darkness. There is also no instance of a demonic spirit inhabiting a son of the kingdom of light. There is a clear demarcation between these two kingdoms. If demons could infiltrate children of light, then the King of light would be unable to defend those in His kingdom. This makes God weak and ineffective in His kingdom. How is it that God cannot inhabit citizens of the kingdom of darkness, but demons can inhabit the citizens of the kingdom of light? If this were so, which kingdom is displaying the greater strength?

> ***Matthew 12:28-29*** *"But if I cast out demons by the Spirit of God, then the kingdom of God has come upon you. Or how can anyone enter the strong man's house and carry off his property, unless he first binds the strong man? And then he will plunder his house."*

The purpose of saying this is that God is displaying His superior power over the power of the devil. In other words, if God is kicking devils out of human spirits thereby making them free, then He is plundering the kingdom of darkness and making these free ones new citizens of the kingdom of God. No one can come into a house without overpowering the strongman. God demonstrates His power over the strongman by kicking him out. Then God moves into that house Himself and are we to believe that the devil can now bind the new Strongman of the house?

There is only one method of entry into God's kingdom and that is through the Son of God.

> ***John 3:3*** *Jesus answered and said to him, "Truly, truly, I say to you, unless one is born again he cannot see the kingdom of God."*

Even though this kingdom of God is spiritual, it is also physical. That is, God's kingdom is enforced spiritually because He won a spiritual victory on the cross. However, the physical kingdom of God is not here yet. It will be realized in the reign of Jesus upon this earth as King of the entire world.

> ***Hebrews 12:28-29*** *Therefore, since we receive a kingdom which cannot be shaken, let us show gratitude, by which we may offer to God an acceptable service with reverence and awe; for our God is a consuming fire.*

The kingdom of God is within us and as a kingdom it cannot be shaken. Would not that kingdom be shaken if minions of darkness were able to penetrate it? There is just too much evidence to the contrary. We have an unshakable kingdom because we have an unshakable King who lives in us. In the beginning of this chapter I quoted a response to the question, "Can Christians be possessed?" Part of the response was, *"There is no real Biblical basis to claim that Christians cannot have demons."* In light of the previous Scriptures I think we can safely say that statement is categorically false.

We do not serve a weak Deliverer. He completed the job He came to do and even declared from the cross, *"It is finished!"* Our God is strong and He is able to keep those who belong to Him free from the molestation of our enemy. In fact, if we look at the meaning of salvation we find that one of its meanings is just that, *"freedom from the molestation of our enemies."*

To say that demons sneak by the blood of Jesus during salvation just diminishes the victory won by our God. When you understand the kingdom of God you understand that God dominates His kingdom and if you are in His kingdom as a citizen you will not be plundered by demonic hordes. You are the one who will do the plundering!

The idea that Satan cannot touch the spirit of man, but he can inhabit the body or mind of man, is again a misunderstanding of both the kingdom and the effect of the Holy Spirit who lives inside the believer.

> **Hebrews 10:22** *let us draw near with a sincere heart in full assurance of faith, having our hearts sprinkled clean from an evil conscience and our bodies washed with pure water.*

Do you not think that when the Spirit of God comes into a temple that temple is cleansed? Our baptism in water is the cleansing of our temples before God. We consecrate ourselves this way. We set ourselves apart unto God and God cleans us.

> **John 15:3** *"You are already clean because of the word which I have spoken to you."*

When you by faith accept God's Word as true you have His Word abiding in you. That faith is what causes you to be clean. You do not and cannot have an unclean spirit in you. You are not infested with demons; you are set free by your Deliverer, Jesus. Think of the temple of God. What part was unclean? Could a demon spirit inhabit the holy place or the outer court? If so, why was the devil kicked out of the temple in heaven as well as all of those that followed Him? Are we to believe that God will dwell in a demonized temple? How do you compartmentalize the temple when it is one? Your soul is not a repository of demonic possession.

When you understand the grace of God and how by faith we are clean because of the word that He has spoken to us, then you will also understand that you cannot be unclean or demonized.

Why then do Christians exhibit signs of demon possession? We cannot deny what we see, can we? Are not these signs enough evidence? Let me ask you, were the signs the magicians performed in response to Moses' evidence of the superiority of the demonic realm? Of course not! We are influenced by our beliefs. If we believe we can be possessed we will develop symptoms of being possessed. It is not unlike a person who believes they are sick will develop symptoms of being sick. Are they really sick? No. Do they look sick? Yes. When we come out of agreement with the lie that we can be possessed, we will never have to deal with a false symptom of being possessed.

I would ask you something. Do you think your experience is superior to the Word of God? Can you not see that this is a trick of the enemy to keep Christians thinking they are in bondage and in this state are unusable by the Spirit of God to minister to the lost? You who espouse this doctrine had better be convinced because you have a date with your Redeemer to give an account for every word that proceeds out of your mouth. I would not want to stand before Jesus having been a proponent of doctrines of demons that have put people in bondage that the Son had set free!

Remember, we become bound when we believe a lie. This is what sets up a stronghold. By applying God's Word to your heart you can break free from all of the symptoms that have come with the lie. Saint, God loves you and He delivered you; He set you free so you could now bear fruit unto Him. The ball is now in your court. I pray that you get a vision of your deliverance by the Great Deliverer! Walk in it because you are already free!

Soul Ties

Chapter Nine

Another doctrine that is prevalent in deliverance type ministries is the doctrine of soul ties. It is my intention to look at things from a biblical perspective and allow the Word of God given by the Holy Spirit to enlighten us to His truth. What is a soul tie?

A soul tie is based in a relationship that you have with a person. This tie could be struck through a casual sexual encounter or a deep heartfelt relationship with someone. I am sure many will agree that one can knit their soul with another individual because they genuinely love them, but we will need more evidence of the casual connection. It is also believed that in the case of the casual or negative soul tie there is a connection between the two souls that allow demon spirits to traverse back and forth by reason of the tie.

Proponents teach that soul ties can be either positive or negative. A good example of a positive soul tie is David and Jonathan, Saul's son.

> ***1 Samuel 18:1*** *Now it came about when he had finished speaking to Saul, that the* ***soul of Jonathan was knit to the soul of David****, and Jonathan loved him as himself.*

The soul of man is distinguished as being the seat of the will, senses, and emotions. It is also called the mind. It is the place from which you take in information, reason, judge, and decide. Those functions then create an emotional response by reason of the sensory data. A soul tie would be some kind of connection between the soul or mind of one person and that of another.

From this basic understanding come many different avenues of belief. The idea is that a good soul tie results in blessings from being in the relationship and that forming a bad soul tie can result in demons being transferred from one to the other. In this idea we find a certain level of truth and we need to acknowledge the truth where we find it. However, as I warned in an earlier chapter, truths can come as Trojan horses with insidious lies buried deep in the heart of it. The lies become difficult to separate from truth because they have been so interwoven with it.

> **Matthew 19:5-6** *"and said, 'FOR THIS REASON A MAN SHALL LEAVE HIS FATHER AND MOTHER AND BE JOINED TO HIS WIFE, AND THE TWO SHALL BECOME ONE FLESH'? So they are no longer two, but one flesh. What therefore God has joined together, let no man separate."*

Here is where I think we need to make some distinctions. There is a connection in the marriage covenant that I think is deeper than any other relationship. This relationship is of such a high order that it is the type of relationship God wants with us. If there were a higher order of relationship, God would have used it. There is a tying together in my estimation, not only the soul, but the spirit and the body as well. I see marriage as a picture of the trinity wherein there can be no distinction where one person starts and the other ends. There is just a whole that is a union of the parts. The parts are not very visible, but the whole is.

I do not want to give anyone a prince and princess mentality though. Humans are fallen creatures with a sin nature that brings with it the capacity for selfishness, hatred, dishonor, and emotional and physical abuses in any relationship. It is not that one should have an expectation of these, but an awareness of them. This means that unlike the Trinity, humans will need to forgive one another and repent of their own failures if they plan to maintain the relationship.

This is why divorce is so painful; there is a tearing away of the spirit, soul, and body. Even though this is so, we must separate fact from fiction. Proponents point to the statement *"For this reason a man shall leave His father and mother…"* as the breaking of a soul tie. Although one could infer such a break, I do not think it rises to the level of breaking a soul tie. For instance, is the relationship severed between the groom and his father and mother?

This deduction on the part of those that propose this reveal a fatal flaw and that is one of control. The belief is that one person can control another person through this mystic soul tie. This is where I believe we start to go down a road that ends in error. Although a person can be controlling, that controlling mechanism cannot be a soul tie for all soul ties would then have that as a component of it. In other words, the control could go both ways.

What I have observed with regard to individuals that have the need to control a spouse is that they use psychological manipulation in order to control the other person. For instance, a controlling personality might say to the person they want to control how stupid they are. Then having convinced them of their stupidity they tell them what to do. Controllers set their own stage in order to manipulate. The husband might tell the wife how ugly she is and then abuse her. When she thinks of leaving, he states that no one else would have her.

These are not soul ties. This is the same thing the devil does to people. He tempts them to sin and then when they give in he accuses them. It is a tactic, not a mystical connection between people. If the one who is controlled ever gets a sense of who they really are, they will not be able to be manipulated any longer. Now let's go back to soul ties. See how easy it was to believe the statement that the groom is breaking a soul tie with his father and mother? Does Jesus break a soul tie with the Father when He cleaves to us the Church, His bride? This clearly shows the fallacy of that statement.

Dr. Michael Lake, whom I highly respect, reveals in one of his teachings that there are different levels of relationship with our Lord and those different levels are revealed by the different covenants. The blood covenant causes us to enter into a relationship with God as a servant. The salt covenant begins our being his friend. The shoe covenant elevates us to inheritance which reveals that we are a son or daughter. Then finally the marriage covenant that is the highest form of covenant between man and God.

In human relationships there are also different levels of relationship and according to the soul tie proponents all of them have a soul tie associated with it. Basically, what we call a relationship, they are calling a soul tie. This can be a bit confusing so I will try to keep it clear. The friendship tie we already saw with David and Jonathan. There is also a believer tie among Christians.

> ***Colossians 2:1-3*** *For I want you to know how great a struggle I have on your behalf and for those who are at Laodicea, and for all those who have not personally seen my face, that their hearts may be encouraged, having* **been knit together** *in love, and attaining to all the wealth that comes from the full assurance of understanding, resulting in a true knowledge of God's mystery, that is, Christ Himself, in whom are hidden all the treasures of wisdom and knowledge.*

The believer is knit together with other believers. The word that keeps popping up is "knit." What is interesting to me is that the Greek Old Testament has this word translated as teach and instruct. It is the teachings of Christ that holds us together as

Christians. We find fellowship with one another based upon those teachings. I think we could also use the term "bonding." As in a father is bound to his children, or a mother bonds with her children. To bond, or be bound to, or knit all have the same picture. There is a relational connection between two or more people. These are meant to be good connections. There is no disagreement with this. Where we disagree is in the area of bad relationships. They speak of a soul tie as a channel upon which demons can transfer from one to the other that is connected by a soul tie.

> ***Proverbs 22:24-25*** *Do not associate with a man given to anger; Or go with a hot-tempered man, Or you will learn his ways And find a snare for yourself.*

Now we get to the proofs they offer to show that demonic activity is transferred over the channel of a soul tie. The statement of this passage should read, *"And take a snare for yourself."* It is their belief that a snare is to take a demon from this relationship. This cannot be the case if one looks at the statement before it. *"You will learn his ways."* This isn't anything to do with a soul tie; it is a revelation of how a person who befriends another who has anger problems will have that trait passed on as a learned behavior. The Bible also states that bad company corrupts good morals.

> ***2 Corinthians 6:14-15*** *Do not be bound together with unbelievers; for what partnership have righteousness and lawlessness, or what fellowship has light with darkness? Or what harmony has Christ with Belial, or what has a believer in common with an unbeliever?*

The admonition to not be yoked with an unbeliever has nothing to do with demons being transferred from them to us, but it has everything to do with peace. What fellowship, what harmony, or what do we have in common with an unbeliever. God wants His people to live in harmony and peace. This is why the apostle Paul stated that if the unbeliever wants to leave, let them leave.

> ***1 Corinthians 7:15*** *Yet if the unbelieving one leaves, let him leave; the brother or the sister is not under bondage in such cases, but* ***God has called us to peace.***

I thank God for my believing wife. What a joy it is to converse about the things of God. I cannot imagine what conversation would look like with an unbelieving spouse. Thus, being yoked with an unbeliever is wrong on the basis that no fellowship is possible. It has nothing to do with demons. This is nothing more than an inference that is not in the text.

> ***1 Corinthians 6:15-17*** *Do you not know that your bodies are members of Christ? Shall I then take away the members of Christ and make them members of a prostitute? May it never be! Or do you not know that the one who joins himself to a prostitute is one body with her? For He says, "*THE TWO SHALL BECOME ONE FLESH.*" But the one who joins himself to the Lord is one spirit with Him.*

This is a valid admonition about treating a sexual relationship so flippantly that no commitment of marriage is entered into first. I would agree there is a bond that takes place as a result of a sexual encounter; however, there is no evidence to support that demonic activity will be transferred over that bond. God's law is being broken in this case, that is enough to cause one to avoid it.

Add to this soul ties with the dead and you have the doctrine known as soul ties. My take on this is somewhat like that of Christians being demon possessed; although demon possession is not inferred in this case, but demonic influence. Yet, there is a cessation of responsibility for behaviors that are ungodly. Just chalk it up as a soul tie. Like I said in the beginning of this writing, it is not easy to nail this down as it is surrounded with some truth. The capability of a relationship to influence me after that relationship has been severed is up to me. I can pine away after that person, or I can mourn the loss of the relationship and move on.

To suggest that a person can control me through a soul tie is without merit. Control takes two. It takes a willing victim and a domineering personality. If a person is domineering but they do not have a victim to dominate, control does not take place. When a person refuses to properly prioritize their relationships, trouble will surface. We are all to put God first. Nevertheless, how many people put their spouse, children, or grandchildren before their Creator? Spouses are to put each other ahead of the children, yet we see spouses putting children before their spouse.

Soul ties might be partially real as in good and bad relationships, but they have no explicit authority to control by means of a channel made possible by the soul tie. How one is supposed to break a soul tie tells us much about what is actually believed. One must break, loose, and untie, if you will, any demonic activity based upon a particular relationship.

Here again, we have the idea of a lack of freedom based in the blood of Christ and we are subjected to the control and whims of demonic spirits. The reality of this teaching puts one in bondage as they come to believe that a demonic power is controlling them and manipulating them beyond their willingness to be controlled or manipulated.

When a person realizes the reality of their freedom in Christ, they are set free from false beliefs that put them in bondages whereby demons are able to produce a desired outcome through faith in that doctrine of demons.

Generational Curses

Chapter Ten

When discussing generational curses in the context of the Biblical text, there is a glaring reality that speaks to us about our protection and our freedom. Namely, that most of the curses mentioned in the Bible are God-uttered. What does this mean? It means that we must be careful when defining these things else we will be found fighting against God Himself. For instance, in Genesis 12:3 God tells Abram that He will bless those who bless Abram and He will curse those who curse Abram. Okay, so God curses, what's the problem? Can you imagine rebuking a curse that God has instituted? Not a good place to be.

Another problem arises when we take a curse that God is speaking and then associate that curse with the devil so we can convince people they need to break that curse through rebuking the devil. Then once the person starts rebuking the devil to remove the curse, they are in essence attributing the work of God to the works of Satan, and are thereby fighting against God as well as blaspheming Him.

Before I tackle this subject on generational curses, I want to reveal the Christian's position with regard to them. When a person comes into covenant with God there is a protection from enemies without. We saw it with Adam and Eve before they disobeyed, we saw it with Job which was identified as a hedge, and we saw it with Israel as a nation in the form of Michael the Arch Angel. But what about the Church and the individual Christian? Are they protected too?

Yes, we are protected. In fact, with regard to cursing, the New Testament is primarily addressing believers not to do any cursing. Consider the following.

> **Romans 12:14** *Bless those who persecute you; bless and do not curse.*
>
> **Matthew 5:44** *But I say to you, love your enemies and pray for those who persecute you,*
>
> **Luke 6:28** *bless those who curse you, pray for those who mistreat you.*

We are cautioned about cursing others, not about curses that can come upon us. This is unambiguous evidence that suggests curses are powerless against us. We are the ones who wield the power to curse else there would not be an admonition against it. Cursing, by the way, is not in and of itself a sin. God curses people and He cannot sin. Cursing someone for the wrong reason or without merit could possibly be a sin. For now, let us consider what James says concerning the tongue:

> **James 3:9-10** *With it we bless our Lord and Father, and with it we curse men, who have been made in the likeness of God; from the same mouth come both blessing and cursing. My brethren, these things ought not to be this way.*

I think this would be a good time to determine what a curse is. The Greek word is a compound word that means, "after the manner of dishonor." Anytime we dishonor someone we are guilty of cursing them. This is why one of the Ten Commandments is to honor your mother and father. To do otherwise is to curse them by dishonoring them. This also suggests that cursing without reason is considered sin. What this means is that if I am having a bad day and I take it out on someone by cursing them, I need to repent of that as I will bring the discipline of God upon myself if I don't.

To get an understanding of this word we will have to go to the Hebrew language because that is the culture that has handed us the Word of God. There is no mystery surrounding this word as it simply means "curse." What we need to understand is how the people defined it.

> *"QUOTE"*
>
> *"Cursing rests on the belief in the possibility of bringing down calamity upon persons or things by the mere power of the spoken word, without any regard to its moral justification. ... but in general the Bible conceives a curse to be merely a wish, to be fulfilled by God when just and deserved."* [42]

Now consider what the book of Proverbs has to say.

Proverbs 26:2 (NCV) *Curses will not harm someone who is innocent; they are like sparrows or swallows that fly around and never land.*

Curses were seen by the Hebraic mind to be powerless unless one was guilty. If one had guilt then the curse might have power. They based their belief on the previous text. I suppose they figured that since this speaks of a curse without cause having no power, that if there was a cause then the curse might land on the person. As New Testament Christians, however, we are instructed to curse not. This is important in light of a shift that takes place in the New Covenant.

An eye for an eye was a legal right established by God. That is, if someone wronged me I had the right of vengeance. Most times that right would take place as a fight in the courts, and at other times under certain conditions it took place at the hand of the one wronged. When Jesus begins to instruct us, we see a shift take place with regard to this law.

---

[42] Jewish Encyclopedia

Matthew 5:38-42

38-39 *"You have heard that it was said, 'AN EYE FOR AN EYE, AND A TOOTH FOR A TOOTH.' But I say to you, do not resist an evil person; but whoever slaps you on your right cheek, turn the other to him also."*

40-42 *"If anyone wants to sue you and take your shirt, let him have your coat also. Whoever forces you to go one mile, go with him two. Give to him who asks of you, and do not turn away from him who wants to borrow from you."*

Why the shift? Jesus is now asking us to go beyond the law. How could this be since we are incapable of fulfilling the law in its current state? The answer is that man was about to have access to a power that he had heretofore no access to. That power was the indwelling of the Holy Spirit. We who were forgiven much would be asked to forgive others of their sins against us. No more need for cursing, no more need for vengeance.

When a person felt powerless to acquire vengeance because of the superior power of the one who harmed them, they would often resort to speaking a curse over that person. But an unjust curse would be considered an unjust act. A just curse, however, would be considered valid. If you want to examine this further look in the Psalms. There were many times that the enemies of Israel were cursed. Now that you are familiar with what a curse is, let's look at what we are hearing from the pulpit today regarding curses.

Generational Curses

What is a generational curse? It is believed that generational curses are judgments that are passed to other generations because of sins committed by a family member. The form of that judgment is defined a couple different ways. According to proponents, one of those ways is that demons hitchhike on this curse and travel from generation to generation. Another thought, however, is that God is the One who is making this judgment. The most often quoted text to support both those theories is actually found within the Ten Commandments.

> ***Exodus 20:4-6*** *"You shall not make for yourself an idol, or any likeness of what is in heaven above or on the earth beneath or in the water under the earth. You shall not worship them or serve them; for I, the* LORD *your God, am a jealous God,* **visiting the iniquity of the fathers on the children, on the third and the fourth generations of those who hate Me,** *but showing lovingkindness to thousands, to those who love Me and keep My commandments."*

First, we need to look at what this means. When a parent sinned there was an effect caused by the sin that would last for at least three and possibly four generations upon that family line. It wasn't that God was punishing the children for the sins of the parent, but that the parent could open an **effect** that would last for a long time.

God is the One who instituted seed time and harvest. That means that if we sow badly we will reap badly. This is a cause and effect stipulation. Reaping is not instantaneous. Thus, the parent is completely responsible for the result that comes upon their children as a consequence of their sins. We do not have to look very far to see the ravages of evil upon the children for a number of generations. Consider David's sin and the effect upon his son.

If we do not read this text carefully we will miss some important principles. First, we need to ask what the conditions are that will precipitate the bad and what the conditions are that will precipitate the good. Two words come to the forefront and they are "hate" and "love." It appears that we are actually very much in control of whether we are receiving God's lovingkindness or suffering a punishment that we deserve.

The question we must get to is, *"Does the 'those that love me' statement refer to the father or the offspring?"* I think that because the text reads *"...on the third and fourth generation of those that hate Me..."* we can with surety say that *"those that love me"* refers also to the offspring of the fathers who sinned. This raises an interesting condition then. If I have a father who sinned and I hate God, I will be reaping the punishment of my hate along with the reaping that my father has sown seeds for. Not only that, but I too am sending this forward onto other generations through my own sin. If I have a father who sinned but I love God, I will receive lovingkindness and I don't have to be under that reaping because I have come under covenant with God. Therefore, I am able to break this so-called generational curse simply by loving God and coming into covenant relationship with Him.

Here is where I have difficulty with those who are proponents of this teaching. In breaking these curses they say, *"I rebuke or break this curse."* Well, if God is the One who initiated it, what right do you have to rebuke it or break it? When people quote this verse and then start rebuking the devil, it becomes utter nonsense.

There are those that also misappropriate the text to say that God visits the sins of the father to the children, meaning that the children will be stuck doing those same sins. There is plenty of evidence regarding sins being repeated by the next generation; nonetheless, God is not the cause of it. What parents do in their sinning is create a psychological environment of *acceptable behavior* whether they like it or not. When a parent commits adultery the children are more likely to as well. This is because one day when they are tempted they will look back to the one in their life who shaped their morality, but was lax in that area thus making it permissible behavior.

As with many doctrines, there are fringe elements that take things to an extreme position. One of those is the illegitimate birth curse. If a child is conceived out of wedlock, these proponents suggest there is a ten generation curse upon that family line that needs to be broken. The Scripture used is the following.

> **Deuteronomy 23:2** *"No one of **illegitimate birth** shall enter the assembly of the L*ORD*; none of his descendants, even to the tenth generation, shall enter the assembly of the L*ORD*."*

What we need to look at is the single Hebrew word translated "illegitimate birth." It is a rare word and it is only used twice. Looking at the other instance will give us some insight.

> **Zechariah 9:6** *And a **mongrel race** will dwell in Ashdod, And I will cut off the pride of the Philistines.*

From the context we see that an illegitimate birth takes on more of the meaning of mixed races marrying and producing offspring. But before you gasp at that, I am only talking about one race; the Jewish people. All other races could mix marriage all they wanted to, but not the Jews. They were to remain pure because of one event that would shake the world. That would be the advent of Christ. He needed to come from the Jews and if that line were polluted enough, it would serve as a way for the devil to defeat the plan of God. In fact, if you read all of Zechariah chapter nine, you will see that it is a beautiful messianic prophecy that would culminate in the reception of that mongrel race.

In light of this, I don't think we can say that there is a ten generation curse on any child born out of wedlock. The parents bear their own sins and those sins are not passed on to the children.

If there is, it could only be the three and four generation curse and that only if the children that are born out of wedlock hate God.

Another thing that annoys me greatly is some of the advertisements from ministries that will break these so-called generational curses. They say things like, *"Are you having things happen in your life that you can't explain? Are there some sins you just can't seem to overcome? You might be suffering from a generational curse."* With as much dignity as I can muster, may I say that, as a child of God, a citizen in the kingdom of God, a saint made holy by the blood of Jesus, you are not under a curse. He who the Son sets free is free indeed!

There is a generational effect. It can be called a curse or a blessing, depending on what the parents pass on to their children. Consider the following story my wife, Kathryn, penned about her family and I think you will get a good idea of what I am trying to communicate.

A Family Revelation

Being the oldest of a dysfunctional family and the only one that was showing any signs of a fruitful relationship with Christ, eventually brought me to question my genealogy. At a very young age, as I attended Sunday School, a preschool teacher took me aside and made sure that I understood who Jesus was. She embedded in me the belief that wherever I go, Jesus goes with me. That carried with me throughout my life, which resulted in what most people would refer to as a "sheltered life."

I never got into the drinking or drug life that others were engaged in during the 60's movement, whether it was my classmates or my family. While others were experimenting with the "sexual freedom" of the time, I was living as a widow of the Vietnam War. Woodstock went right over my head, I did not know it even existed. It was during this time that God got my attention through the death of my husband.

I had my first prophetic dream and knew that Joseph was killed in the war before I got word from the Pentagon. That dream changed my Christian life by the revelation that God speaks to His children! The fact that He warns us and guides us was so overwhelming to me that it comforted me in Joseph's death and impacted how I handled it. What a gift from God! He knew by revealing this information to me, not only would I be cushioned by the shock, but it would change in a greater way my relationship with Him.

My relationship with the Lord grew tremendously through the years, thus leaving behind close relationships with my friends and my family. It seems to be that one cannot be walking with Christ in Spirit without it changing relationships with others that are not on the same path as you. As I grew with the Lord I came to know truths about myself and my purpose for being. It had the effect of driving a deeper and deeper hole within the dysfunctional family ties. Most times, I felt like the black sheep in the family, but I was not about to give that role up!

Throughout the years, being separated from my family in spiritual things made me take a look at our family and wonder if I was the only one in our family line that had a call to ministry. My father has always talked about his family tree, and because I enjoyed history, I would listen to his stories about his family and how his great-grandfather was killed in the Civil War. For years my father would search for members of his family and waited patiently for the production of the Colton family genealogical book that contained the names of his father, brothers, and sisters; hoping to add his own children to this book and carry on the tradition.

One day, after my husband and I had become so frustrated with trying to grow our ministry, I told God that I needed to know if at least one Colton family member in the past was ever a minister. For as far as I have ever seen my family was set apart from me in their vision for our lives. As far back as I looked all I could see was alcoholism, drug addiction, and an occasional "good" person. Just knowing if there was one more minister other than myself in my family, would give me motivation to go on. What God made available to me was absolutely remarkable and has totally changed my outlook and my fight to run this race without wondering if I am really supposed to do this!

I knew there was a genealogical record of the descendants of Quartermaster George Colton that was first published in 1912 and subsequently updated. After some time of searching the internet, I was able to come across the book which was carefully researched and printed by George Woolworth Colton and John Milton Colton. Little did I know when I first received this book what a treasure it would become to me! I bought myself this book as a Christmas present in December of 2006. When I received it, I carefully went through the book searching for answers at what had become of my forefathers.

It was not until I got to the very back of the book that I not only realized how God was using my family line from the beginning of our time, but I found the understanding of generational curses. The Lord had opened the door for me and showed me the purpose of my family line. He showed me that the Colton's were actually Spirit filled and even prayed for me as a future generation! I saw the names of Colton's that loved God and dedicated their lives to the Church as deacons and church builders! I was amazed! Allow me to quote a piece of this writing that has become such a revelation to me:

"As to the parts the Colton's have played and are playing in the field of the world. True we cannot point to one as chief executive of the nation—no matter – we stand well on the roll. One or two governors, one or two presidents of colleges, several college professors, educators not a few, positions many, and clergymen a goodly number. But after all, our grand distinction and boost is of our deacons." [43]

The writings also include a note as the people were building their first church in Longmeadow, Massachusetts;

"Of the sixteen persons joining to organize this Church, six were Coltons, four women and two men." [44]

You must understand my shock. My husband and I have been working for ten years together to open a Bible institute so we may teach and equip ministers for their calling. What an awesome gift to know that I am doing exactly what God has called my family to do for at least the past 390 years! Words just escape me; I cannot explain how it feels to know that I am following God's will for my life and I have written confirmation to prove it!

After all this amazement, I began to wonder what happened to my family. Where did this call on our lives get cut off? I carefully began to look backwards from my immediate family on up the line.

---

[43] A Genealogical Record of the Descendants of Quartermaster George Colton

[44] A Genealogical Record of the Descendants of Quartermaster George Colton

> ***Deuteronomy 5:9-10*** *'You shall not worship them or serve them; for I, the LORD your God, am a jealous God, visiting the iniquity of the fathers on the children, and on the third and the fourth generations of those who hate Me, but showing lovingkindness to thousands, to those who love Me and keep My commandments.'*

There it was standing right in front of me on those white pages. It all began with my great-great-grandfather, Luther Colton's family. As it is written, Luther Colton (43 years old) and two of his sons, Hartwell Henry (17 years old) and Franklin (16 years old) committed themselves to fight in the Civil War. They were all killed in the war. Luther left behind his wife, Roxy Jane, with their remaining eight children and the farm. The youngest baby was Russell at 5 months old, my great-grandfather. This was four generations away from me.

I believe that Roxy Jane had much heartache from the loss of her husband and two sons. Not long after she lost them Roxy faced the death of another one of her babies. Orville died at the young age of 3 ½ years old. Roxy ran the farm and took care of the remaining seven children until her death. She never remarried. The pressure and heartache of all this hardship on her I imagine was overwhelming, to say the least. I do not know what became of the other siblings, but Russell, my great-grandfather, succumbed to alcohol, and from there it went down the family line, including the use of drugs.

Perhaps the loss of a father figure in the home left a void in the foundation and upbringing of this family, especially the youngest members who would have no memory of their father. Not many women alone could fight off Indians and work a farm and tend to children; meeting all their needs with only two hands and a broken, depressed heart. Therein lays the answers to the questions

I have asked many times as a young child. "How come we are not like other families, how come our relatives do not get together for the holidays?"

Even aside from the ravages of substance abuse, living life within a dysfunctional family can leave many depressed because you hear the lies from the enemy like, "you will never amount to anything," and that, "good things will never come upon you because it never has before." Coming from a background similar to this leaves an open door for the enemy to make sure that you never discover who you really are and that you never fulfill God's purpose for your life.

We hear these lies in our spirit that men need to find a job so they can support a family. Nothing fancy! Any job will do, as long as the pay is good enough. They can never be more than that. Men believe the lie that they will never fulfill their dream of owning their own business, or entering into a professional career, or fulfilling a ministerial call "knowing" that they do not qualify for it. Don't misunderstand me. I am not saying that one should not take any job to support their family. I am saying that men from dysfunctional families are often conditioned to believe that they can never advance to better careers.

The women grow up knowing that if they want to have a good quality life, they had better find a husband with an advanced career to provide shelter and support for the family. This is primarily because the women envision themselves as inadequate to pursue a calling that would provide for themselves and members of their family. Alas, the signs and symptoms of a dysfunctional family living under the umbrella of the generational curse!

What struck me about my wife's family is that here is a picture of the generational curse and it is just as the Bible describes it. Russell Colton may have had thoughts of rejection brought on by the lack of a father figure. I am sure the devil whispered his serpent-like thoughts to get this family line off track. After all, they are too much of a threat. The Coltons are a distinguished family and successful on many fronts. This dysfunctional behavior brought on poverty and lack that has lasted four generations. But take note that this curse stopped when little Kathryn accepted Jesus.

Her love for God brought her under covenant and under covenant there is no curse. Her children have had nothing to do with drugs or alcohol. I watched as her mother received Christ. Then one family member after another; each one breaking any kind of a curse because they were willing to come into covenant with God. But something greater is revealed in this story than generational curses. It is generational callings.

I have always believed that God puts a calling on a family. What a blessing to know that God wants to use a family to accomplish His will. How could we have overlooked this? Why is it that mankind seems to gravitate toward the negatives of life? To Abram He said, *"Kings will come out of you," "All the nations of the world will be blessed through you."* Abram became Abraham and is the father of the Jewish nation of Israel. Think this out for a moment. The seed of Abraham, some alive today, are living under a calling that began with one man and one woman.

Consider the disciples Peter and Andrew, his brother. When Jesus called one, He also called the other. How could this be? Is there more evidence? Yes, look at James and his brother John. Jesus called one and then the other. Two sets of brothers called to be disciples and apostles of Jesus. Don't tell me that God does not call families! Even in our Biblical institute we see evidence of a call upon families as we have brothers and sisters called to ministry.

Saint, I want you to be set free from this notion that you are under a curse as a Christian. You have covenant with God and you have calling. Quit believing that you are under the spell of the enemy and put him under your feet. Take up your calling and fulfill your destiny! Enter in and take the kingdom of darkness by storm! That is your calling! That is your legacy!

Word or Spoken Curses

Chapter Eleven

In this chapter we are going to be dealing specifically with curses that are spoken against another, primarily a Christian. I learned much about word curses from Derrick Prince who based much of his evidence upon experience. I am not besmirching Mr. Prince and I consider him a good example of ministry leadership. I just happen to disagree with him on some of the spiritual warfare issues.

I want to start out by relaying a story that took place back in the early 1990's. At this time I was in the testing phase of the doctrines that I had studied and adopted into my life. I wanted to make sure they were defendable. I found that an effective way of doing that was to debate with a group that disagreed with it to see if I could actually defend that particular doctrine with the Word of God. In the middle of these debates we would often be crashed by witches and warlocks.

I remember one of these encounters as they began to blaspheme our God, I resisted them. They got so angry with me that they said they would cast spells on me and my family if I did not stop resisting them. I told them I would not stop and that I needed to give them a warning before they actually cast these spells. I warned them that whatever spell they cast upon me would come back upon them and their families so be careful in what you are doing.

Well, they did not take me serious and began all of these incantations. They finished and left. About one or two weeks later one of the warlocks came back and revealed to us that the very curse he had spoken to harm me and my family came upon him and his family. At that point he said, *"I want to know your God."*

We led him to Christ and we inflicted loss upon the kingdom of darkness!

Although this story has a great ending, there are thousands of others that do not. With all humility I am asking of those who believe curses can come upon you as a Christian to hear my argument. I believe that you can have an epiphany that will totally make you free. I believe that you can walk in freedom without fear as a warrior of Jesus, being free yourself and able to set others free.

Can word curses work on Christians? They are not supposed to, but yes! What I mean by this is that you hold the key to whether they can work or not. This is found in the proof text used by Derrick Prince to suggest that they do work. Here is the text.

> ***Ezekiel 13:17-18*** *Now you, son of man, set your face against the daughters of your people who are prophesying from their own inspiration. Prophesy against them and say, 'Thus says the Lord G*OD*, "Woe to the women who sew magic bands on all wrists and make veils for the heads of persons of every stature to hunt down lives! Will you hunt down the lives of My people, but preserve the lives of others for yourselves?*

In this passage we have women who were using magic to hunt down lives. The implication of this is that they were using magic to kill people. That is why this text is used for a proof text to support the working of word curses upon Christians. After all, are Christians not God's people too? On the surface this looks air tight with regard to what the proponents of word curses are saying. Yet, we need not stop at verse eighteen.

Ezekiel 13:19-23

*19 "For handfuls of barley and fragments of bread, you have profaned Me to My people to **put to death** some who should not die and to keep others alive who should not live, by your **lying to My people who listen to lies."***
20 Therefore, thus says the Lord GOD, "Behold, I am against your magic bands by which you hunt lives there as birds and I will tear them from your arms; and I will let them go, even those lives whom you hunt as birds.
21 I will also tear off your veils and deliver My people from your hands, and they will no longer be in your hands to be hunted; and you will know that I am the LORD.
*22 Because you **disheartened the righteous with falsehood** when I did not cause him grief, but have encouraged the wicked not to turn from his wicked way and preserve his life,*
23 therefore, you women will no longer see false visions or practice divination, and I will deliver My people out of your hand. Thus you will know that I am the LORD."

When we read the whole story we see that the people of God were ensnared by these women. But notice **how** this trapping took place. THEY WERE LIED TO! Notice the end of verse nineteen, *"...by your lying to My people who listen to lies."* It wasn't that these women had any real power, but they were able to convince people that they did and by convincing them, they were able to even bring death. But only if they believe the lies. Do you understand how important faith is to the equation of spiritual warfare? If you have faith in the power of the enemy to kill you, you have given Him the road to kill you.

But, by faith in God, if you put to rest those things the enemy says, he stands before you powerless and defeated. He has nothing else to harm you with. Look at verse 22. *"Because you disheartened the righteous with falsehood..."* That is what the enemy is doing to the Church right this minute. He is disheartening them through his lying to them. Pastors, you are victorious in the name of Jesus! Stand upon the solid rock of His Word and proclaim the riches of His glory! God has delivered you and He will watch over you and He will protect you. You will overcome; you will be victorious if you keep faith with Him! Even in death we are victorious in faith. We are victorious even in persecutions, beatings, and slanders. God will not abandon His people!

Blessing and Cursing

But if you choose to believe the lies of the enemy you will find yourself walking in dejection and feeling lost. You will be disheartened by the lies. Remember that we are warned about paying attention to seducing spirits and doctrines of demons. Many who tout this doctrine of being cursed list all of the sins and curses found in Deuteronomy. They then instruct the people to renounce and pray to break the effect of the curse upon your life.

First, the way to break those curses from an Old Testament perspective, according to God's instructions, is to repent and return to following the Lord. Second, as Christians we are set free from the curse of the law. Where can we find the curse of the law? In Deuteronomy. Consider the following, however.

Galatians 3:10-14

10 For as many as are of the works of the Law are

under a curse; for it is written, "CURSED IS EVERYONE WHO DOES NOT ABIDE BY ALL THINGS WRITTEN IN THE BOOK OF THE LAW, TO PERFORM THEM."
11 Now that no one is justified by the Law before God is evident; for, "The righteous man shall live by faith."
12 However, the Law is not of faith; on the contrary, "He who practices them shall live by them."
13 Christ redeemed us from the curse of the Law, having become a curse for us—for it is written, "Cursed is everyone who hangs on a tree"—
14 in order that in Christ Jesus the blessing of Abraham might come to the Gentiles, so that we would receive the promise of the Spirit through faith.

What a glorious promise! I have no need to break a curse that was broken by my Big Brother Jesus on the cross! I am under the blessing of Abraham by faith. Saint, you have to take what is yours. *"Forget none of His benefits"* as the Psalmist put it. You can live in defeat or you can live in victory. Defeat can only come by His people listening to falsehoods. Victory can only come by faith in God and what He says.

The Power of Words

None of us would diminish the effect that words can have upon a person. Many of us have suffered from stinging statements of failure. What I would like to do is look at the mechanics of this. This will release you from the fear of what someone might be saying about you or to you that you deem a word curse. Before we do that I want to say this to you.

No doubt you have been told that you were this or that - fill in the negative blank. Some of it may be true, some of it may not. The exciting thing about the Word is that it protects us even if some things said about us are true. If we have sinned, we have an Advocate with the Father. If we are just being persecuted, Jesus tells us that we are blessed when people say all manner of evil against us. We are delivered either way!

Let's take the statement, *"You are so stupid."* What is the power of those four words? Do those four words have power to put you into bondage? Of themselves they can do nothing to you. Think about that for a moment. There is something those words need to be empowered; something that will make them real. What is it? Faith! Those words are only able to harm you when you believe they are true. If you did not believe them, they could have no effect. This is why faith is so important.

What we need to keep in mind is that our enemy is watching us and knows what he needs to say to reinforce a lie in your life at the right time. If he has you on the ropes and someone happens to say that you are so stupid, he will then reinforce that statement with thoughts in your mind. What I have noticed is that he casts thoughts to look like they are coming from me. For instance, after hearing someone say that you are so stupid, you will then hear something like, *"Yeah, I am so stupid. I don't know why I even try."* Although those thoughts could come from you, if you guard your mind you will find them just spontaneously appearing, which means that they may not be from you.

Faith is what the enemy needs you to have in him so that he can dishearten you and cause you to give up or become ineffective in God's kingdom. This is where you need to employ the mighty weapon placed in your hand to destroy that lie. You could reply, *"Not many wise are called, not many noble…" "His strength is perfected in my weakness." "I can do all things through Christ*

Jesus who strengthens me." God's Word is your weapon to defeat the enemy.

Harmless Idioms

I must address this idea that every little word that you say will harm you. I will never forget the gasps that I once heard when in response to something that was funny, I said, *"That just tickles me to death."* That statement was met with gasps as if I had just signed my own death warrant. I was told that I just cursed myself. Excuse me, but my death will not come at the hand of ticklers. That is just an idiom to express how funny something is.

Words without faith have no power. Did they actually think that I believe a band of ticklers will hunt me down and tickle me to death? That is why this doctrine can be so dangerous. What if I have faith in the words I speak? Is that opening a window for the enemy to torment me? What if I believe I am cursed to die because I said, that tickles me to death? The devil is looking for every opportunity to kill you and God is looking for every opportunity to give you life.

Even God's Words meant for human consumption, without faith, will have no power in your life. *"God so loved the world...,"* means nothing to the man or woman who has no faith in God's Son. It does not benefit them at all. I have no access to eternal life without believing in the Word of God. To clarify this statement, **I am not saying that God has no power**. He spoke the world into existence with a word. He is all powerful and His words demonstrate His power. I am speaking only of those things He has given to us to empower our lives.

Another incident was when my wife told another ministry couple that she was going to put her "bumming" around clothes on. The response was one of unbelief. It was as if she had just announced a curse of poverty upon us. No, it was just another harmless idiom. There are words that are dangerous and can do damage and those are the words you speak out of faith.

Powerful Words

Make no mistake; we are in a battle on a daily basis until we pass from this earth. The battlefield this conflict is waged on is in the area of your mind. When you accept information coming into your mind as truth, you had better make sure the source is God. The devil has thousands of Christians under his spell because he was able to get them to believe his lies.

Especially children. How many children who are not equipped to deal with spiritual warfare believe the lies that a person will tell them. There are teachers who have done so much damage to children by the things they say. Why? Because the child believes the lies. The enemy is very involved in this as well. I also have noticed that the enemy often attacks along the line of your calling. To the teacher, they will hear how stupid they are. To the pastor, they will hear how insensitive they are. To the evangelist, they will hear what a terrible speaker they are. To the prophet, they will hear how out of touch they are. To the apostle, they will hear how they destroy everything they touch.

The child endures so much because if their parents are not aware of these negative influences they will not be able to undue them. This is why we wind up with sick adults. They are only damaged children that grew up. This is where we the Church should be ready and able to set them free with the Word of God!

How many Christians are walking in ignorance to their calling? How many Christians are so defeated they feel disqualified to walk in their calling? How many Christians are walking on a path that is not even theirs? Now compare that with how many Christians you know who are fulfilling their created purpose. These are only some of the things the enemy tries to do in order to neutralize us in the fight.

Your enemy will try to shipwreck your faith. That is where his fight is concentrated. It was that way in the Garden of Eden and it is still that way today. Every atrocity committed by man can be analyzed and found to have been caused by a belief. Ideology based upon anything other than the Bible is dangerous. I am somewhat confident that Charles Darwin never anticipated his ideology of evolution being used by Hitler to exterminate the Jews. Everyone has a belief structure or framework from which they live their life. The question is, *"How much of that worldview is based in truth and how much is based in deception?"*

Do not become smug and arrogant about this. Those who think that they are full of only truth are the ones walking in the greatest deceptions. What our attitude should be is that of the truth seeker. The truth seeker is on a quest to find truth at every turn. Even though they are convinced of the truth that is in them, they are not opposed to someone testing it. In fact, they enjoy it. They do not trust, however, that they are walking completely in truth. They are on the prowl for any deception that might be lying beneath the surface of their consciousness.

When a deception is found, the truth seeker will rejoice because they are able to replace that deception with the truth. They realize that they are able to walk in a greater freedom as a result. They live their lives in courage because they have a God who is absolute and cannot lie. Theirs' is the life of warfare because they are able to see deception and deal with it. Just as God would raise up a deliverer to rescue His nation Israel, the truth seeker becomes the deliverer, able to bring freedom to the Church and the World!

The devil wants you to fail. If he is to bring that about he must deceive you in some way. None of us want to admit that we have been tricked. Please, rest assured that we have all been tricked at some time. Have an attitude that you are going to find every one of them and root them out. To the degree that you rid yourself of them is to the degree that you will have freedom. Consider the following:

- I am no good
- I will not amount to anything
- I am too stupid
- I can't do it
- I am too weak
- I am not smart enough
- I don't have enough talent
- I can't speak
- I can't read
- I can't learn
- I am unworthy
- I am a sinner
- I have done too many things wrong
- God wouldn't want me
- God could not use me
- God hates me
- I made God mad
- I disappointed God
- I am too scared
- I am afraid I will fail God
- I have failed already
- It's too hard
- I won't make it
- God can't use me
- You don't know what I have done
- There is someone else who will do it
- I need to live for myself
- I deserve to have fun

- I have too many things to accomplish
- I have needs
- I don't have time
- I am too busy
- I have a job
- I have pets
- People don't listen to me

All of these excuses I have heard as to why a Christian cannot do what God has called them to do. There is one common denominator between every one of them. The devil has convinced them of a lie! All of these people are unable to do what God called them to do because of something they have believed about themselves. The reality is, YOU ARE CREATED. THEREFORE, YOU HAVE PURPOSE AND ABILITY TO ACCOMPLISH GOD'S GOAL FOR YOUR LIFE!

To use any of those excuses is to make God appear as if He is weak and ineffective in empowering you to fulfill your created purpose. They are lies. In fact, if you believe any of those, and this may shock you, you believe that God is weak and ineffective in carrying out His will in your life. So yes, words believed are powerful for they will direct your life. You will act upon them and you will also do them. Your success is tied to believing the words God has given to you.

> ***Joshua 1:8*** *"This book of the law shall not depart from your mouth, but you shall meditate on it day and night, so that you may be careful to do according to all that is written in it; for then you will make your way prosperous, and then you will have success.*

It astonishes me that we are so easily taken from the only thing that will make our way prosperous. We rely upon our wits, we rely upon trusted friends, we rely upon professionals, we rely upon periodicals, magazines, books, and many other things, but rarely do we rely upon the Word of God.

Speaking something does not make it true, nor does it cause anything to come to pass. I know, you are going to say, *"Yeah, but doesn't the Word say to speak to the mountain and it will be removed and cast into the sea."* Yes it does, but it also says, *"...and you do not doubt in your heart..."* Speech without faith is powerless. So much emphasis has been put on speaking, while ignoring believing.

What is in your heart? What have you inculcated into your belief framework? That framework is the model you have developed to measure your world. Are you seeing the world through God's eyes? Do you see the love He has for a person? Do you feel the anger He has for injustice? Do you agree with His terms of morality or have you fashioned your own? Can we say that we will prosper in our way if we are unwilling to come into agreement with any of His truths?

If you want the right things coming out of your mouth, then you need to have the right things in your heart. Am I saying that you can modify behavior simply by modifying belief? Absolutely! That is exactly what I am saying! If that were not true why would the devil want you to believe what he is saying? He knows that he can modify your actions by getting you to believe something.

The cost of ignoring this is great. I know some dear sweet souls who, because of a lie, are paralyzed in their life. They are swept off of their feet on the road to destiny. Oh, God! There is so much more to their life than what they can see. It is hidden. Lies always hide truth; they always hide reality. If we are ever to walk in the light we will have to expose the darkness.

My wife and I were invited to lunch with a couple and as they were about to sit down, one of them grabbed their back and said, oh man, someone must be speaking a word curse over me. I thought at that moment how simple it was for them to believe that another person could control pain in their body simply by saying something negative about them. This is no different than voodoo. They may as well had an effigy of him poking it with pins. How is it that we have come to have faith in these things when it is clear that Jesus has made us free?

This is all I need to know. God says, "I WILL BLESS THEM THAT BLESS YOU AND I WILL CURSE THEM WHO CURSE YOU." That truth causes me to walk in freedom knowing that if anyone does try to curse me, it is at their own peril. Let's read a Psalm.

Psalm 59:12-17

***12** On account of the sin of their mouth and the words of their lips, Let them even be caught in their pride, And **on account of curses** and lies which they utter. Destroy them in wrath, destroy them that they may be no more; That men may know that God rules in Jacob To the ends of the earth. Selah.*

***14** They return at evening, they howl like a dog, And go around the city. They wander about for food And growl if they are not satisfied. But as for me, I shall sing of Your strength; Yes, I shall joyfully sing of Your lovingkindness in the morning, For You have been my stronghold And a refuge in the day of my distress. O my strength, I will sing praises to You; For God is my stronghold, the God who shows me lovingkindness.*

Saint, you are in God's army. The reality is that no one can curse you without it returning to them. What will happen to your future when you believe that truth? Every attempt to stop your prosperity will result in their poverty. Every attempt to attack your health will result in their sickness. Every attempt to close your open doors will result in their opportunities being lost. God is on our side! Really, who can be against us! We need to quit being wimpy Christians thinking the devil is more powerful than we are. He is not! We represent his defeat. What can he do to us?

> ***Proverbs 26:2*** *Like a sparrow in its flitting, like a swallow in its flying, So a curse without cause does not alight.*

Do you understand what this means? It means that the only one who can bring a curse upon your head is you. But since you have been removed from the curse of the law the only thing left is God and you. What might look like a curse to you and others could be God's discipline. In fact, look what the New Testament writer states.

> ***Hebrews 12:7*** *It is for discipline that you endure; God deals with you as with sons; for what son is there whom his father does not discipline?*

We are told by the author of Hebrews that we are to endure for discipline. I think we can suggest that in the mind of this author they looked at all hardships, not as curses, but as discipline. If word curses were so powerful why is it that there is no real doctrinal treatment of it in the New Testament? For the most part, we are just told to bless those who curse us. That is a position of power! We are not told what to do to break those curses spoken over us. Why? Because they have no power over us!

Oh, how the Body of Christ has been duped to walk in bondage. I see one group of Christians who think and speak of the devil's name more than they do of God. Then on the other side, I see a group of Christians who don't even acknowledge the devil exists. What we must do is hold to the biblical record. We are told that we have an enemy, and we are witnesses of how he has worked. Therefore, we are not left without knowledge of his ways.

So much more power has been ascribed to the devil than he actually has. He appears as a huge Goliath towering over and tormenting the Church. Where are the David's among us? Those that look at the devil and state, *"Who is this un-baptized demonic spirit who taunts the armies of the Lord!"* He does not have covenant with God, you do! Put him under your feet where Jesus placed him. He is not a doll to take out and play with.

To sum up, we have the Word of the kingdom (Matthew 13:19), we have the Word of the Lord (Luke 22:61), we have the Words of eternal life (John 6:68), we have the Word of His grace (Acts 20:32), we have the Word of the gospel (Acts 15:7), we have the Words of the Prophets (Acts 15:15), we have the Words of sober truth (Acts 26:25), we have the Word of promise (Romans 9:9), we have the Word of faith (Romans 10:8), we have the Word of Christ (Romans 10:17), we have the Word of reconciliation (2 Corinthians 5:19), we have the Word of life (Philippians 2:16), we have the Word of God, we have the Word who became flesh, and we have the Word Who is God (John 1). How can we possibly have a word that is a curse?

The Fruit of Adultery

Chapter Twelve

We have shown how the enemy twists scriptures and discourages us with lies. Now I want to show you how he uses temptation, accusation, and judgment. As you can see by the title we are going to be discussing adultery. Not just in the sense of the sin itself, but from the beginning to the end.

You might be tempted to think that adultery starts with temptation. It does not. The sin of adultery is based in much more than temptation. Temptation becomes a part of the process, but it does not initiate it. What initiates it is the voice of the enemy. It could be that you got into a fight with your spouse and in your anger you allow the enemy to suggest reasons for committing adultery. (It is not my intention to consider all of the possible reasons for adultery and for this please keep in mind that I am concerned with the fruit of adultery.)

What about the person who has such low self-esteem they are easily tempted to commit adultery because they need to feel worthwhile. The enemy has tricked them into thinking that a sexual encounter will help support their self-worth. I think this was the problem of the woman caught in adultery found in John chapter eight. In this story we find a woman brought out into the public square to be accused of adultery. Was she guilty? Yes, she was, but notice the conspicuous absence of the other party.

One cannot commit adultery without a partner in crime. Why was it if she was "caught" that just the woman was brought out to be stoned publically for her sins? Something else to consider is what did the accusers see in Jesus that would make them think they could test Him by facing Him with stoning a woman caught in adultery? Did they think Jesus was so passive that faced with a law that demanded stoning, He would break the law? Or were they tempting Him to forgive a sin which only God could do so they could accuse Him of blasphemy? Either way, Jesus did what God does. First, He rescues her from her accusers. Sound familiar?

At first Jesus ignores the accusers. He simply stoops down and writes in the dirt. Perhaps this was done to give the accusers time to think about what they were doing. Then when they kept pressing Him about this issue He responded. He appeals to the conscience in each one by simply saying, *"He who is without sin, cast the first stone,"* then He stooped back down and began writing in the dirt again. Notice the reaction Jesus got to this simple statement. The older ones dropped their stones first. Consider what it took for them to pick up the stone in the first place.

They would have already had the idea in them that they were doing a righteous act by stoning this woman. That must have been hard upon their conscience. They were about to make the ultimate judgment with regard to a human being. Since it was early in Jesus' ministry that He said, *"He who lusts after a woman has committed adultery with her in his heart already,"* it is likely that these men who had picked up stones to hurl at one caught in adultery had heard this and are now feeling the pains of their consciences.

The oldest of this group dropped their stones first. The older ones always represent the wiser in a group. It was only then that the younger ones thought that they too should follow in kind and drop their stones as well. As they did, they also walked away. What happened to them? They were convicted of their own sins and unable to make a judgment of another's sin. But, *"What about the law!"* you say. And I say, *"What about repentance!"* Does God allow for repentance?

Does that mean we release all murderers who are repentant? Of course not! Jesus is not setting the law aside; He is only making those men aware of their decision. He did not force them to put down their stones. He did not stop the execution; He persuaded the accusers that perhaps there were things in their life that required a death sentence as well and for them to participate in this death sentence would make them the ultimate hypocrites.

What would the woman be thinking at this point? She is guilty. Notice the first thing Jesus says to her, *"Woman, where are your accusers?"* He could have said just as well, *"Woman where are those who represent your worthlessness?"* When the woman responded, *"Lord, I have none,"* God in the flesh, the only one able to judge righteously, raised her esteem of herself when He said, *"Neither do I accuse you..."* What a glorious statement to hear from God. Now, for the first time, she is free to do what Jesus commanded her to do, she is free from those voices telling her she is worthless, she is free to *"sin no more."*

Adultery does not start with a temptation; it starts with demonic discouragement of some kind. There must be an open atmosphere of a sort before the temptation can be effective. In other words, this is a set up. This is what the enemy does. He sets you up for failure and then tempts you to fail. After falling, he accuses you hoping to bring God's judgment upon you, thus taking you out of the plan and destiny of God for your life.

There is a cause and effect at work here. This is the message of the Old Testament. If you do these things, this is what will happen. I think the cause and effect of sin is lost on this generation. How many people cry out to God when hardship comes and state, *"What have I done to deserve this?"* The problem with not understanding cause and effect is that you never stop doing the thing that is causing the effect. You are unable to correct behavior. Instead, one becomes bitter and disillusioned with God and likely forsakes Him altogether.

On the other hand, when you understand cause and effect and are tempted to do wrong, you are able to reason within yourself that the effect is not worth it. Ask anyone who has committed adultery if it was worth it. Ask them if they could go back in time would they make a different decision in light of the consequences.

David is a good study with regard to this subject as he exhibited a heart that God desired, but he also exhibited some considerably bad traits as well. David did some atrocious things and God did not overlook them. David paid a price for his mistakes. As Christians, I think we can sometimes become smug with regard to our sins as if nothing will come of it. The woman caught in adultery might have been set free, however, that does not guarantee that you will be.

God does not judge as a man judges for God judges after the heart of man. His judgment is true and right. He may let one go free and He may put another in prison. It does not matter what we can see for God looks upon the heart. One crime may have been committed out of hatred for another and another crime may have been committed out of being deceived. Which one deserves the greater punishment?

> ***2 Samuel 11:2*** *Now when evening came David arose from his bed and walked around on the roof of the king's house, and from the roof* ***he saw*** *a woman bathing; and the woman was very beautiful in appearance.*

David is the king of Israel. He is in a position of power. With that position is a responsibility not to abuse that power to acquire to himself things or persons that are not his. When "he saw" he should have turned away; however, something would not let him do that. That something is lust of the flesh. The sexual appetite of David's body exerted its power to persuade the mind to take the next step.

Bathsheba also is not without guilt. I am sure she was aware of the line of sight. In her defense, however, it was at night so we can't read too much into that.

> ***2 Samuel 11:3-4*** *So David sent and inquired about the woman. And one said, "Is this not Bathsheba, the daughter of Eliam, the wife of Uriah the Hittite? David sent messengers and took her, and when she came to him, he lay with her; and when she had purified herself from her uncleanness, she returned to her house.*

Temptation is not a sin. Jesus was tempted in all ways, yet He was without sin.

> ***James 1:14-15*** *But each one is tempted when he is carried away and enticed by his own lust. Then when lust has conceived, it gives birth to sin; and when sin is accomplished, it brings forth death.*

That Greek word "conceive" means "to bring together." When temptation and lust come together it gives birth to sin. Sin is the action. When David's lust came into contact with the temptation (seeing Bathsheba bathe) it produced sin (had her brought to him and he lay with her). How was the devil involved in this?

> ***1 Thessalonians 3:5*** *For this reason, when I could endure it no longer, I also sent to find out about your faith, for fear that the tempter might have tempted you, and our labor would be in vain.*

The devil is the tempter. But I am sure that he also tried to arrange the meeting. Could it be that he was tormenting David in his sleep and out of restlessness he arose to walk on the roof knowing that Bathsheba was taking a bath? We don't know what happened in the spirit realm, but this has the devil's signature all over it. Do you not think that he tries to arrange these same types of meetings today?

> ***2 Samuel 11:5-6*** *The woman conceived; and she sent and told David, and said, "I am pregnant." Then David sent to Joab, saying, "Send me Uriah the Hittite." So Joab sent Uriah to David.*

Having been found out in one sin, now instead of repentance, David looks for a way to hide his sin. David sends word to the commander of his army and has Uriah, Bathsheba's husband, sent back to give a report of the battle to the king. The plan is to get Uriah in his home and into relations with his wife so that the child she is pregnant with could be seen as Uriah's child.

David gets his report from Uriah and then tells him to go to his house and wash his feet. Uriah left the king's presence, but he did not go in unto his wife. Instead, he slept at the steps of the king's palace. When David questioned Uriah the next day as to why he did not go home, Uriah said that it would not be right to go to the comfort of his home when his fellow soldiers were in the battlefield camping out in the open air.

Then David hatches the second part of his plan to hide his sin. He invited Uriah to eat and drink in an attempt to get him drunk, figuring that in a drunken state he will surely go home to his wife. That too failed. David then set part three of his plan into effect. David composes a letter to Joab the commander of his army. Here is what was in the letter.

> ***2 Samuel 11:15*** *He had written in the letter, saying, "Place Uriah in the front line of the fiercest battle*

> *and withdraw from him, so that he may be struck down and die."*

Unable to hide his adultery, David now resorts to murder. Yet, Uriah was not the only casualty. There were other soldiers that died as they withdrew from the fight. There were other husbands that would not come home to their wives because a man made the decision to commit adultery. Sin has an ugly consequence. It is followed by trouble of all sorts. Sin has a fruit.

When Bathsheba learned of her husband's death, she mourned him. Then David took her for his wife. She bore David a son, yet the sin is not hidden as David had thought. There is a God who sees all things.

> **2 Samuel 11:27** *When the time of mourning was over, David sent and brought her to his house and she became his wife; then she bore him a son.* **But the thing that David had done was evil in the sight of the LORD.**

God has given David ample time to repent, but David has only gone deeper into his sin by murder. God is about to challenge David with what he has done by sending a prophet to confront the king. The Lord sends Nathan. Nathan gets an audience with the king and begins to tell a story about a poor family with a beloved sheep and a rich neighbor with a whole herd of sheep. Read the story and you will see that the rich man takes that beloved sheep from the family and slaughters it for his own use. Let's pick up where David reacts to this story.

> **2 Samuel 12:5-9** *Then David's anger burned greatly against the man, and he said to Nathan, "As the LORD lives, surely the man who has done this deserves to die. "He must make restitution for the*

> *lamb fourfold, because he did this thing and had no compassion."*
>
> *7 Nathan then said to David, "You are the man! Thus says the LORD God of Israel, 'It is I who anointed you king over Israel and it is I who delivered you from the hand of Saul. 'I also gave you your master's house and your master's wives into your care, and I gave you the house of Israel and Judah; and if that had been too little, I would have added to you many more things like these!*
>
> *9 'Why have you despised the word of the LORD by doing evil in His sight? You have struck down Uriah the Hittite with the sword, have taken his wife to be your wife, and have killed him with the sword of the sons of Ammon.'"*

David is now confronted with the awfulness of his sin. I am sure Satan was also accusing David. The devil hopes these accusations will bring poverty, destruction, and death. The plan of the devil is to bring you into a place where God will have to deal with your sin. By doing this you cannot be as effective in your destiny as you could have been. From this point we begin to see the fruit of adultery.

> ***2 Samuel 12:10*** *"'Now therefore, the sword shall never depart from your house, because you have despised Me and have taken the wife of Uriah the Hittite to be your wife.'"*

I have actually had Christians tell me that they were going to commit this sin or that sin because God would forgive them anyway. Yes, God will forgive, but these Christians are ignorant to the damage that they bring into their lives and the lives of their loved ones. David could have had any single woman in the whole of Israel for his wife. The choosing of this one would come with serious consequences. Violence would never depart from David's posterity. I wonder if David was thinking about his posterity when he called for Bathsheba to be brought to his bed. Many Christians have not thought the consequence of their sin through.

When we look at the line of David, indeed the sword did touch them and has not departed as God said it would. How many times have you heard, *"Oh, I am not hurting anyone else, this is my life and I will do with it what I want."* Yes, it is your life, if you want, but you are not just hurting yourself.

> ***2 Samuel 12:11-12*** *"Thus says the LORD, 'Behold, I will raise up evil against you from your own household; I will even take your wives before your eyes and give them to your companion, and he will lie with your wives in broad daylight. 'Indeed you did it secretly, but I will do this thing before all Israel, and under the sun.' "*

The seed of sin might be buried deep under the soil out of the sight of men, but rest assured that seed will grow and it will pierce the soil into the light of day for all to see. They may not understand what the seed is, but they will surely see its fruit. What we do in the darkness will be brought out into the light.

> ***2 Samuel 12:13-14*** *Then David said to Nathan, "I have sinned against the LORD." And Nathan said to David, "The LORD also has taken away your sin; you shall not die. "However, because by this deed you have given occasion to the enemies of the LORD to blaspheme, the child also that is born to you shall surely die."*

What did the child do that was wrong? Did the child commit some sin that he had to die for? By your behavior you can bring blessing or trouble to your children. This is what is meant by God visiting the sins of the fathers unto the third and fourth generation. It isn't that the children have done anything wrong, but that there is a fruit of sin, and that fruit is consequently eaten by others as well as yourself. We must understand that our actions are paving a road upon which we and our posterity will have to walk. You choose whether that road will be fraught with danger or paved with safety. The life of the child was taken because of the sin of the parents. That is the ugly revelation of the fruit of adultery.

> ***Proverbs 20:7** A righteous man who walks in his integrity— How blessed are his sons after him.*

Oh, God! Would that we walk in integrity to bring a blessing unto generations after us. God, help us to confess our sin before you and repent that we might begin a life of integrity to bless our children. We see that our actions affect more than ourselves.

This child of David and Bathsheba became ill and in seven days he was dead. David and his wife were faced with the hideous consequence of their sin. There before them lay the lifeless corpse of their only child. A morose reminder of that night this child was conceived. That night that sin was also conceived. I can imagine that David would have said, *"Take me, I am the one who sinned."* No, David, you do not understand destiny. God's plan will not be halted and David was a big part of that plan.

David would not shake his fist at God because of this tragic loss. He realized that he had brought this upon his own head. When David heard of his son's death, he arose, anointed himself, dressed and went to the house of the Lord and worshiped. I have ministered to those who have lost a grandchild and as a result have given up on God. I cannot imagine the pain of losing a child or a grandchild, but I cannot imagine giving up on God either. In a sad event like this we should run to God and tell Him we understand that His nature is intact and that He is right, good, and holy. That He has every right over life and death, that we thank Him for His righteous decision.

> **Proverbs 6:32-35** *The one who commits adultery with a woman is lacking sense; He who would destroy himself does it. Wounds and disgrace he will find, And his reproach will not be blotted out. For jealousy enrages a man, And he will not spare in the day of vengeance. He will not accept any ransom, Nor will he be satisfied though you give many gifts.*

There are doctors who commit adultery, as well as professors, business men and women, scientists, presidents. All of them intelligent I am sure, yet they lack sense because they have engaged in adultery. It is self destructive behavior. It will only produce wounds and disgrace. What about the spouse whose marriage is violated? Even the most mild mannered of persons are filled with rage and vengeance.

> **Jeremiah 3:13** *Only acknowledge your iniquity, That you have transgressed against the Lord your God And have scattered your favors to the strangers under every green tree, And you have not obeyed My voice,' declares the Lord.*

God requests of us that we expose our sins by acknowledging them. This is not what David did at first. This is also not what most people do. They make excuses and begin to justify their sin. They say things like, *"You don't know what I have had to put up with at home." "I've been under a lot of stress." "I can't stand being alone."* There is no good excuse for adultery. Just admit it, turn from it, repent of it, but for goodness sake don't justify it.

Ezekiel 16:36-42

36 Thus says the Lord God, "Because your lewdness was poured out and your nakedness uncovered through your harlotries with your lovers and with all your detestable idols, and because of the blood of your sons which you gave to idols, 37 therefore, behold, I will gather all your lovers with whom you took pleasure, even all those whom you loved and all those whom you hated. So I will gather them against you from every direction and expose your nakedness to them that they may see all your nakedness.

38 Thus I will judge you like women who commit adultery or shed blood are judged; and I will bring on you the blood of wrath and jealousy. 39 "I will also give you into the hands of your lovers, and they will tear down your shrines, demolish your high places, strip you of your clothing, take away your jewels, and will leave you naked and bare.

40 They will incite a crowd against you and they will stone you and cut you to pieces with their swords. 41 "They will burn your houses with fire and execute judgments on you in the sight of many women. Then I will stop you from playing the harlot, and you will also no longer pay your lovers. 42 So I will calm My fury against you and My jealousy will depart from you, and I will be pacified and angry no more."

So often is the case that when a man or woman commits adultery, the one whom they commit this sin with eventually turns on them and exposes them to their spouse. This is a fruit of this sin. Do you think the enemy would like that? Yes, he would. Why do you think he tempted you in the first place? He wants to see the end result—the fruit of adultery take root in your life. The person thought it was just a one night stand. But then infatuation sets in and this person starts exposing their nakedness through contacting the person's spouse.

We have only explored adultery. There are many different behaviors that the enemy would like you to engage in; each one of them having a fruit that will be a result. Do you think the devil wanted Adam and Eve to become like gods? Of course not. He wanted them dead. He wants you dead, too. That is why I think this book is so important. I want you to live. I want you to become all that God has created you to become. I want you to see the pits so that you do not fall into them. I want you to see the freedom Jesus has brought to you. I want you to be successful in your walk. Refuse the fruit of adultery by not planting its seed.

The Jezebel Tactic

Chapter Thirteen

2 Corinthians 2:10-11 (ESV) Anyone whom you forgive, I also forgive. What I have forgiven, if I have forgiven anything, has been for your sake in the presence of Christ, so that we would not be outwitted by Satan; ***for we are not ignorant of his designs.***

In a Christian culture that focuses on life after death, there is a lack of understanding concerning the enemy's tactics with regard to life before death. In Paul's day the Corinthian church was taught how Satan works. I am troubled that we cannot say the same for the modern church. The effect of this is that we, as Christians, unwittingly come into agreement with our enemy, and we become unwilling pawns in his plans for our destruction. In this chapter we are going to expose the most dangerous of these strategies, the Jezebel tactic, to the end that you would be able to recognize the enemy's working in your own life.

I would like to preface this chapter with a clarification. No doubt you have heard of the term Jezebel spirit. This has caught on in the Body of Christ. I want to suggest to you that this is not a singular Jezebel spirit, but it is a name that we place upon a set of tactics that all demonic spirits use. It is for this reason that I do not use the term Jezebel spirit; rather, we use the term Jezebel tactic which I believe brings clarification to this subject.

Now, before you ask any questions, let me alleviate one of them right up front. Even though Christians can be used by the devil, as you have read, they **cannot** be possessed by the devil. In fact, the only way that Satan has access to Christians is through deception. He deceives us into carrying out his plans when we come into agreement with his suggestions or thoughts. What joy that must bring Satan when we, the sons and daughters of the kingdom of God, do his bidding for him. It is my desire that this chapter will reveal to you Satan's tactics so that you will know them and reject them in your life.

Jezebel Tactic Revealed

> ***Revelation 2:18-25 ~ESV~*** *"And to the angel of the church in Thyatira write: 'The words of the Son of God, who has eyes like a flame of fire, and whose feet are like burnished bronze. " 'I know your works, your love and faith and service and patient endurance, and that your latter works exceed the first. But I have this against you, that you tolerate that woman* **Jezebel***, who calls herself a prophetess and is teaching and seducing my servants to practice sexual immorality and to eat food sacrificed to idols.*
>
> *I gave her time to repent, but she refuses to repent of her sexual immorality. Behold, I will throw her onto a sickbed, and those who commit adultery with her I will throw into great tribulation, unless they repent of her works, and I will strike her children dead. And all the churches will know that I am he who searches mind and heart, and I will give to each of you as your works deserve.*
>
> *But to the rest of you in Thyatira, who do not hold this teaching, who have not learned what some call the deep things of Satan, to you I say, I do not lay on you any other burden. Only hold fast what you have until I come.*

This revelation was given by Jesus to John from heaven. It must be noted that I do not speak of this tactic in a gender sense. Both men and women have fallen prey to this tactic. Here are some points to note.

- There was a spirit of toleration in this church
- Jezebel was self proclaimed
- She is teaching the saints to compromise with the world
- She was engaged in sexual immorality
- She was teaching the deep things of Satan

Who is Thyatira

> *"QUOTE"*
>
> *The church of Thyatira (a flourishing manufacturing and commercial city in Lydia, on the site of which now stands a considerable Turkish town called Ak-Hissar, or "the White Castle," with nine mosques and one Greek church) was very favorably distinguished for self-denying, active love and patience, but was likewise too indulgent towards errors which corrupted Christianity with heathen principles and practices.*[45]

How this church relates to us today is that we oftentimes put emphasis on **love** to the **quenching of truth**. Indeed, Paul says in 1 Corinthians 13:1 that if we have all knowledge and do not have love we are nothing. Yet, if you love and do not have knowledge, you will compromise the truth into a lie. This is what the church of Thyatira was doing.

---

[45] Schaff, P., & Schaff, D. S. 1997. *History of the Christian Church.* Logos Research Systems, Inc.: Oak Harbor, WA.

Jezebel's argument might go like this:

*In order to win this city for Jesus, we must relate to the people or they will not hear our message. The Thyatirians will not listen to our message unless we become their friends first. We need to go to **their** temples and their restaurants so that we can relate to the worship of **their** gods. If we become like them, partake of their culture, then you will be able to convince them of Jesus. God understands that we have to engage in the same things in order to win them to Jesus.*

This is the lie that Jezebel was teaching the church. Consequently, members were having sex in the temples with the temple prostitutes and partaking of feasts by eating meat that had been sacrificed to **their** idols. They were doing all of this in the name of Christ and evangelism.

Toleration Leads to Compromise

The most notable result of this tactic is that of compromise. What we mean by this is that we willingly **relinquish** part of the message of the Bible for a so-called *"noble cause."* When a person or church does this, it will destroy them. People find themselves compromising:

- To get attention or to get noticed
- To be popular, acceptable, and liked by those in prominence
- To secure their jobs
- To get promotions
- To get good grades
- To get more money
- To get bigger houses
- To live in a better neighborhood
- To get more power [46]

---

[46] Preacher's Outline Sermon Bible, "Revelation"

The point is made, but the list is incomplete. There are many reasons for compromise, but there is only one outcome. Anytime you compromise a truth, it ceases to be the truth any longer. Jesus said that knowing the truth will set you free (John 8:32). It then becomes obvious that not knowing the truth will put you in bondage. Your actions are forged from what you believe. If what you believe is false, your actions become the evidence that you are walking in bondage. Compromise always produces actions that are opposed to the truth. We see this in the church of Thyatira.

When we read this account we only see a snapshot of where they have come to, not the road they traveled to get there. For instance, Jesus says that He has this against them, that they tolerate… What must happen in a church before they are willing to relinquish the truth by tolerating false teaching? Before we look at this I also want to note that if Jesus is correcting them for tolerating this false teacher, it also tells us that we should not tolerate false teachers in the church.

At one time or another we have all been faced with an opportunity to compromise our position with regard to morality. This tactic of the enemy will get you into one of his traps to cause you to compromise what you know to be true. The enemy will use the acceptance of the group to get you to compromise. In other words, if you are unwilling to compromise you will become an outsider with regard to the group. The enemy will use labeling to suggest that you are somehow inferior morally because you won't compromise. You will be labeled as a prude, mean, insensitive, and I love this one, intolerant, bigoted, narrow minded, fanatical, obsessive, crazy, and our all-time favorite, fundamentalist.

The enemy uses these labels to marginalize the person so he can marginalize the message. In philosophical circles this tactic is called ad hominem. It is a Latin expression that means "to the man." The idea is that when one has a weak argument they resort to character assassination to hide their weak argument and to undermine their opponent's argument. It is a tactic that works most of the time so it is employed often. However, it is sinister.

If a person is a lover of truth, to be bested in an argument would be a favor done for then they would have a greater range of truth in them. If the goal is to win at any cost, then there is an immoral component now injected into the process. With that immorality there will also come compromise or toleration of something that is not right.

A good example of this is a job promotion. You can have the promotion, but it requires that you fudge the reports once in a while. The pay is great and you won't have to fudge often, just once in a while. You take the job thinking that compromising your values in this small area is no big deal. After all, the company headquarters requirements are too stringent. After proving yourself worthy as one who will lie on the reports, you are then asked to make a presentation of numbers that are false. Now the ante just went up. But you find you are in a catch 22 because you already proved you would fudge on paper, so why wouldn't you fudge in person?

The enemy will always seek to get you into a situation where he can ramp up the compromising. Watch yourself by refusing to compromise in the first place. If you show yourself honest, then you will not be called upon to be dishonest. Also, if you show yourself to be dishonest, you will not be called upon for a position that requires honesty. In other words, what you show you are willing or unwilling to do will dictate what you are asked to do.

The Bishops or Overseers Failed the Church

The overseer of a church is responsible to maintain sound doctrine in that church. This is the office of the bishop or overseer. If you study that Greek word, you will find it has to do with investigation and judgment. Namely, the bishop should investigate what is being taught to make sure the teaching is sound.

Because Jezebel is already seated and teaching it shows a failure of leadership to deal with this. Compromise is already being allowed. The leaders are tolerating things that should not be tolerated. This is the ultimate goal of this tactic; to undermine and neutralize leadership, gain access to power and begin to deceive. It is apparent that this has already happened in Thyatira.

When compromise creeps into a church, it is the overseer's responsibility to apply the Word of God to those who brought the compromise into the church. Church members in our own period of technology hear many different teachings from many different sources. It is easy, therefore, for a false teaching to come into a church. The overseer is to point the flock of God back to Christ and to what Christ says.

No one in the church is supposed to compromise with the world. The apostle John tells us that the love of the world is hostility toward Christ. Everything we as believers characterize is opposed to the world system. We are bought with a price and we owe our allegiance, love, and life to Christ.

> ***Luke 9:23 (ESV)*** *And he said to all, "If anyone would come after me, let him deny himself and take up his cross daily and follow me."*

> ***1 John 2:15-16 (ESV)*** *Do not love the world or the things in the world. If anyone loves the world, the love of the Father is not in him. For all that is in the world— the desires of the flesh and the desires of*

the eyes and pride in possessions—is not from the Father but is from the world.

"Q*UOTE*"

"Jesus sees all that we do. Notice that in the first part of the message to the Church at Thyatira, His eyes are like a flame of fire. He sees, and He rewards or disciplines according to thoughts and actions. He sees the faithful; He sees those who refuse to compromise His message and He helps them to stand firm in the faith."[47]

Jeremiah 16:17 (ESV) *For my eyes are on all their ways. They are not hidden from me, nor is their iniquity concealed from my eyes.*

Hosea 7:2 (ESV) *But they do not consider that I remember all their evil. Now their deeds surround them; they are before my face.*

Thyatira's Works

Notice also that the church at Thyatira was involved in many good works. This church is commended for the many good things they are doing right. Jesus describes them as having works of:

- Love
- Service
- Faith
- Patience [48]

Many of us would look at this type of church and say that they must be doing things right. Look at their love, faith, service,

---

[47] Preacher's Outline Sermon Bible, "Revelation"

[48] Preacher's Outline Sermon Bible, "Revelation"

and patience. This was an active growing church. From all appearances things were going quite well. Think about how this church is described.

- Dynamic
- Vibrant
- Alive
- Exciting [49]

This church met the needs of the community. It was a church that was bursting at the seams with activity, yet from within it was corrupted with compromise. Even today when we look at some of the mega churches that have compromised with the world, we find they have embraced worldly ideas like secular humanism, moral relativism, or universalism. Some have given up on the singular message of Christ and have opted instead for a more broad view of salvation. Often these churches are filled with members who seem to be happy and excited about their church. To the world the church at Thyatira looked like a colossal success story, **but to Jesus it was full of corruption.**

Thyatira's Breakdown

What were the components of Thyatira's breakdown? What can we learn from their failure? If we are to learn a lesson that will keep us from repeating the failures of this church, we must define the problems associated with their failure so we may avoid them in our church. Again they were:

- Allowing a spirit of toleration in this church
- Allowing Jezebel who was self-proclaimed
- Allowing her to teach the saints to compromise with the world

---

[49] Preacher's Outline Sermon Bible, "Revelation"

- Allowing her to maintain leadership even though she was engaged in sexual immorality
- Allowing her to teach the deep things of Satan

We have sufficiently dealt with the toleration and compromise issue so let's move to the next flaw.

Allowance of False Prophets

Jezebel was a self-proclaimed prophetess. Observe in verse 20 that she called **herself** a prophetess. Those who are influenced by this tactic will claim that their message is from God and will proclaim their own spirituality. Thus, the church will position such a one where they will have access to teach. They will not only feign themselves as prophets, but as teachers, apostles, pastors, and evangelists as well. The prophet seems to be easier for them to fake since they will often appeal to *"God said to me."*

Once given a platform from which to teach, Jezebel will begin to seduce those in the church. We must remember that gender is not important here. Both men and women can be influenced by Satan to operate under his direction. There is a lesson for us to learn from this. When someone has to make self-proclamations to qualify their ministry, something is wrong. One's ministry should validate them. Just as Apostle Paul said to the Corinthian church, *"You are my seal of apostleship."* Anytime someone proclaims their own spirituality, be careful of him or her.

True spirituality is marked by humility and bringing attention to Jesus; true spirituality does **not** seek to bring attention to self. True spirituality is marked by the fruit of the Spirit; love, joy, peace, patience, long suffering, gentleness, kindness, goodness, and faithfulness. It is important to understand that this church was allowing Jezebel to seduce them. They were allowing her to shift from sound doctrine delivered to the church by the apostles, to teaching fornication and idolatry and the deep things of Satan. What she was teaching we still find alive today.

Allowance of False Teaching

"QUOTE"

Jezebel was teaching: that believers could not separate themselves from the world, not entirely, not without becoming exclusive and snobbish.

That believers needed to be sensible in dealing with the world and its functions: they needed to be participating in "some of the world's" functions in order to be friendly, keep their jobs, secure promotions, help their businesses, keep from being considered "fanatical," and win the lost.

That believers could reach the world more easily by associating and fellowshipping with the world.

That if a person really worshipped God, he/she would be acceptable to God even if he did not know about Jesus Christ; that Jesus Christ is not the only way to God; that He is not the only Savior.

That believers should attend the social functions of neighbors and fellow workers and not be exclusive and separatists. [50]

Jezebel was teaching believers to commit idolatry. Remember that idolatry can be anything that we place in

---

[50] --*Preacher Outline Sermon Bible*

importance over Jesus and His will for us. That means that idols can be:

- A job
- Money
- Position
- Possessions
- Pleasure
- Sports
- Business
- Family
- Self
- Sex
- Knowledge
- Power
- Church
- Ministry
- Hobbies

When false teaching is allowed in the Church, it opens the door for deceiving spirits to begin plundering the congregation. This is in accordance with the warnings that we already have for our time period.

> ***1 Timothy 4:1** But the Spirit explicitly says that in later times some will fall away from the faith, paying attention to deceitful spirits and doctrines of demons...*

Why is the Church paying attention to deceitful spirits and doctrines of demons? It is because it is being taught from the pulpit! It's not like the demons appear as a special guest! Do you actually think it would be that easy to spot them? **When those in the Church refuse to study the Word and learn, they offer themselves upon the altar of deception and by their lack of knowledge they are destroyed.**

Allowance of Seduction

> ***2 Timothy 3:13-14** But evil men and impostors will proceed from bad to worse, deceiving and being deceived. You, however, continue in the things you have learned and become convinced of, knowing from whom you have learned them...*

To avoid seduction you have to continue in the things you have learned and become convinced of them. How are you going to do that when you don't apply yourself to learn the Word of God in the first place? What does it mean to be seduced? It means that one is led astray, they are deceived. The goal of the devil is to deceive you. This tactic of Jezebel is a way to complete that goal. There is a leadership problem in this church. They have allowed a self-proclaimed prophet access to leadership position while also allowing them to teach seductions from that place of honor and respect.

Allowance to Teach the Deep Things of Satan

Jesus commended one group who were not listening to Jezebel's teaching to continue not to hold to them. But note that He called the teachings *"the deep things of Satan"* then added *"as they call them."* This means that a lot of what might be passed off as demonology or spiritual warfare might actually be puffing up the devil. We do not need a deep understanding of the devil. We need to understand his tactics, but we do not need to understand him in a deep way. I think that Jesus said "so-called" because Satan actually is not deep at all. We know this, he is a liar, he is a murderer, and he is a destroyer. Everything he does has at its root one or more of those natures involved. How deep is that?

Warning to the Church

Jesus gives Jezebel a time to repent. This shows us that Jezebel was a person who belonged to the church. She was just operating in error. This should cause concern for ourselves that we don't fall into being used by this tactic. Jezebel was cast upon a bed of sickness. Notice also that those who come into agreement with her are thrown into tribulation. We have to be careful with what we come into agreement. If we are not careful we can bring tribulation into our own lives and become influenced by demonic spirits which influence others.

> ***Galatians 6:7-9*** *Do not be deceived, God is not mocked; for whatever a man sows, this he will also reap.* ***For the one who sows to his own flesh will from the flesh reap corruption****, but the one who sows to the Spirit will from the Spirit reap eternal life. Let us not lose heart in doing good, for in due time we will reap if we do not grow weary.*

We also see Jesus saying that He will strike her children dead. Even as children of God we can become more of a threat to our own family than a blessing. Jesus has in the past and will in the future remove those who will not bear fruit unto His name. Those children of God who enter into compromise endanger their own lives.

Look at the example of Israel. Look at Ananias and Sapphira. There are numerous accounts in which God removed rebellious people from the earth even though they were His people. It does not mean they went to hell. It only means they will harm the rest of His family if they are allowed to remain.

Characteristics of Jezebel

First Things First

The underlying factor of this tactic is that it destroys families, churches, businesses, relationships, jobs, and lives. This is why God will not just let this run rampant in His Church. God will give time for repentance, but it is only for a time. Then He will judge and discipline.

There are some things that I need to set forward before we continue. First, we should not use the following attributes as a reason to treat someone harshly. Just because you may have identified someone who may be influenced by this tactic does not mean that God wants you to confront them. **It must always be remembered that we are to fight for one another, not against one another.** Second, it is not right to pick one or two traits out and say that the person is being used by the enemy. Only when a number of these traits are present can we conclude that they are in a spiritual battle. Third, the person himself may not understand what he is dealing with, so criticism should not be employed.

Dangers

The biggest danger in dealing with people who have come under the influence of the Jezebel tactic is **coming into agreement with their accusations**. When you hear accusations and come into agreement with them without doing the research to find out if they are true, you open yourself up to the same influencing spirits by which that person is influenced. Then, without notice, your life begins changing. You begin to dislike yourself. You can't figure out why you feel the way you do. You find it hard to hear and understand teachings from the Word of God. It becomes harder to read the Bible and understand it. You are more open to deceiving spirits and your belief structure may begin to change.

If this has happened to you, trace it back to when it started and you might find that you came into agreement with someone who was talking bad about someone else, especially those in leadership. I am talking about an attack that gets personal and assaults the character of a person in leadership. Later, we will deal with how to separate yourself from this spiritual attack.

Now we have come to the place where I ask each of you to make mental notes of the following characteristics. This is not so you can see them in someone else at first, but rather so you can see them in yourself. Every one of us has been influenced in at least one of them at some point in his or her life, so don't be afraid to face the truth. It is important that you be honest with yourself.

You are going to be doing an **internal audit** so that you can identify and destroy the work of the enemy in you. As Jesus taught us, *"How can you see to get the sliver out of my eye when you have a plank in yours? First, get the plank out of your eye and then you can see to get the sliver out of your brother's eye"* (Matthew 7:5 and Luke 6:42).

Common Characteristics of the Jezebel Tactic

Looks to Rub Elbows With Leadership

In order to get to a place of power, the person who is influenced by this spirit must get access to the leadership. When people come into a church and expect right away to begin hobnobbing with leaders in that church, be careful. They have a thirst for power and control.

Erodes Current Leadership

Since they seek positions of power, they will undermine those who hold the positions they are after. Quite often they do this through the use of what I call the evil power twins. These twin powers are the **power of suggestion and the power of assumption**. This tactic works because of our psychological construction. When we take in information, we accept it, reject it, or file it because we do not have enough evidence to support it one way or another. The problem lies in the filing processes of the mind.

For instance, someone in the church comes to you and says that he or she thinks that the pastor's wife is being unfaithful to the pastor. You do not have enough evidence to support or reject the information, so you subconsciously file it away. At this point, your mind begins to search for information to support or reject the original data. Often this happens on a subconscious level. That means you are not aware of it taking place. It is no different than when you cannot think of a person's name and it pops up hours later out of nowhere. Your mind was searching for it unawares to you.

You may see the pastor's wife giving another church member a hug and that causes your mind to file data in support of the suggestion of unfaithfulness. At the time this is taking place, demonic spirits are whispering accusations against the pastor's wife into your mind as well. As this so-called evidence grows, there is a point where you accept it as a fact and you come into agreement with the accusation based upon assumption, not empirical evidence. Now you have just opened yourself up to influence by the same spirits.

In short, someone *"suggested"* information, and at some point *"assumption"* is employed to make that information factual when in reality it may not be. There are thousands of stories with the same sad ending just because someone took a suggestion and allowed it to fester into an assumption. This tactic is so successful that we have an American idiom concerning it. I am sure you have heard the phrase, *"The Power of Suggestion."*

It really is powerful because it acts upon our subconscious mind and we are not aware of it under normal circumstances. Once information is suggested, it sets in motion the subconscious to look for evidence. The problem is that if you are looking for evidence to support something you will likely find it, but it hardly will be empirical evidence. Why? Because the suggestion was leaning in one direction.

How can we defeat this tactic? We do it by refusing to accept anything as factual without real evidence to support it and by being aware of how we work psychologically so we can be on guard. Let's take a look at some scriptures that deal with this.

> ***1 Timothy 5:19 ~JNT~*** *Never listen to any accusation against a leader unless it is supported by two or three witnesses.*

> ***Deuteronomy 19:15*** *"A single witness shall not rise up against a man on account of any iniquity or any sin which he has committed; on the evidence of two or three witnesses a matter shall be confirmed."*

Jezebel Opposes the True Prophetic

Since the true prophet is able to spot this tactic in operation first, he or she is relentlessly attacked by those influenced by this spiritual attack. Note that those influenced by the Jezebel tactic will try to destroy the true prophets as they themselves often make claims to being a prophet. Watch out for those who show a striking dislike for the prophetic!

They Need to Know Everything

The reason they need to know is that they see information as power. They can leverage themselves with it to access the reins of power through their manipulation of information. This causes them to be nosy with a need to know everything. They constantly barrage people with questions comparing answers with answers to find out what the leadership is up to.

Controls and Manipulates People

This is probably their most notable trait. They sneak their way into friendships and subtly begin to manipulate and control them. They always like to have a plausible alibi if something goes wrong. Because of this, they use their friends to do their dirty work. They turn them into spies to gather information.

Cause Division

This spirit will spread division, factionalism, and sectarianism everywhere they go. They divide and conquer. The Bible is not silent concerning these things.

> ***Romans 16:17-18*** *Now I urge you, brethren, keep your eye on those who cause dissensions and hindrances contrary to the teaching which you learned, and turn away from them. For such men are **slaves**, not of our Lord Christ but of their own appetites; and by their smooth and flattering speech they deceive the hearts of the unsuspecting.*

Deceptive

In order to further their aspirations of leading, they employ the greatest tool available to the dark forces of the demonic realm. Deception, or lying, is a big part of the Jezebel's life. They use it to destroy people so they can gain access to the seat of influence. They also use deception to inflate or deflate people's egos to accomplish their ultimate goals.

They are excellent liars and as such, it often takes the gift of discernment to see through their ruse. They can force themselves to cry or laugh just to get what they want. This is their primary way of manipulating and controlling people. They can look you straight in the eye and lie with not so much as a tinge of guilt.

Mystic

Anyone who uses manipulation and control to get what he wants is using tactics of demonic spirits. It is the use of witchcraft. In witchcraft spells are formulated to get people to do certain things. To lie, use emotional outbursts, manufactured affection, anger, or any other method to get someone to do what you want is a form of witchcraft. Those who use demonic methods to accomplish their goals will open themselves up to other demonic influences as well. It seems that they are always projecting an air of super spirituality. This is used to keep them from being found out.

Spiritualizes Everything

When confronted, this tactic will take a spiritual road. They will emphasize God in the decisions they made. By doing this they are hiding the true motive of undermining leadership. The use of implication is a way they have of shifting the focus that is on them to another.

Incapable of Logical Communication

It is impossible to converse with a Jezebel in logic. I remember when I would write letters to a person who was being influenced by this tactic. They would twist everything I said. They would make implications that would completely change the meaning of my original letter. Finally, I told my wife, Kathryn, that I could not communicate with this person. This is a way to maintain control and domination. Anytime you get too close to discovery they will barrage you with multiple questions on varied subjects. Confusion keeps them unexposed.

An Incomplete List

This is an incomplete list. I don't have the room to reveal all of the characteristics of the Jezebel tactic, but I want you to understand those most prominent. There are good books out there devoted entirely to expose this tactic.

We Recognize It, Now What?

Now that we recognize how this tactic is employed, what do we do about it? The answer to that question is determined by whether you see these characteristics in yourself or another. First, let's deal with what to do if we see it in another. What we do in this case is determined by our positional authority. If you are under that person's authority, then you will be most effective by praying for them. Remember to fight for them in your prayers, not against them. If you fight against them, God will open your life to discipline.

If you are in authority over that person or on the same level of authority, then again prayer is your greatest weapon, but in this case you can also confront them. In fact, if you are the leader in that organization it is your duty to deal with it. The longer you let it go unchallenged the more damage that can occur to that body of believers. However, it must be dealt with in love. Recall that the person you deal with may not even realize the extent of influence demonic spirits have in his life and revealing this can make him defensive.

> *"QUOTE"*
>
> *Can this person come to repentance? Yes, this person can repent, but the person must recognize the pattern and motive of control. Those influenced with a Jezebel tactic must be confronted by someone who is not afraid of a*

reaction. If that person is confronted about his actions in firmness and love, he may be able to recognize the spirit and seek freedom. Without confrontation, the person no doubt will remain in the pattern of control, as it has become a lifestyle and there is no motivation to change.

Even following confrontation, the person may repent and acknowledge that he or she has a problem. Since much of the behavior traits become habitual, it must be dealt with on a continuous basis, or there will be no change.

There must be a willingness to allow the Holy Spirit to bring change in one's personality. Patterns of control are often deeply entrenched in the personality by demonic thoughts forming a stronghold over time. Therefore, there must be not only the resistance of the devil, but a continual renouncing of all thought patterns that lead to control.[51]

If you recognize any of these traits in your own life, begin by praying.

1. **Repent** of having faith in what the enemy was saying over what God has said.
2. **Renounce** the use of any of the characteristics revealed in this chapter that you find in yourself.
3. **Refuse** to operate in them any longer.
4. **Request** God's help in overcoming these things.

---

[51] --*Confronting Jezebel* by Steve Sampson

5. **Require** accountability of yourself so that when others raise an issue you do not react negatively to it.

What is a Stronghold?

A stronghold is a way of believing that is contrary to the way God wants us to believe concerning any given subject. For instance, God said that we are not to commit adultery. Any belief that tries to change this in our thinking can become a stronghold. We may try to justify adultery by saying that our spouse committed it first. That is a stronghold. We might try to justify adultery by saying our spouse treats us bad and doesn't love us. That is a stronghold.

Anything that disagrees with what God says is a stronghold. When we have strongholds in our lives they become **access points** whereby the enemy can plunder us. This is why it is important that we come **out of agreement with the enemy** and thereby arrest the enemy's ability to plunder our lives.

God is always right. He is always just. He is always love. If there is something that annoys you about what God has said or done, agree with God that you know His nature is just, right, and loving. Agree with God that you don't understand why He said or did something, and that you are in agreement with His will to do so.

What we do when we question God's motives is that **we make ourselves His moral judge,** and this places us in a dangerous position. God will not be dethroned…not by Satan and certainly not by us. Resolve to admit to your inability to understand and **refuse to bring an accusation against God.**

2 Corinthians 10:3-5 (NKJV) For though we walk in the flesh, we do not war according to the flesh. For the weapons of our warfare are not carnal but mighty in God for pulling down strongholds, casting down arguments and every high thing that exalts itself against the knowledge of God, bringing every thought into captivity to the obedience of Christ...

What will cast down an imagination? What will cast down a thought that exalts itself against the knowledge of God? What will bring every thought into captivity to the obedience of Christ? Only the Truth will! Only the Word of God is called a sword! Our spiritual warfare is waged on the battlefield of ideas, concepts, speculations, suggestions, and assumptions!

When a person is operating under the influence of demonic forces, **he is blinded to the truth**. When the tactic of the enemy is exposed, we need to take note of it so that we are not fooled into Satan's deceptions. We should not be ignorant of his devices against us.

When a person becomes influenced by demonic spirits **he does things that he doesn't understand.** This is because he came into agreement with a spirit and as a consequence he started taking on the nature of that spirit. He may experience anger, rage, depression, anxiety, fear, bondage, and so on.

You can rebuke and demand these spirits leave until you are exhausted, but they will still be there. The only way to free yourself of their activity is through recognizing their work in your life, repenting of coming into agreement with them, and continuing to do soul maintenance. How do you do soul maintenance?

- **Humble yourself** *because the enemy is always proud.*
- **Fill yourself with truth** *because the enemy is filled with deception.*
- **Cultivate the fruit of the spirit which is love, joy, peace, patience, kindness, goodness, faithfulness, gentleness, and self-control,** *because the enemy is full*

> *of hate, depression, conflict, impatience, rudeness, crookedness, unfaithfulness, un-tactfulness, and panic.*

- Remember that we pick up this influence when we come into agreement with the accusations of someone else that is fighting this influence.
- To overcome, all we need to do is come out of agreement with that same spirit and the door of access is then closed; repent for engaging in this in the first place.
- When you recognize yourself being used, stop. Change your course; change your mind; put on the mind of Christ, that is seeing things as He does; and rejoice for you have just defeated the enemy of your soul!

Pastors need to be especially careful when people come into their group who seem overly chummy with leaders. We need to watch carefully. I also like to make my folks aware of this tactic so they can see it in operation because they are more likely to observe it before the leadership does. In effect, this deputizes each member to arrest this tactic as soon as it begins to operate. The end goal is not only to defeat this tactic, but to set the person free who is operating in it.

Preparing for Warfare

Chapter Fourteen

God did not leave us defenseless against the wiles of the devil. He made it clear in His Word how the enemy attacks us and how we can counter that attack. We have four thousand years of historic biblical record of his actions against humanity. We have another two thousand years of historic observation. We have no need of a deep understanding of satanic nature. We need to save that energy to know our Creator. We do have a need for a deep understanding of God's nature.

I want this chapter to be one of victory, hope, and power. The instructions of our God are perfect, they are flawless. They require, however, our diligence and our cooperation to implement. This leads us to the armor our God has provided for us to put on. So much of the time God provides, but we do not implement.

> ***Ephesians 6:10** Finally, be strong in the Lord and in the strength of His might.*

Every Christian wants to be strong. We implement many different plans to affect that end result, nevertheless, we find ourselves failing again and again. That is why I raise this verse for us to ponder. We are called to be strong, but we do not have strength with which to be strong. We are actually weak. Now, before you accuse me of using negative speech, let me remind you that I have agreement from the Word of God.

Why would we be commended to be strong in the Lord if we already possessed strength? That statement presupposes weakness on our part. At least we see that we can BE strong—if we are willing to cooperate. It is easy to tell someone to be strong in the Lord, but how does one actually do that?

Ephesians 6:11 *Put on the full armor of God, so that you will be able to stand firm against the schemes of the devil.*

The wide perspective is to put on the full armor of God. To "put on" demands a decision on your part to take what is available to put on. This is not a decision whether to enter the battle. The fight is coming to you whether you want it to or not. You are thrust into this fight against your will. The question then becomes, *"Are you willing to engage your enemy or are you going to be a casualty of war?"*

The Greek word for "put on" is *enduo* and it means to clothe one's self. A person does not get up in the morning and find clothing flying off the hook and dressing them. Nor will the Christian find that they are automatically clothed with God's armor. You have to press into the armor. It is there for you to use, but you will have to put it on. If you do, then, and only then, will you be able to stand against the schemes of the devil.

Why does the text say "full armor?" How many Christians go into the battle with partial armor? The inclusion of the word "full" would indicate the importance of taking each part and putting it on. **The inference would be that anything less than full armor could end up in defeat.** How serious do we take this?

The Greek word for "against" is *pros* and it expresses the idea of moving toward. How many of us see our warfare as moving toward the enemy. So many of us have been duped into thinking we are in a defensive posture rather than a posture of aggression. This means that with the full armor of God you will be able to not only stand firmly, but you will be able to stand firmly while advancing against your enemy.

I am reminded of the Roman army tactic where they lock arms and with shields in front they take very small steps forward so as to maintain sound footing. With the full armor of God you can take ground from the enemy. Remember, the kingdom of God is not measured in geography but in souls. There is, I think, an allusion to this when Jesus said:

Matthew 11:12-19

12 "From the days of John the Baptist until now the kingdom of heaven suffers violence, and violent men take it by force."

This is a verse that has been treated in many different ways. I have pondered it in the context of many different views. I think the problem with understanding it is that we over complicate it and think it is obscure. It is obscure only if read by itself. When we read it in context and we understand our enemy it begins to make sense.

One of the most popular interpretations on this verse is that we Christians are the ones taking the kingdom by force. Why would we Christians need to take the kingdom of heaven by force if the kingdom of heaven has been given to us? If anything we are taking the kingdom of darkness! If the idea that the violent men are Christians, then I ask you to open your mind to hear another view and test it to see which is right. So let's keep reading.

13 "For all the prophets and the Law prophesied until John."

The inclusion of the word "for" shows us that the previous verse is about to be explained. Before you can understand verse thirteen you need to take note of the time frame first. *"From the days of John the Baptist until now…:"* The kingdom of heaven is suffering violence from violent men during this time period only. In verse thirteen Jesus now points to the time frame before that by saying that all the prophets and the Law prophesied up to John.

This is the clue that unlocks this passage. Jesus is telling us that there is a vast amount of truth available by the time this violence begins to take place. Why would He say this unless He expects that generation to understand what is taking place and the time period that they are privileged to witness?

What information is Jesus referring to regarding the prophets and the Law? Since the time periods have been divided between the coming of John the Baptist and all of the time previous to that event, then it is fair to say that this time period is the time prophesied that the Messiah would come. Keep reading:

> **14** *"And if you are willing to accept it, John himself is Elijah who was to come.* **15** *He who has ears to hear, let him hear."*

There it is! The prophecy of Malachi about Elijah coming to be the forerunner of the Messiah! Jesus establishes WHO John is. In other words, we have arrived at a point in time that was foretold by the Law and the prophets. The forerunner is here so that means the MESSIAH must also be here! The statement, kingdom of heaven is suffering violence, could not be in keeping with the idea that the violent men are Christians.

What was the first message John preached? Repent, for the kingdom of heaven is at hand. The reason that the time period that the kingdom of heaven suffered violence was only from the days of John the Baptist until now is that it was not available until the beginning of the ministry of John the Baptist. Keep reading!

> **16** *"But to what shall I compare this generation? It is like children sitting in the market places, who call out to the other children,* **17** *and say, 'We played the flute for you, and you did not dance; we sang a dirge, and you did not mourn.'"*

What does this mean? This generation was marked by not being satisfied by anything God was doing. The comparison is between a marriage and a funeral. The dance was done at weddings with a flute playing and mourning was done at funerals when they sung a lament. Neither one was satisfactory to them. How does this play into this section of Scripture? First, you will need to keep the characters straight. John and Jesus were the children in the market place calling out to the other children. The term "children" speaks of the seed of Abraham to whom the promise of the Messiah was made. KEEP READING!

> **18** *"For John came neither eating nor drinking, and they say, 'He has a demon!'* **19** *"The Son of Man came eating and drinking, and they say, 'Behold, a gluttonous man and a drunkard, a friend of tax collectors and sinners!' Yet wisdom is vindicated by her deeds."*

Notice the inclusion of the word "for" again. It again is to be an explanation of the previous text. Again there is a comparison. This time it is John who did not come eating or drinking, to which the children of Israel responded with complaint that he had a demon, and Jesus who did come eating and drinking they complained that He was a drunk!

Who were the men of violence? We have two groups. Jesus and John represent one group who came preaching the kingdom of heaven was at hand. Then you had another group, represented by the rest of Israel, who were resisting this message and even criticizing it. Which group did violence to the kingdom of heaven and which group advanced the kingdom of heaven?

It becomes clear that those who lie and deceive people with regard to the message of the prophets and the Law are the ones who are violent men doing violence to the kingdom of God. Their father, the devil, is violent and they are revealing that nature in their actions. The violent men, therefore, are those who refuse to accept what God is doing, and by slandering the work of God they are preventing souls from entering the kingdom of heaven and are even convincing some who have entered to come out of it.

Recall that the kingdom of God does not come with observation. It is not measured in geography; the kingdom of God is measured in souls. Think back to the beginning of this book where my wife, Kathryn, was so upset by the violent and hateful nature of those demonic creatures. Think of the violence and hatred with which the people of Israel treated John and Jesus. John was beheaded and Jesus was crucified. The enemy is violently attacking people in the kingdom of heaven to take them out of that kingdom and that is how the kingdom of God suffers violence!

Look at our present day circumstances. That same violence is at work in our nation. Men and women who are so filled with violence and rage toward Christians and the Christian message that they are trying to erase every vestige of Christianity from the public square. Look around you! Wake up! Survey the land! We are right in the middle of the battle! It is warfare! Take your shield, take your sword, and start fighting the fight of faith!

If we can determine WHAT are the schemes of the devil then we are able to identify his actions in the world through knowledge of his methods. The Greek word for "schemes" is *methodia*. As you can see our English word "method" comes from this. It is a compound Greek word composed of *meta* which means "with" and *hodos* which means way or road. Put them together and you have "with a road." Apply to that idea a negative denotation and you have, as most the translators have rendered the word, "deceitful scheming." Everything we have learned about the devil so far reveals deceit.

> **Ephesians 6:12** *For our struggle is not against flesh and blood, but against the rulers, against the*

powers, against the world forces of this darkness, against the spiritual forces of wickedness in the heavenly places.

In this passage we have the identification of four types of foes. Some have suggested that this is a hierarchical order. It may be, but we do not have enough evidence to support this completely. That is subjective at best. However, I think there is some ranking going on here. The four foes are:

1. Rulers
2. Powers
3. World Forces
4. Spiritual Wickedness

Looking at these four foes will give us insight into the battle. Rulers are no doubt the top ranking demonic spirits. This word is also used for "beginning." The Greek word is *arche* and is used for first in time or first in rank. Thus, when referring to time it is translated beginning, but when used of rank it is the highest rank in a set. What we should take away from this is that we are able to stand against these primary leaders and we can advance on their kingdom by taking souls from them.

"Powers" is the Greek word *exousia* and simply means ability or right. Since a right must be given it denotes a rank lower than a ruler. "World forces" is the Greek word *kosmokrator* and denotes a lord or god of the world. When darkness is added to this term it completes the idea that this is Satan who is the god of this world and the progenitor of the kingdom of darkness. This verse is the only place this word is found in the New Testament.

Spiritual wickedness is actually two separate Greek words. Spiritual is the Greek *pneumatikos* and simply means to be of spirit. We know that demons are spirits so no surprise here. Wickedness is the Greek *poneria* and it has at its root the meaning of being poor. When one is poor in morality they are wicked. Spiritual wickedness is demonic spirits who are morally depraved doing evil in the heavenly.

This is not only what we are fighting against, but it is what we are able to overcome. With the full armor of God we can advance against this kingdom of rulers, powers, god of this world, and spiritual wickedness in the heavenly. The apostle now goes back to the armor.

> ***Ephesians 6:13*** *Therefore, take up the full armor of God, so that you will be able to resist in the evil day, and having done everything, to stand firm.*

Compare this verse with eleven. Whereas eleven tells us to put on, verse thirteen tells us to take up. The reason for taking up and putting on the armor of God is to cause us to stand firm in verse eleven and to resist the devil in verse thirteen. Notice the opening of the next verse is "Stand firm therefore…" Three times this word has been used in this passage. Do not forget that "standing firm against" is not only holding your ground, but advancing as well.

> ***Ephesians 6:14*** *Stand firm therefore, having girded your loins with truth, and having put on the breastplate of righteousness...*

"*...girded your loins with truth*" The first thing mentioned with regard to armor is truth. Without truth we have no armor at all. Note that you have to take it up (verse 13) and put it on (verse 11). Truth will not magically attach itself to you. You have to acquisition it. As Proverbs 23:23 states, *"Buy truth and sell it not..."* Do you recall that I told you that faith is the primary component of spiritual warfare? You will find that every part of the armor of God has to do with faith. Without truth there is nothing to have faith in. What does it mean to take up and put on truth? It means that you are getting knowledge and putting it on. You are growing your faith.

> **Isaiah 11:5** *Also righteousness will be the belt about His loins, And faithfulness the belt about His waist.*

Speaking of the Messiah who will rule earth, this verse gives us a picture of what was in Paul's mind when he penned Ephesians 6:14. Because of Messiah we are able to put that same belt upon our waist. This is how we will be able to stand firm. Keep in mind that the belt covers to protect the loins. The loins of a man represent his ability to reproduce himself. Truth protects your ability to reproduce others as well. The Christian needs the truth to convert the souls of others that they too might be transformed through the born again experience.

> *"…having put on the breastplate of righteousness"*

The breastplate covers and protects the heart. There are those who believe in their own righteousness. But this is something you put on. It represents the righteousness of God through Jesus. It is not your righteousness but His. Without truth we would not know what is right. Righteousness is that action of right judgment. Right judgment takes place in the atmosphere of truth. We are completely ill-suited to righteousness as humans consigned to our senses. It is something that must be put on or applied to us by faith. *"The righteous man shall live by faith."*

> **Isaiah 59:16-17** *And He saw that there was no man, And was astonished that there was no one to intercede; Then His own arm brought salvation to Him, And His righteousness upheld Him. He put on righteousness like a breastplate…*

The Messiah is again pictured. If you read this in context you find that justice and truth were lacking. To this God is saying that He will do it Himself. He will become a man and He will put righteousness on like a breastplate. Righteousness, therefore, can only come by faith.

> ***Ephesians 6:15*** *and having shod your feet with the preparation of the gospel of peace;*

I have heard many say to someone who was going through a rough time, *"You need to put on your shoes of peace!"* This is not the meaning of this piece of armor. It is the PREPARATION of the gospel of peace. This is calling you to supply the time and effort to study to know what you believe. Bear in mind, this is so you can stand and resist the devil. He is going to be undermining the gospel message constantly. If you do not know why you believe what you believe, you will be destroyed in your faith.

The shoes are a protection to your feet. Your feet represent your ability to move. Those that do not have a clear understanding of their faith are paralyzed in their movements. We could even say they are not able to pursue destiny nor can they pursue their enemies. Every piece of armor is important. It takes the full armor to stand.

> ***Ephesians 6:16*** *in addition to all, taking up the shield of faith with which you will be able to extinguish all the flaming arrows of the evil one.*

The shield is very important. When we understand why it is called the shield of faith, it will become clear. The apostle probably had this verse in mind when writing about the shield. Faith cannot exist without faithfulness.

> ***Psalm 91:3-5*** *For it is He who delivers you from the snare of the trapper And from the deadly pestilence. He will cover you with His pinions, And under His wings you may seek refuge; His faithfulness is a*

shield and bulwark. You will not be afraid of the terror by night, Or of the arrow that flies by day.

What does "fiery dart" refer to? The Hebrew word for "teach" means to shoot an arrow. But note the addition of fire.

Psalm 120:2-4 *Deliver my soul, O LORD, from lying lips, From a deceitful tongue. What shall be given to you, and what more shall be done to you, You deceitful tongue?* **Sharp arrows** *of the warrior, With the* **burning coals** *of the broom tree.*

If we put all of this together we see that when you add deceit you get the mention of fire. This means that the fiery darts are arrows of deceit shot at you to discourage and deceive you. The shield of faith is able to extinguish every one of these flaming arrows. This points us back to 2 Corinthians again. Also 1 Timothy should come to mind.

1 Timothy 4:1-2 *But the Spirit explicitly says that in later times some will fall away from the faith, paying attention to deceitful spirits and doctrines of demons, by means of the hypocrisy of liars seared in their own conscience as with a branding iron...*

Observe that these doctrines of demons are presented by human beings. Also, notice that these human beings are liars. Liars are deceivers. This is the warfare we are engaged in whether you accept it or not. Deceitful spirits are spreading their lying doctrines through the teachings of men. They are flaming arrows aimed at the Christian to deceive and wound them. Consider the following:

2 Corinthians 11:14-15 *No wonder, for even Satan disguises himself as an angel of light. Therefore it is* **not surprising if his servants also disguise themselves as servants of righteousness**, *whose end will be according to their deeds.*

This is so important for you to understand. If you think that you can walk into a place that calls themselves a Church and expect that minister is a minister of God you are deluding yourself. This passage clearly states that these servants of Satan will disguise themselves as ministers of righteousness. What do you think these disguised ministers will be teaching? Doctrines of demons! How would you identify a doctrine of a demon? It would only be indentified through knowing and believing the Word of God. At the risk of repeating myself, let's read 2 Corinthians again.

> ***2 Corinthians 10:3-5 (KJV)*** *For though we walk in the flesh, we do not war after the flesh: (For the weapons of our warfare are not carnal, but mighty through God to the pulling down of strong holds;) Casting down imaginations, and every high thing that exalteth itself against the knowledge of God, and bringing into captivity every thought to the obedience of Christ.*

What brings every thought into captivity to the obedience of Christ? The weapons of our warfare. What are the weapons of our warfare? It is the Word of God. When you have studied the Word of God and believed it, it becomes a shield that will take captive every fiery arrow of doctrines of demons to the obedience of Christ.

> ***Ephesians 6:17*** *And take the helmet of salvation...*

Since the battlefield is in your mind and the helmet covers this area, then we need to pay special attention to it. The primary sense of the word "salvation" is deliverance. What have we been delivered from? What comes into the mind that causes us to be delivered of it? We see again a connection back to the idea of deceptions being thrown into our mind like flaming arrows. We have the capacity for deliverance through the helmet of salvation.

1 Peter 1:9 *obtaining as the outcome of your faith the salvation of your souls.*

The devil will also try to get you to misunderstand your salvation. He will try to get you to think that you have to do something to get it or do something to keep it. He wants to hide the fact that salvation is a gift of God. All it requires is faith. Once you are confused about your salvation then the enemy can rock you from side to side with regard to many different things.

Ephesians 6:17 *…and the sword of the Spirit, which is the word of God.*

The Word of God will be used to advance the kingdom of God. One question, however. How much of it do you actually know? How long is your sword? Are you aware that without understanding the Word of God you are left to be pulled around by your nose in any direction the enemy chooses? Do you realize that without understanding the Word you have become an unwilling pawn of the enemy to espouse his false doctrines? Without an understanding of the Word you have no way of testing what you hear. You are left with making a decision without knowledge.

This is the danger that thousands of Christians walk around in every day. They have rejected the notion that they need to study the Word of God. They have rejected the notion that they were called by God to become a disciple. Then they hear things like there are more paths to heaven than Christianity. They accept homosexuality as an alternate lifestyle, but not a sin. They accept the slaughter of innocent babies still in the womb as a right of choice. They are clouds without water. They may look like a Christian, they may talk like a Christian, they even go to church like a Christian, but they are far from being a Christian.

Jesus had an encounter with Satan and in the encounter He demonstrated the power of the Sword of the Spirit. Every time the enemy attacked him with a false statement, Jesus countered with *"it is written."* Why then have we abandoned this powerful weapon as we are engaged in warfare by the enemy? God has given us everything we need to win the battle.

You are in the battle whether you think you are or not. What secret beliefs of the enemy have you picked up without knowing it? How would you know if you are not skilled in the Word of God? Your pastor may give you truth, but if you cannot understand it, that truth it is stolen by the enemy.

This is warfare! Your enemy does not fight based on the rules of the Geneva Convention. He is a sick, maniacal, twisted being that seeks your destruction. Those who fight for the enemy take on the characteristics of his nature. He cares nothing about offending someone, he only seeks their destruction. He is full of hatred for you, and if you do not take him seriously you put yourself in danger. Will you engage in the fight or will you become a casualty of war? How much of your faith has already been undermined because you did not study the Word of God? The choice is yours. No one can fight your battle for you. Get involved and fight the good fight of faith!

About the Author

Bishop Mark Shaw and his wife Kathryn, are co-founders and directors of *Five Fold Ministries Training Academy (FFMTA)* and *Collegium Bible Institute* where the next generation of ministers is being equipped for God's service around the world. Bishop Shaw is the author of *"Is God Calling You to Ministry?," "The Glory of Kings,"* and *"The Government of God."* Shaw is the senior editor of *A Voice in the Wilderness* newsletter, which is published quarterly. He is also founder of Collegium Books, which is a publishing and distribution firm that seeks to offer educational materials for the equipping of the saints for the work of God. Shaw has been in ministry for thirty-two years. He was vice-director of Five Fold Ministries for twelve years and has been director for the last nine years. Shaw and his wife, Kathryn, preside as pastors over *Adonai Worship Center* in Cannon Falls, Minnesota.

Shaw teaches on the structure and government of the Church with emphasis on divine order. He brings clarity to the Scripture by revealing a Hebraic understanding and emphasizes the causes and conditions upon which we develop our faith. His desire is to return true discipleship back to the Church so that true leaders are being forged with truth and integrity. He has a vision for the Church that is cutting edge and Spirit mandated.

In 2008 Shaw founded the Five Fold Ministries on-line E-learning center. The E-learning center is designed to distribute world class learning to students through internet technology that brings the school into the living room. The purpose is to develop leaders nationally and internationally that are willing to arrange the Church and its leaders in such a way that validates the Church as a voice in a secular society.

Called to the office of ministry, Kathryn Colton Shaw has a heart and a voice to teach those that are hungry to walk in the ways of the Lord, and awaken them to do what God has called them to do. It is Kathryn's desire to bring healing to the whole person in order that they may be released to accomplish the destiny for which they were created. Kathryn has a gift for networking and hosting seminars and educational programs. She is also gifted in administration and is a valuable asset in giving direction to the Church. Pastor Kathryn is the co-founder of *FFMTA* and *Collegium Bible Institute* where she serves as Academic Dean/Counselor and continues to develop curriculum to impact the next generation for Christ. The Shaws reside in Minnesota and they have six children and ten grandchildren that live in California and North Carolina.

Collegium Bible Institute

The International Equipping School of the Five Fold Ministry

Collegium Bible Institute is a four year biblical institute where students are prepared for ministry and receive a deep sense of awe for the Scriptures. For more information on our ordination program at the local campus, write us at 410 Dakota Street W, Cannon Falls, MN 55009 or call us at 888-808-5455. Our website is: www.collegiumbibleinstitute.com

If you are interested in the Online E-Learning Center visit us at: www.5fold.org.

The Lord commanded His disciples to go into all the world and make disciples of all nations, teaching them to observe all that He said. The question then is have you been discipled yet?

Available on CollegiumBibleInstitute.com

Available on CollegiumBibleInstitute.com

Available on CollegiumBibleInstitute.com

www.ingramcontent.com/pod-product-compliance
Lightning Source LLC
Chambersburg PA
CBHW070722160426
43192CB00009B/1286